MARGERY KEMPE

Covering one of the most fascinating yet misunderstood periods in history, the MEDIEVAL LIVES series presents medieval people, concepts and events, drawing on political and social history, philosophy, material culture (art, architecture and archaeology) and the history of science. These books are global and wide-ranging in scope, encompassing both Western and non-Western subjects, and span the fifth to the fifteenth centuries, tracing significant developments from the collapse of the Roman Empire onwards.

SERIES EDITOR: Deirdre Jackson

Christine de Pizan: Life, Work, Legacy *Charlotte Cooper-Davis*

Margery Kempe: A Mixed Life *Anthony Bale*

MARGERY KEMPE
A Mixed Life

ANTHONY BALE

REAKTION BOOKS

For Tim and Benny, with love

Published by Reaktion Books Ltd
Unit 32, Waterside
44–48 Wharf Road
London N1 7UX, UK
www.reaktionbooks.co.uk

First published 2021
Copyright © Anthony Bale 2021

Printed and bound in India by Replika Press Pvt. Ltd

A catalogue record for this book is available from the British Library

ISBN 978 1 78914 470 3

CONTENTS

NOTE ON TEXTS AND TRANSLATIONS   7

Foreword: A Note on this Book   9

1 Creature   13

2 The Town of Bishop's Lynn   25

3 Places   47

   INTERLOGE: 'my weddyd wyfe', Rome, 1414   82

4 Friends and Enemies   86

   INTERLOGE: 'fals strumpet', Leicester, 1417   121

5 Things   131

   INTERLOGE: 'a gret fyer', Lynn, 1421   154

6 Feelings   158

7 Old Age   182

8 Writing and Rediscovery   193

   Envoie   207

CHRONOLOGY 211

ABBREVIATIONS 213

REFERENCES 214

FURTHER READING 239

ACKNOWLEDGEMENTS 240

PHOTO ACKNOWLEDGEMENTS 241

INDEX 242

NOTE ON TEXTS AND TRANSLATIONS

Quotations from *The Book of Margery Kempe* are taken from *The Book of Margery Kempe* ed. Lynn Staley, which is available online at https://d.lib.rochester.edu. References are given in brackets by book and line number according to this edition. Where the Middle English requires translation into modern English, I have followed *The Book of Margery Kempe*, ed. and trans. Anthony Bale (Oxford, 2015). Biblical quotations are from the Douay-Rheims version, via www.drbo.org.

Foreword:
A Note on this Book

Lock up your libraries if you like; but there is no gate, no lock, no bolt that you can set upon the freedom of my mind.
VIRGINIA WOOLF, *A Room of One's Own* (1929)

To write an autobiography is to assume responsibility for one's life. Telling one's story may involve selective memory, but this story also becomes the lasting version one presents of oneself. In *The Book of Margery Kempe* (written 1436–8), often called the first autobiography in the English language, Margery Kempe gave a partial account of her life, but one in which she assumed responsibility for those things that had, at times, put her in danger and made her both celebrated and disliked.

Our main source, *The Book of Margery Kempe*, survives in a unique manuscript (British Library, London, Add. MS 61823), copied in the 1440s from a lost original; parts of Kempe's *Book* also survive in two highly abbreviated early printed editions (of c. 1501 and 1521). *The Book of Margery Kempe* is a written document replete with historical fact and context; however, it is certainly not 'reliable'. Kempe herself could not have written her book without assistance, since she states that she could neither read nor write. However, she was highly 'literate' in the sense of having a deep, allusive and supple knowledge of the Bible and of popular religious texts that had been read to her. Kempe's *Book* was written down over a period of time by scribes and amanuenses shaping Kempe's oral recollections, but the fictionality of the *Book* has often been overstated. It is a *partial* piece of writing but it is also a valuable historical source. It would not be possible to narrate Kempe's life entirely chronologically (the *Book* itself admits errors in its chronology), and so in what follows I have introduced Kempe, her life and her *Book* chronologically where possible but also thematically. This book is not a 'complete' account of Kempe, but rather puts moments of Kempe's life into historical and interpretative contexts and introduces some key themes in her *Book*. I include three 'interloges' – a word used in Norfolk in the fifteenth century for an interlude, a performance between parts – which describe three specific and dateable moments in Kempe's life. The book closes with an 'envoie', a concluding message. Through Margery Kempe one can build a kind of highly personalized history of fifteenth-century England, and investigate the identity and subjectivity of one of its most voluble and fascinating individuals.

Hermione Lee begins her exploration of biographical writing with two dominant and striking metaphors of biography: the autopsy and the portrait. On the one hand, an autopsy 'invokes biography as a process of posthumous scrutiny', a 'forensic process' that 'can have nothing or little to say about the subject's thoughts, intelligence, emotions, temperament, talents, or beliefs'. On the other hand, a portrait should 'seem to make the subject alive, breathing, present in all the totality, thereness, and authenticity of their being', but with its attendant pitfalls of 'flattery, idealization, flatness, inaccuracy, distortion' and dependence on the artist/biographer.[1] In this book I seek neither to perform an autopsy nor paint a portrait. This study is conceived as an 'analytical biography', alighting on significant moments in Kempe's *Book* to enrich our understanding not only of its contexts but of its language, its protagonist, and our own engagement with it. Kempe can tell us much about fifteenth-century England but also how any person's life is mediated, rendered and transformed into a narrative.

The Book of Margery Kempe is a book about the writing of a book and about the making of a testament. When I write about the narrative of *The Book of Margery Kempe* and incidents from it, I use the present tense. When I write about Kempe's life and historical context, I use the past tense. Readers who have not yet read *The Book of Margery Kempe* are advised to read that remarkable text, perhaps the most vivid surviving account of a medieval English person's life.

1 Margery Kempe's Europe.

ONE

Creature

*. . . this creatur went owt of hir mende and was wondyrlye
vexid and labowryd wyth spyritys*

Ｉn the bustling town of Bishop's Lynn, Norfolk, around the
year 1394, a young woman is going through a difficult pregnancy. The woman has many advantages in life. She is from
a well-off background, a daughter of the town's elite. She has
a good house in the town centre and many material comforts.
This is her first child, and she became pregnant shortly after
marriage. But the pregnancy has been utterly wretched, and
fever and sickness ravage her body.

At the same time her mind is in a state of torment. There's
a guilty secret on her conscience. She knows she should have
been absolved by going to confession and revealing her sins to
a priest. In the fourteenth century, it was considered especially
important for pregnant women to confess; a guide for parish
priests says that when the mother is close to giving birth she
must 'schryve hem clene' (make her full confession), because
of 'drede of perele that may befalle' (fear of the physical injury
that may happen).[1] For the same reason, medieval women often
wrote their wills before going into labour.

This thing on the woman's conscience is tearing at her, causing her intense agony. Yet she has declared that she will see no
confessor, that she can do her own penance. So on some days

she will punish her ailing body further, eating only bread and water, while on other days she gives small donations to beggars, or devotes hours to long and fervent prayers. All this she does in order to avoid confessing her terrible sin. Indeed, in all her long life she will never disclose this secret to anyone. One can still only guess at the nature of this terrible, unspeakable, unredeemed sin, but it changed fundamentally the course of her life.

Sickness and severe illness in childbirth are nothing new to the young woman: she has seen many pregnant women suffer, and some die, often in a state of shame because of the private, intimate nature of their ailments. Local women have tried cures, following medical recipes, taking herbal baths, drinking expensive juices and making complicated powders, syrups and suppositories out of the recommended ingredients. These include acorns, goat's milk, mint leaves, poppies, Armenian earth, the stomach of suckling hare, acacia sap, mastic gum, dragonwort, dove's droppings in wine.[2] But such cures do nothing to stem the expectant mother's sickness, and she has known women suffer atrociously, from unstoppable bleeding, from problems with the uterus such as prolapse, wind or inflammation, from ulcers of the womb, and similar painful and often mortal illnesses. Medical knowledge of the time holds that one reason for sickness in pregnancy is due to 'the feblenesse of the moder' – that is, the frailty or weaknesses of the mother's womb. This may be because she has been compromised by sickness, or because of her 'gret thought' – her anxiety or her distress. Alternatively, a pregnancy may be difficult because the mother is overweight, her fatness blocking the mouth of the uterus, holding back blood which would otherwise have been purged. Or, it could be because the unborn infant is itself ill, failing or even dead.[3] Medieval medical guides recommend the keeping of an exotic jasper-stone about one's person to relieve all the pains of pregnancy.[4] These books also say that a mixture of iris, hyssop, rue and savory crushed

in the best white wine promises a quick and easy delivery of
the baby.[5] The young Norfolk woman can afford anything that
would help (or her father could pay for it all). But nothing has
been able to stop the wretched feelings she has had during her
pregnancy.

When her baby is born – a little boy named John, after his
father – the young woman's health, in both body and mind, gets
much worse. For the first eight months of her little boy's life,
the woman is frantic and frenzied. At times she seems bewil-
dered, at others hugely vexed. She receives horrifying visions of
devils, visions as real to her as the pains in her belly and womb.
The devils creep round her, opening their mouths, breathing
scorching flames, snarling and snapping as if to swallow her
whole, sometimes pawing at her, sometimes threatening her,
sometimes pulling and dragging at her. They cause her to flail
and throw herself about the room. This happens day and night,
almost constantly. The devils scream at her, telling her to forsake
Christianity, to deny God, Mary and all the saints. They tell her
to reject her father, her mother and all her friends. For periods
of time during this ordeal, the young woman lies thrashing in
her bed, or she roams around the house, screaming in torment,
succumbing to the devils' instructions: she slanders everyone
she knows, screams curses at them, swears blasphemous oaths,
uses the foulest language. She slanders her own husband and her
friends, and she slanders herself. She scratches in a frenzy at her
skin with her fingernails. She would take a knife to herself, if
she could find one. She would so love to join the devils in hell
– which is where she is sure she is going. She is, as she would
later describe it, 'owt of hir mende' (1.149) – out of her mind.

Eventually, when her family can take it no longer, the young
woman is bound and restrained at all times, night and day, locked
in a room at home. Warders are employed to guard her. She
knows that her husband still cares about her. Her family says they

are only trying to stop her from causing more harm to herself or those around her. What they are doing is indeed the standard treatment for someone who has gone out of her mind. Diagnoses of mental illness were numerous, as they are today. Terms like 'annxumnesse' (anxiety), 'frenesie' (delirium), 'langour' (mental suffering) and 'misconfort' (mental distress) conveyed different kinds of illness. London's Bethlem ('Bedlam') Royal Hospital has, around this time, started to receive such patients, 'to maintain those who have lost their wits and memory'. The binding and confinement of the insane was seen as a good way to care for (or deal with) them.[6] The mad were worthy recipients of charity and prayers, but they were also considered possible victims of demonic possession and in need of exorcism.

About eight months after giving birth to little John – and after eight months of being highly disturbed in body and mind – the distraught young woman has still not stopped screaming and raving. At one point, as a sign of her desperate misery and, she will later say, a token of her damnation, she bites her hand with incredible violence, tearing into the flesh with her teeth. She will bear this scar for the rest of her long life. It is for her an everlasting and authentic mark of the depth of her torment and sinfulness.

One day, probably at some point in 1394, the woman's warders are elsewhere. She lies alone in her bedchamber. Suddenly, she has a vision different from those demonic apparitions with which she had been struggling. She describes it thus:

> owyr mercyful Lord Crist Jhesu, evyr to be trostyd, worshypd be hys name, nevyr forsakyng hys servawnt in tyme of nede, aperyd to hys creatur, whych had forsakyn hym, in lyknesse of a man, most semly, most bewtyuows, and most amyable that evyr mygth be seen wyth mannys eye, clad in a mantyl of purpyl sylke, syttyng upon hir

beddys syde, lokyng upon hir wyth so blyssyd a chere that
sche was strengthyd in alle hir spyritys, seyd to hir thes
wordys: 'Dowtyr, why hast thow forsakyn me, and I forsoke
nevyr the?' And anoon, as he had seyd thes wordys, sche
saw veryly how the eyr openyd as brygth as ony levyn, and
he stey up into the eyr, not rygth hastyli and qwykly, but
fayr and esly that sche mygth wel beholdyn hym in the
eyr tyl it was closyd ageyn. And anoon the creature was
stabelyd in hir wyttys and in hir reson as wel as evyr sche
was beforn, and preyd hir husbond as so soon as he cam to
hir that sche mygth have the keys of the botery to takyn hir
mete and drynke as sche had don beforn (1.167–79).

our merciful Lord Christ Jesus – ever to be trusted,
worshipped be His name, never forsaking His servant in
time of need – appeared in the likeness of a man to His
creature who had forsaken Him, the most handsome, the
most beautiful and the most affable that could ever be seen
with human eye, clad in a purple silk mantle, sitting upon
her bedside, looking upon her with so blessed an expression
that she was fortified in all her spirits, and He said these
words to her: 'Daughter, why have you forsaken me, and
I never forsook you?' Then at once, as He had said these
words, she truly saw the air open up as bright as any lightning, and He stepped up into the air, not very hastily and
quickly but elegantly and steadily, so that she could easily
behold Him in the air until it closed up again. And then
the creature was steadied in her wits and in her reason as
well as she had been before, and pleaded with her husband
as soon as he came to her that she might have the keys
to the buttery to fetch her food and drink as she had
done before.

This strikingly beautiful piece of writing marks the end of the woman's first crisis and the beginning of her spiritual conversion and physical revival. She is visited by her own personal Jesus: a good-looking *Christus medicus*, a friendly healer, in utter contrast to the threatening devils that have beset her. He wears a purple cloak, the garment of majesty in which He was mockingly dressed at Calvary.[7] Her Christ utters just a few words – 'Dowtyr, why hast thow forsakyn me, and I forsoke nevyr the?' – echoing the Psalms and Christ's distressed cry at Calvary: 'My God, my God, why hast thou forsaken me?'[8] So even though Christ appears very much as an incarnate man, He also appears as the loving God who has still not forsaken His own favoured daughter.

The bright flash of air as Christ departs is neither violent nor intimidating. Christ ascends into the air calmly, elegantly, steadily, as he rises out of the woman's chamber and from her field of vision.

This moment of communication is, for the young woman, transformative: it steadies her wits, brings her back to her reason. She successfully pleads to be released from her confinement and is allowed to collect her own food and drink from her household buttery (a pantry or larder). She has commenced a journey of transformation, from tormented wretch to exemplary recipient of grace, from inconsolable misery to the consolation of finding, or discovering, oneself. This will not be an easy or straightforward path, but it is in this moment – at which Christ erupts into her anguished world – that her special story emerges.

This young woman is Margery Kempe. We know about her crisis in childbirth because of the remarkable book she dictated about forty years later, in the 1430s. *The Book of Margery Kempe* is truly a unique and intimate story of a woman's life. It is fitting that it opens with a portrait of its protagonist's sin and sickness, disorder and desire, and a description of her individual and distinctive spiritual travails. These are themes that will recur throughout Kempe's life.

Medieval women's voices often emerge through male-authored documents: damning, biased indictments such as court records and inquisitorial documents, or idealized fictions of impossible models of conduct, such as saints' lives. *The Book of Margery Kempe* is valuable and unique because, even though it was written down by Kempe's amanuenses, it follows her life and version of events. In what follows I take Kempe's *Book* as an unrivalled source for understanding her experience as a woman in fifteenth-century England, for understanding the England and Europe through which she indefatigably travelled, and for understanding what it means to give an account of oneself, to write one's own life, to turn one's life into a book. Throughout her *Book*, Kempe is referred to in the third person, as the 'creature'. This does not imply that she is a beast or animal, but describes her as being made, shaped and created by God: as Kempe's contemporary, the English poet John Gower (d. 1408) wrote, 'God . . . is creatour, And othre ben Hise creatures' (God is the creator, and others are His creatures).[9]

'thys creatur': This creature

Margery Kempe (née Burnham) was born in about 1373, in the bustling town of Bishop's Lynn (now King's Lynn) in Norfolk. Her father was John Burnham (d. 1413), a successful merchant and local politician, and her mother, or possibly stepmother, was Isabella. Some 160 km (100 mi.) north of London, Lynn was then an important trading port, situated on the northern coast of East Anglia at the mouth of the River Great Ouse (illus. 1 and 2).

The contours of Margery Kempe's life are as follows. In about 1393 she married John Kempe and shortly afterwards had her first child, and this was the pregnancy and labour in which she was afflicted by devils and eventually calmed by a vision of Jesus. The child was named John, after his father, as was common. She subsequently had thirteen more children. Around 1403 to 1408, when she must have been having a child every year or so, John went into business, as a brewer and a miller. In about 1409, Kempe, by then in her mid-thirties, began to abstain from eating meat and showing more public signs of religiosity. She also began to pray for an end to sexual relations with her husband. In 1412 she received a divine directive to visit Jerusalem, Rome and Santiago de Compostela, three pre-eminent pilgrimage sites in medieval Latin Christendom. By this point, Kempe was developing a public identity as a pious visionary, and around this time she spent several days with the celebrated mystic Julian of Norwich in the latter's anchorhold (a hermit's cell). In midsummer 1413, Kempe began to live chastely, having made an agreement with her husband to do so (in a remarkable roadside conversation near York, 1.520). She became a 'vowess' – a chaste bride of Christ – even as she remained married to John. Kempe shows the clear influence of the late medieval religious movement known as *devotio moderna* (modern devotion), emphasizing individual piety and humble penance, and focused especially on the imitation of Christ and the Virgin.[10]

In the second half of 1413, around the time of her father's death, Kempe set off for the Holy Land, travelling via Bologna and Venice. She visited Jerusalem, Bethlehem and other sacred sites. At Calvary she underwent her first bout of divinely ordained crying, a feature of her religiosity that was particularly conspicuous and bothersome to those around her. Returning to Italy, Kempe spent many months in Rome, meeting various patrons and supporters, undergoing a mystical marriage to the Godhead (the unified Christian deity, rather than the individual members of the Trinity), and becoming voluntarily destitute.

She returned to England around the middle of 1415, and in 1417 went from Bristol to Santiago de Compostela. Upon her return to England Kempe was held, threatened and interrogated on suspicion of heresy, at Leicester, York, Beverley and at Hessle on the banks of the River Humber.

In 1418, back in Lynn, Kempe started to suffer from an unidentified illness, which she endured for eight years. Her *Book* describes how, at this time, she was abandoned by at least two priests and publicly attacked by a Franciscan friar. In 1421 she observed, and intervened, in a great fire at Lynn. Otherwise, for most of the 1420s Kempe seems to have been in isolated contemplation in Lynn, focusing on her spiritual development, through 'holy meditacyons' with Jesus, the Virgin and the saints.

In the early 1430s Kempe's husband had declined, after a bad fall, into ill health and a kind of dementia. Kempe tended him. Around 1432 he died, as did her eldest son, John Kempe junior, who had been living in the port city of Gdańsk with his Prussian wife and had only recently returned to England. The following year, the widowed Margery Kempe, now aged around sixty, boarded a ship at Ipswich and sailed to Gdańsk with her daughter-in-law, during which journey the ship was blown off course to Norway. After reaching Gdańsk, Kempe made a pilgrimage to the important shrines of Wilsnack and Aachen, and then returned to England via Calais.

On 23 July 1436, the feast of the death of St Bridget of Sweden, the process of writing Book I of *The Book of Margery Kempe*, as we know it today, began, continuing for about two years. In April 1438 a woman named 'Margeria Kempe', who can confidently be identified as our Margery Kempe, was recorded as a member of the Lynn Guild of the Holy Trinity, the town's most prestigious and influential confraternity. Around the same time (on 28 April 1438) the writing of Book II of *The Book of Margery Kempe* commenced. A further mention of Kempe in the

Guild's records for 22 May 1439 provides the last evidence that she was alive. One assumes that Kempe died around this time, when she would have in her mid- to late sixties.

Kempe's life was immensely varied but some patterns emerge in her biography. Kempe oscillated between home (the town of Lynn) and abroad. She became an inveterate and dedicated pilgrim and her travels took her across the entire continent of Europe, yet at all times she remained deeply anchored to Lynn, where she was born and where, most likely, she died. Kempe's life moved on an upward trajectory towards holiness, but worldly concerns were never far away, whether in the form of detractors' attempts to silence her or her own pursuit of recognition. Kempe never transcended her earthly surroundings or friction with other people and she was followed by (or courted) controversy. Then there are the periodic illnesses and crises; not only was the distressing period following the birth of her first son a pivotal moment of change, there are other moments of affliction which prove transformative. Kempe very effectively placed herself apart from her family at times, and says little about her fourteen children, but she tended her husband and it was with her daughter-in-law that she embarked on her final pilgrimage. Family ties do not always sit easily with her religious calling but they remain key coordinates of her identity.

Overall, Kempe's life can justifiably be called a 'mixed life'. As well as evoking varied fortunes and diverse roles, the 'mixed life' was a medieval ideal of a life that bridged the sacred and the secular. The author Walter Hilton (d. 1396), whose writings were known to Kempe, wrote an 'Epistle on the Mixed Life' in which he urged readers to follow whatever route to holiness was practical for their own circumstances. Hilton encouraged his readers to accept that withdrawal to a contemplative life was not possible or desirable for everyone. Instead, many should seek to achieve the 'mixed life', combining worldly engagement (what

Hilton calls 'bodili werk', or physical action) with spiritual contemplation ('goostli werk').[11] The mixed life, 'bothe actif and
contemplatif', was a model for combining work, family, politics
and pleasure with an intense, individual and mystical relationship with God. Hilton urges the lay reader to 'breke doun, as
moche as thou mai, fleschli likynges', such as 'glotonie' and 'lech-
erie', and only then to attempt 'goostli', spiritual labour.[12] His
letter is a luminous exhortation to lay people just like Margery
Kempe: those who felt they had earthly responsibilities but
were also called to devotion. Using the biblical story of Leah
(Jacob's weak-eyed but fecund wife, who 'bitokeneth actif liyf')
and Rachel (Leah's beautiful but barren sister, who 'bitokeneth
liyf contemplatif'), Hilton says that since God has sent these two
lives, we should use them both, as both active and contemplative
lives are 'needful' (necessary) and 'speedfulle' (profitable).[13] To
achieve the mixed life, according to Hilton, is a slow, gradual and
uneven process, and requires patience, self-knowledge and hard
work. Such a model of living gave Kempe and her peers a way of
experiencing daily life as a sacred journey. For Kempe, spiritual
development and divine revelation went alongside work, illness,
intimidation, guilt and embarrassment.

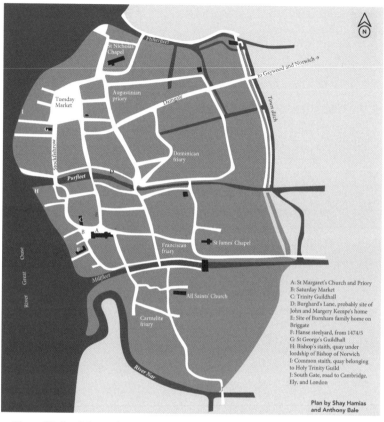

Plan by Shay Hamias
and Anthony Bale

A: St Margaret's Church and Priory
B: Saturday Market
C: Trinity Guildhall
D: Burghard's Lane, probably site of
John and Margery Kempe's home
E: Site of Burnham family home on
Briggate
F: Hanse steelyard, from 1474/5
G: St George's Guildhall
H: Bishop's staith, quay under
lordship of Bishop of Norwich
I: Common staith, quay belonging
to Holy Trinity Guild
J: South Gate, road to Cambridge,
Ely, and London

2 Plan of Bishop's Lynn (Norfolk) in the fifteenth century.

TWO

The Town of Bishop's Lynn

The town of Lynn is where Kempe's story begins, returns to and ends. It is the urban context in which Kempe grew up and in which, throughout her life, she tried to prove, assert and craft a lasting image of herself.

Kempe's father, John Burnham, was from a well-to-do local family that originated in the beautiful region of north Norfolk, in the cluster of small towns known as the Burnhams (about 34 km (21 mi.) northeast of Lynn). Norfolk was one of the wealthiest and most cosmopolitan parts of England, due to its proximity to commercial sea routes to Flanders, northern Europe and the Baltic. The region of East Anglia – the eastern counties of England, especially Norfolk and Suffolk – had become rich on the export of linen and wool, and the import of copper, fish, furs, grain, lumber, pitch and wax. The Burnham family had moved to Lynn by the 1320s, and by the time Margery was born in the 1370s the family had established itself there, with land and property throughout the town and members of the family active in trade. Lynn was a densely populated place, characterized by the proximity of the town centre to the port. Lynn was the main conduit for goods to and from northern Europe and to substantial towns such as Ely, Huntingdon, Cambridge and Bedford. In the later fourteenth century, the population of Lynn can be estimated at around 5,000 people, among the larger towns of England (London, by far the biggest city in the country, had about 50,000 to 60,000 people).[1] Numerous monasteries and friaries – most of which would feature in Kempe's life in one way or another – were dotted through the town.

John Burnham was a merchant burgess, importing and exporting cloth, fish and lumber.[2] He also held a range of high offices in local and regional government, most important of which were his periods as mayor of Lynn (in 1370–71, 1377–9, 1385–6 and 1391–2). He was alderman of the Guild of the Holy Trinity by 1393 until at least 1402. Therefore throughout his daughter's youth, Burnham held positions of great prestige and a high level of political and financial responsibility. The town's mayor was the most important and powerful secular official and had legal and financial jurisdiction within the town, responsible for collecting royal taxes, imposing local taxes, safeguarding the borough's liberties and regulating the town and its trades. The mayor recorded wills relating to property in the town, regulated apprenticeships and undertook to provide a water supply and to maintain the town's walls and fortifications. Each town had different customs relating to the mayoralty, but often the mayor also enforced policies concerning town trade, charity and commerce, covering issues such as the dumping of waste, the selling of diseased meat and the quality and price of bread. In the event of a war – and during Kempe's lifetime England was at war with France and her allies, Aragon, Castile and Scotland, and against Welsh rebels – the mayor was also responsible for provisioning the army. Being mayor of a busy commercial town like Lynn was a complex and often controversial post, and Kempe would have witnessed several outbursts of violence against the town government, such as the riots of 1404–6, and in 1414–15, when a group of local men tried to introduce new procedures for the election of a mayor.[3]

At the head of Lynn society were the *potentiores* (literally, the powerful ones, potentates), a cabinet of local government usually made up of the 24 merchant jurats.[4] Several Burnham and Kempe men were *potentiores*, including John Burnham. As well as being mayor, John Burnham was a Member of Parliament for Lynn some six times between 1364 and 1384, including during the 'Good Parliament' of 1376.[5] Burnham attended the Westminster Parliament as a burgess (a representative of the town), one of two representatives from Lynn. Prior to this point the House of Commons existed mostly to support the Crown and to confirm or endorse royal policy; the Commons negotiated tax and similar levies required by the Crown, and it developed and passed legislation. The House of Commons was neither politically independent of the king nor was it party political. That said, John Burnham would have received generous expenses for his parliamentary duties, and he was probably party to some pivotal political decisions in the reigns of Edward III and Richard II. The 'Good Parliament', of which Burnham was a member, fundamentally changed the way in which English governmental power operated by effectively becoming prosecutors and state auditors, in developing the process of impeachment, and in first electing a Speaker who spoke for the House.[6] The Commons of the 'Good Parliament' asserted a voice that, if not exactly democratic, gave more opportunity than previously for non-aristocratic opinions. Moreover, such a parliament made space for regional involvement in national government, so the citizenry of towns like Lynn could make itself heard.

Burnham was married to a woman called Isabella (who was either mother or stepmother to Margery Kempe), about whom little is known. Isabella was almost certainly from local burgess stock, the Trussebut and the Lok families.[7] In 1408–9 the Burnham family's neighbour in Briggate, Margery Lok, bequeathed a coral rosary and 40 shillings to 'Isabelle de Brunham' and 20 shillings to a goddaughter named Margery (possibly Margery Kempe); Margery Lok may have been Isabella's sister.[8] In the

period around 1411–13, John Burnham may have lost much
of his fortune and fallen from political favour; in the first part of
1413 he died.[9] Isabella remarried, to a man named Geoffrey de
Sutton, events that are not mentioned in *The Book of Margery
Kempe*, although this period, of Margery Kempe's father's death
and Isabella Burnham's remarriage, is precisely when Kempe
was visiting Jerusalem, Rome and Santiago and undergoing the
bouts of noisy crying that became her defining behaviour.

Lynn was one of a handful of English ports closely linked
to the Hanse, the league of trading ports centred on Lübeck.
Lynn, Boston and London were the only ports in England at
the time to have a Hanse *kontor*, a kind of trading complex
known in English as a 'steelyard' (translating the German *stahl-
hof*, a courtyard for merchants' samples in which the merchants
lived and worked, at once lodging, depot, warehouse, office,
tavern and shop). The Hanse had similar *kontor* outposts in
towns from Edinburgh to Bergen to Novgorod, providing a trans-
continental trade network. Hanse merchants were active in
Lynn from at least 1310 and possibly set up a steelyard in Lynn
in 1428.[10] Lynn's later fifteenth-century steelyard still stands,
located in St Margaret's Lane (which runs between Kempe's
church at St Margaret's and Lynn's port);[11] it is the only surviving Hanse building in England, although it dates from a couple
of decades after Kempe's time (illus. 3).

Lynn had particularly close relations with the Baltic port
of Gdańsk, relations that are described in *The Book of Margery
Kempe*. 'Dewch' (German-speaking) people of the Hanse,
sometimes known in Middle English as 'esterlings' (literally,
easterners), visited Lynn and settled there in the fourteenth
and fifteenth centuries. Kempe's eldest son, John junior, lived
in Gdańsk for many years, involved in Anglo-Baltic trade.[12] In
Kempe's own account, she meets an expatriate 'marchawnt of
Lynne' (a Lynn merchant; 2.286) by chance as she is negotiating

for a ferry in Gdańsk; this man uses his local knowledge to help her on her way. Kempe's husband's family had long been involved in trade with the Baltic ports, and John Kempe's father had been imprisoned in the Hanse port of Stralsund in 1389 in a trade dispute.[13] In the 1420s, Margery Kempe's mother or stepmother, 'Isabelle de Brunham', had a 'duchman Taylour' (a German tailor) as a tenant in one of her houses, attesting to the kinds of links that existed between Kempe's Lynn and the Hanse communities.[14] Many such Continental people intermarried and assimilated rapidly and Hanse merchants and artificers frequently appear in the late medieval Lynn records. For example, immigrants to Lynn included Deryk and Isabella Ducheman (their surname showing their origins), Clemens, Hans and Matthew Berebruer (the surname reflecting their occupation) and other 'esterlings' such as Geffard and Gysberd Hatmaker, William Vandepar and Henry Vantoter.[15] Relations between English traders and the Hanse were not always harmonious. For instance, in 1406 the sheriff of Norfolk made an inquisition on attacks at sea on English merchants by Hanse merchants of various Hanse towns including Gdańsk, Lübeck and Stralsund.[16] Around the same time a Hanse merchant, John Gyscowe, complained that merchandise from his ship, the *Mary Knyght* of Gdańsk, had been cast ashore in Norfolk after a pirate attack.[17] In 1432 at Lynn a group of local merchants – some of whom were related to Margery Kempe – had Henry VI intervene after the confiscation of their ship, the *George*, and its merchandise by the Hanse.[18]

   The Burnham family lived in the centre of Lynn, probably in a house on Briggate (now 115–116 High Street).[19] Most houses in Lynn built at this time were carefully designed to have commercial premises facing onto the street, with domestic rooms behind and, usually, warehousing to the rear.[20] The Burnham 'house' (at the northern end of the High Street, and now a

dentist's practice) would have been two or perhaps three sto-
reys high and would likely have combined warehouse and shop,
with its own bread oven and brewing facilities, and is about a
minute's walk from the door of St Margaret's Church.

John and Isabella Burnham had a number of children. In
addition to Margery there was a son, John, who was a Lynn
burgess and member of the town's Corpus Christi guild and the
guilds of St Giles and St Julian.[21] A kinsman, Robert Burnham,
probably Kempe's brother (or perhaps stepbrother), became very
wealthy as a Lynn vintner, merchant and shipowner, and also
served as MP for Lynn in 1402 and 1417 and alderman of the
Holy Trinity Guild in the late 1410s.[22] Neither this John nor
Robert Burnham (who had an especially turbulent public career)
is mentioned in *The Book of Margery Kempe*. Indeed, during the
second decade of the fifteenth century, the period impressionisti-
cally described in *The Book of Margery Kempe*, the Burnham and
Kempe families were well established in the town and its hinterland, although Margery Kempe barely mentions them.[23] This
context of bourgeois wealth and municipal influence in which
Margery Kempe grew up is presented in her *Book* as something
from which she sought but struggled to escape, her spirituality
and outspokenness sitting awkwardly with her elite, mercantile
and materialistic background.[24]

At about the age of twenty, around 1393/4, Margery married
John Kempe, the younger son of a Lynn skinner and merchant
(also called John; d. c. 1393). John Kempe had been admitted
to the Freedom of the town of Lynn in 1393 (giving him the
protection of the town's charter, and the right to trade and to
own land), and was a chamberlain of Lynn in 1394. He was
recorded as being involved in brewing around 1403–5.[25] John's
brother, Simon Kempe (d. c. 1409), seems to have been more

3 The Hanse *kontor* (built c. 1474) at King's Lynn.

successful, owning a large amount of property in central Lynn
and occupying a number of key roles in Lynn's government.[26]
John and Margery Kempe probably lived in Lynn's commercial
heart on Burghard's Lane (now New Conduit Street), in a ten-
ement owned by John Kempe;[27] it is just a few minutes' walk
from St Margaret's Church.

Shortly after her vision of Christ softly entering her bedchamber in around 1394, Kempe was seduced into materialistic
competition with her neighbours in Lynn. She describes how
even after Christ steadied her wits,

> sche wold not leevyn hir pride ne hir pompows aray that
> sche had usyd befortym, neithyr for hyr husbond
> ne for noon other mannys cownsel (1.191–2)

> she would not put aside either her pride or her pretentious
> costumes that she had been used to, neither for her hus-
> band not on any other person's advice.

She wore luxurious and extravagant outfits, with gold piping on
her headdress, hoods with tippets, and cloaks lined with many
colours, 'that it schuld be the mor staryng to mennys sygth and
hirself the mor ben worshepd' (so that it would be more striking to people's eyes and she herself should be more admired;
1.195–6).

Luxury clothes were thought of as prideful and inimical to
godliness. The fourteenth-century *Book of Vices and Virtues* contains strict injunctions about women's attire at church, aimed
at socially ambitious people like Kempe. It says women should
have 'honest clothinge' and 'not to moche', but qualifies this
by saying that finer attire is more suitable for a queen 'than to
a burgeies wif', that is, a burgess's wife, like Kempe. Women
should look 'simpliche', 'loweliche', 'meke and schamefaste';

they should not 'caste aboute here eien on every man' or 'atire here hevedes with gold and silver other perles and precious stones' (dress their heads with gold and silver or pearls and precious stones). Such luxury, worldly items ('smale goodes') are not 'true' goods (like grace, virtue and charity); the author of *The Book of Vices and Virtues* says that 'who-so hateth pride, he loveth poverté', a sentiment that resounds throughout Kempe's spiritual conversion.[28]

Kempe's prideful pursuit of ostentatious finery continues, even once she has started her journey towards godliness. As Kempe describes it,

> Sche had ful greet envye at hir neybowrs that thei schuld
> ben arayd so wel as sche. Alle hir desyr was for
> to be worshepd of the pepul (1.201–2).

> She was hugely envious of her neighbours, that they were
> dressed as stylishly as she. Her every desire was that she
> should be admired by the people.

Envy, the second Deadly Sin, is described in *The Book of Vices and Virtues* as 'the modre of deeth' (the mother of death), because the envious person delights in seeing harm done to others. It was because of envy and the pursuit of worldly glory that Kempe embarked on two business ventures, both of which would fail.

First, probably around 1403–5, she begins to brew. She has a few years of great success but then, despite her best attempts, the head on the beer keeps collapsing; her brewing business falls into such bad shape that no servants will work with her. After this failure, likely around 1407–8, she develops a horse-mill, grinding corn by using two horses to power the mill.[29] The horses, though otherwise healthy, resolutely refuse to pull at the mill. Kempe interprets the failure of these two businesses as divinely ordained, a sign that Christ is beckoning her from 'the pride and vanyté of the wretthyd world' (the pride and vanity of the wretched world; 1.236).

Kempe describes brewing and milling as 'huswyfré' (1.216), a term that translates as 'housewifely jobs', occupations particularly suitable for housewives. Milling was an urban service trade open to men and women, although it was not characterized as a stereotypically female occupation like spinning, laundering, embroidery or brewing.[30] Ale (made from malt, water and yeast) was a staple drink in England and commercial brewing was a frequent occupation for married women. Ale could not be transported easily and went sour quickly, so the brewing industry tended to be highly localized and, relying on household utensils and skills, lent itself to women's work.[31] The kind of English ale that Kempe would have brewed was weak, an essential part of the daily diet. Ale formed the basis of liquid refreshment at a time when water was rarely drunk (due to its impurity) and milk and wine were more luxurious products than they are today. But brewing, as Kempe suggests, was also a relatively high-status occupation for women and her early success would have brought Kempe money, recognition and contact with suppliers, clients and civic officials.

However, Kempe's business ventures also laid her open to insults and misogynistic slanders about the morality of alewives. Writing in East Anglia during Kempe's lifetime, John Lydgate (c. 1370–c. 1451), a monk of Bury St Edmunds (Suffolk) and the period's most voluminous poet, wrote a poem about a Cambridge alewife defined by her deception and her ability to lead men astray. She calls men to drink and, with her kisses, makes them pay for more than their beer: 'Thus with your ale, and with your cheer so slye,/ Ye them disseyve [deceive], that in yow moste affye [trust].'[32] This alewife uses ale to 'disseyve', luring 'trusting men' into her trap. Lydgate's poem exemplifies the bind in which Kempe, as a woman with a degree of independence and ambition, found herself. As she would discover time and again, to assert herself as a woman could as easily bring ridicule as it could bring acclaim. Indeed, in the roof of the nave of Norwich Cathedral Kempe might have glimpsed the remarkable boss depicting the triumph of a fraudulent alewife (illus. 4). It shows the Devil pushing a soul in a wheelbarrow as the naked alewife holds a flagon of ale, riding joyously, drunkenly, on the Devil's shoulders.[33]

Kempe's life develops in this urban context, riven with political and social competition, but also a place of material comfort, a godly, goodly, well-connected town. Kempe has a degree of independence, but she is also defined by the men

4 The triumphant alewife rides the Devil, who pushes a soul in a wheelbarrow. Roof boss sculpture, Norwich Cathedral, late 15th century.

5 Trinity Guildhall, King's Lynn. In the foreground is the
commemorative bench to Margery Kempe (installed 2018).

6 St Margaret's Church, now Lynn Minster, King's Lynn.

around her; she feels herself to be connected to an elite, but it
is a precarious status. Opportunity and mutability go hand in
hand, slander and disparagement come in many forms. Kempe's
key challenge is to negotiate sacred *and* worldly categories of
judgement and esteem in order to establish a lasting reputation,
on earth and in heaven.

At Lynn's centre are two institutions that dominated Kempe's
experience of the town and provided the stage for key moments
in her self-transformation: St Margaret's Church (now King's
Lynn Minster; illus. 6), and the Trinity Guildhall (illus. 5). St
Margaret's, close to the oldest part of the river port and adjacent to where Kempe's family lived and worked, functioned in
Kempe's time both as a priory (a cell of Norwich Cathedral) and

as a parish church for the whole borough of Lynn.[34] Just outside St Margaret's Church, the Trinity Guildhall, the meeting place of the town's influential Holy Trinity Guild, with its dazzling frontage chequered in flint and stone, was rebuilt in the 1420s after a fire that is described in *The Book of Margery Kempe*. Both buildings are spaces in which God is reported as having wrought miracles for Kempe.

Kempe's earliest experiences of divine communication were her vision of Christ as she lay fettered in her bedchamber and then an experience of heavenly melody as she 'lay in hir bedde' (1.241) with her husband. These took place in domestic interiors. Early in her spiritual conversion, Kempe took a coarse cloth, a 'hayr', from her brewing days (1.277–8) to wear beside her skin, renouncing entrepreneurialism in favour of intimate self-mortification. From these highly personal moments, Kempe's religious journey works centrifugally, starting in the bedchamber and home, moving outwards to her church and the town of Lynn, and eventually finding its expression in far-flung sites of Christendom. Early on in her account of temptations and self-reform, the *Book*'s first three key moral examples all happen at St Margaret's Church.[35] First, Kempe is tempted at evensong at the church one year on the eve of St Margaret's Day (19 July), by a handsome neighbour with whom she decides to have sex. Second, on a Friday just before Christmas, possibly later the same year, Kempe is 'ravysched [in] hir spyryt' (1.368) by Christ in the church, receiving a commandment from Him to desist from eating meat. Third, it is in St Margaret's Church that Kempe receives her first 'miracle', when, on the Friday before Whitsun (the date seems to be 9 June 1413), a stone and a beam collapse from the church's roof, hitting Kempe, who miraculously emerges unscathed.

These three incidents are described in quick succession, and are structured around the devotional calendar: St Margaret's

Day (celebrating the dedicatee of Kempe's church and Kempe's namesake, St Margaret of Antioch), Christmas (celebrating Christ's birth) and Whitsun (commemorating Pentecost, when the Holy Spirit descended upon Christ's disciples). A history of salvation is repeated for Kempe as her parish church becomes the stage for her trials and conversion.

The scene of sexual temptation on the eve of St Margaret's Day is introduced as a 'snar of letchery' (snare of lechery; 1.314–15) set by the Devil, to test Kempe's movement towards God. Despite going frequently to confession, wearing the hair-cloth beside her skin, and renouncing marital sex, Kempe remains open to temptation, and at church no less. A man 'whech sche lovyd wel' tells her that 'he wold ly be hir and have hys lust of hys body, and sche schuld not wythstond hym' (he would do anything to sleep with her and indulge his bodily lusts, and she should not resist him; 1.322–4). The *Book* says that 'he dede it for to preve hir what sche wold do, but sche wend that he had ment ful ernest as that tyme and seyd but lytyl therto' (he did this to test her, to see what she would do, but she believed that he had meant it in earnest and she said very little about it to him; 1.325–7). Far from a seduction, this is an aggressive test – 'he dede it for to preve hir'. Kempe's unnamed suitor relies on Kempe's inability to 'wythstond' him and, like many literary seductions, this is a transaction of power, powerlessness and shame. Lechery was often perceived as a specifically female vice and is depicted as a woman, riding a ram, a symbol of virility, and with a chained lock on her wrist, in an East Anglian manuscript of circa 1420 (see illus. 7).

Following the man's declaration of desire for Kempe, both go to hear evensong (the evening prayers), and Kempe finds herself entirely occupied with the man's words, so much so that she cannot say her Paternoster. This is an important detail because lechery in church or in holy places was considered a kind of sacrilege.[36] Kempe finds herself led by the man's words, and she tells him that he can indulge his lust with her. Then her troubles really start:

> This creatur was so labowrd and vexyd al that nygth that sche wyst nevyr what sche mygth do. Sche lay be hir husbond, and for to comown wyth hym it was so abhomynabyl onto hir that sche mygth not duren it, and yet was it leful onto hir in leful tyme yf sche had wold. But evyr sche was labowrd wyth the other man for to syn wyth hym inasmech as he had spoke to hir. At the last thorw inoportunyté of temptacyon and lakkyng of dyscrecyon sche was ovyrcomyn, and consentyd in hir mend, and went to the man to wetyn yf he wold than consentyn to hire. And he seyd he ne wold for al the good in this world; he had levar ben hewyn as smal as flesch to the pott (1.337–44).

> This creature was so troubled and vexed all that night that she had no idea what she might do. She lay beside her husband, and to have sexual contact with him was so abominable to her that she could not endure it, even though it was a permitted time and permitted for her to do it if she had wanted. But all the time she was troubled by the other man, to sin with him in the way in which he had said to her. In the end, through the importunity of temptation and a lack of discretion, she was overcome, and consented in her mind, and she went to the man to know if he would then consent to take her. But he said that he would not for all the wealth in this world; he would rather be hacked as small as meat for the pot!

7 'Lecherye' alongside 'Chastite', as women, *Canterbury Tales* (c. 1420), Cambridge University Library.

attemparuce that holdeth the meene in alle thyngis.
& schame that escheweth al disoneste. & suffraunce that
sekith no ryche metis ne drenkys ne doth nofors of to
outragious apparaylyge of mete. mesure also that res
streynyth by reson the dissaue spirit of etynge. Sobir
nesse also that restreynyth the outrage of drynk. Spa
rynge also that restreynyth the desiat man. as is to
sitte longe at his mete & softely wherfore some folk sto
dyn of here owene wil to ety at the lasse sepser.

Sequitur de peccato luxurie.

lecherye   chastite

Aftyr glotonye cowyth lecherye
for these two synys been so nygh
cosynys that ofte tyme thei be
le not departe god wot. This sy
ne is ful displesaunt thyng to god
for he seyde by self & no lech
rye and therfor he mitte grete
peynys ageyn this synne in the olde sawe. & if woman
that weren takyn in this synne sche schulde been beth
wt stonys to the deth. and if sche were a gentil
woman sche schulde be slayn wt stonys. and if sche we

This is a unique description of a medieval woman's internal desire, sexual temptation, marital disharmony and her processes of reaching a decision. Kempe describes that hinterland between masturbatory desire – she is lying in bed, contemplating sex with the other man – and the sex available to her as a married woman. Her comment that it was a permissible time for her to have sex (with her husband) reflects the church's requirement that Christians abstain from sex at certain times, such as major feast days and during menstruation and pregnancy. Kempe *can* have sex with her husband, but does not wish to do so. What eventuates is a devastating moment of rejection and humiliation; Kempe has consented in her mind to have sex with the other man, she has revealed her desires to him and rejected her husband in his favour. Then she is thoroughly and violently spurned. The confrontation here is between Kempe's (private) guilty desires and her (social) sense of shame, a collision between the intimate and the public that would cause problems for Kempe throughout her life.

The setting of this scene of sexual humiliation, in church, foregrounds how Kempe fails to live up to the standards set by her patron saint. St Margaret, said to have been martyred in Antioch in 304 CE, was one of the most popular saints in later medieval England. Her *vita* describes her as a remarkably beautiful virgin who is cruelly and violently tested by a spiteful, sadistic provost. St Margaret defends herself by stating 'that she was noble of kynne and of Cristen religion'.[37] Later, when imprisoned, Margaret is visited by the Devil who 'transfigured hym in forme of a man for to deceive her';[38] but St Margaret, unlike Margery Kempe, is able to withstand and overthrow the Devil and, before being beheaded, is able to convert thousands to believe in Christ. The St Margaret's eve temptation story shows us how Kempe is still far from emulating the sanctity and steadfastness of a role model like St Margaret.

Kempe's reaction is thoroughly and memorably abject: 'Sche went away al schamyd and confusyd in hirself, seyng hys stabylnes and hir owyn unstabylnes' (seeing his steadiness and her own unsteadiness; 1.344–5). Kempe's fleshly desires, combined with her own sense of inconstancy, catch up with her not in her bedchamber but in church, at evensong, as her spiritual conversion is tested within her community in Lynn.

Just before Christmas, perhaps later in the same year following the July temptation, Kempe receives a very different masculine encounter, and a spiritual breakthrough, in the church.[39] This occurs in a side chapel, the now-vanished Chapel of St John the Baptist. This chapel was used by Lynn's Guild of Young Clerks so Kempe may be representing herself as a childlike recipient of divine knowledge, or the recipient of a new baptism. As this scene takes place in the season of Christ's nativity, Kempe may also have sought to evoke the imagery of new life. Advent and Christmas were considered to be a time for humility, penance and the forgiveness of sins. As Christ's Nativity was moralized, it was in Bethlehem that God showed mankind 'humilité . . . in his incarnacion', through which 'the stynk of oure pride shulde be heled', a sentiment that resounds throughout Kempe's pre-Christmas encounter, as her own earlier pride is healed.[40]

Kempe is described as kneeling in the chapel, weeping 'wondir sore' (astonishingly bitterly; 1.366), and asking 'mercy' and 'forgyfnes' for her sins (1.367), when she is suddenly 'ravysched' (1.368) in her spirit by Christ. This encounter is a reversal of the earlier sexual test; this time, Kempe is willingly and graciously 'ravished' in a dazzlingly sensual encounter with her living God. Kempe's Christ asks her why she is weeping so bitterly, and assures her that, in the twinkling of an eye, she shall go straight to Heaven, and grants her contrition (complete repentance for her sins) until her life's end. He then says: 'Therfor I bydde the and comawnd the, boldly clepe [call] me Jhesus, thi love, for I

am thi love and schal be thi love wythowtyn ende' (1.374–6).
This loving, human Jesus tells Kempe to put aside her hair-shirt
and stop eating meat. He assures her that, even though she will
be 'knawyn of the pepul' (gnawed at by the people; 1.383), she is
assured victory over her enemies and that He, Jesus, shall never
forsake her. It is a full and loving endorsement of Kempe. Finally,
Jesus commands Kempe to go to a recluse, an anchorite, at the
Dominican priory. This anchorite becomes Kempe's first key
confessor, and reappears at several points not only as confessor
but as friend, prophet and a fervent believer in Kempe and her
visions.[41] The Christmas scene in St Margaret's rewards Kempe's
penitential weeping and offers a morally positive version of her
'ravishment', reversing the shameful and violent humiliation
that took place there before.

A third key scene at St Margaret's is one of Kempe's first
miracles, which occurred 'on a Fryday befor Whytson Evyn'
(Whitsun Eve) as Kempe is 'heryng hir messe' (1.480).
Whitsuntide (Pentecost) commemorates the descent of the
Holy Spirit to Christ's disciples, when 'the holy goste was this
day sent to the Aposteles in tongges of fire'.[42] It therefore mirrors
Kempe's own reception of Christ as a fire of love. In the Middle
Ages, Whitsun was marked by a week's holiday and the wearing
of white garments by the newly baptized. It is an especially aus-
picious moment for a miracle because it was at Pentecost that
the Holy Spirit was made manifest; 'the sending of the holi goste
visibly is whanne he is shewed by sum token visible',[43] and the
miracle received by Kempe at this time is precisely such a *visible*,
public token.

One Friday, in St Margaret's Church, she hears a 'gret' and
'dredful' 'noyse' (1.481). Public opinion has made her dread
that God will take vengeance upon her, and she thinks this is
it. She kneels, holding her book in her hand, bows her head,
and prays to Jesus for mercy.

Sodeynly fel down fro the heyest party of the cherch
vowte fro undyr the fote of the sparre on hir hed and on
hir bakke a ston whech weyd three pownd and a schort
ende of a tre weyng six pownd that hir thowt hir bakke
brakke asundyr, and sche ferd as sche had be deed a lytyl
whyle. Soone aftyr sche cryed, 'Jhesu mercy', and anoon
hir peyn was gon (1.485–9).

Suddenly, from the highest part of the church's vaulted
ceiling, from under the base of a rafter, a stone weighing three pounds fell down onto her head and her back,
and a short end of a wooden beam weighing six pounds,
so she thought her back was broken into pieces, and
she was afraid that she would be dead in a little while.
Quickly she then cried, 'Jesus, mercy!' and at once her
pain was gone.

The miracle boldly asserts Kempe's divine protection and reception of God's grace. It is also a solid, inelegant version of the
tokens – the dove, the cloud, the flame – in which the Holy
Spirit appeared at Pentecost. The detail that Kempe was holding a book in her hand – probably a psalter or a prayer book,
like a book of hours or missal – suggests that the Christian book
is a protective talisman for her, and echoes Christ's disciples'
reception of God's word at Pentecost. Likewise, calling out the
name of Jesus ('Jhesu mercy') functions as a physical remedy,
a vocative easing of pain, reflecting late medieval devotion to
the Holy Name.

Here, Kempe's spirituality goes public: the inner world of
domestic torment during and after pregnancy is repudiated in
the painless miracle. More importantly, the marvel is witnessed
by a well-off local man, 'a good man' (1.489), John of Wereham,
a Lynn guildsman and a local mercer (a dealer in textiles).[44]

Immediately following the miracle of the falling beam, the spirit of God says to Kempe's soul:

Helde this for a gret myracle, and, yyf the pepyl wyl not levyn this, I schal werkyn meche mor (1.494–5).

Take this for a great miracle, and if the people will not believe in this, I shall work many more.

So after being visited by an intimate grace in her bedchamber, Kempe proves herself at St Margaret's, culminating in a public miracle. Her spiritual development follows the year's liturgical festivals, mapping her individual life onto cosmological Christian time, as she represents herself as an exemplary and specially favoured parishioner.[45] Her church is a place in which she can no longer be hurt and in which she will forge and prove herself.

THREE

Places

After Lynn, the city of Norwich is the place most frequently evoked and described in *The Book of Margery Kempe*. It is some 66 km (41 mi.) east of Lynn and was one of England's largest cities, and the region's main centre.[1] Kempe's church, the Benedictine priory of St Margaret's at Lynn, was a dependent priory of Norwich's magnificent Benedictine cathedral and the two institutions were very much intertwined, although their relationship was frequently fractious. The Bishop of Norwich was Kempe's local bishop (and is the bishop to whom the place name Bishop's Lynn refers), although Kempe does not mention Bishop Despenser (appointed 1370–1406), with whom her father had been in conflict,[2] Bishop Tottington (1407–13) or Bishop Courtenay (1413–15), and only fleetingly mentions Bishop Alnwick (1426–36; 1.1360), all of whom were active during her lifetime. The bishops of Norwich were the overlords of Lynn (and thus local courts belonged to the bishopric), and Kempe describes the occasion on which Bishop John Wakering (d. 1425, appointed 1416–25) came to preach in St Margaret's and bore Kempe's crying with patience (1.3965–6).

Norwich itself was a place of great 'religious energy and creativity', influenced especially by Flemish and northern German religious cultures.[3] The city had numerous anchorites and charismatic preachers and was a well-known centre for 'Lollard' heresy, the proto-Protestant reformist movement inspired by the theology of John Wycliffe (d. 1384). Kempe's familiarity with Norwich's religious culture has been evinced from her description of the Despenser Retable, an altarpiece (*c.* 1382) from Norwich Cathedral. One of Kempe's Passion meditations describes how she saw Christ 'bowndyn to a peler . . . hys handys wer bowndyn abovyn hys heved (head)' (1.4526–7);[4] this unusual pose also occurs in the Retable. Kempe very likely saw this particular artefact, and it was certainly in the right place at the right time for her to have done so. Other than making an offering there on her way to Jerusalem (1.1393), Kempe says little about Norwich's cathedral priory itself. She had been investigated by

8 St Stephen's Church, Norwich.

'certeyn offercerys' (1.920) of the bishop in 1412–13, and this may well have caused her to keep her distance.

Early in her spiritual conversion, Kempe received a commandment from God to visit St Stephen's Church at Norwich where she met the vicar, Richard Caister (d. 1420). Caister had been a vicar near Lynn and later moved to Norwich.[5] He was a noted preacher and Kempe had been stirred to go to him in Norwich, first around 1412–13 (1.868), when she was still having children and clad in black, and then again in 1415 (1.2406). At their first meeting Kempe 'schewyd' Caister 'all the wordys' (1.879) that God had revealed to her soul, describing her meditative experiences focused on Christ's Passion. She tells Caister how some people 'slawndryd hir', believing her vexed by illness or an evil spirit (1.1909–10). Nonetheless, Caister acts as Kempe's confessor at Norwich and supports her against her critics (1.913).

Richard Caister was a significant presence in Kempe's religious development. Kempe describes her return to Norwich's St Stephen's Church (illus. 8) in the summer of 1420, following Caister's death on 29 March of that year. The church is situated on Rampant Horse Street where, in the 1420s, the horse market met: a busy, bustling space, a public but also spiritual arena in a vibrant, highly urban environment. When Caister died (as foretold by Kempe; 1.924) he proved to be a holy man (also predicted by Kempe; 1.912), leaving his money to Norwich's poor, saying that 'the goods of the church, according to canon law, belong to the poor'.[6] Caister was locally regarded as a saint and a cult developed around his church at St Stephen's, with local people leaving legacies to the church because of Caister's sanctity.[7] A fourteenth-century alloy pilgrim's badge (illus. 9) shows Caister preaching from a pulpit, a dove (the Holy Spirit) by his head, surrounded by a border aflame with the words 'soli Deo honor et gloria' (glory and honour to God alone; 1 Timothy 1:17). God's

9 Lead alloy
pilgrim's badge of
Richard Caister,
c. 1420, Museum
of London.

hands reach out of the badge's top frame, showing His palms
in judgement. Kempe may very well have bought such a badge.

Kempe luridly describes how at St Stephen's churchyard 'sche
cryed, sche roryd, sche wept, sche fel down to the grownd, so fervently the fyer of lofe brent in hir hert' (the fire of love burned
in her heart; 1.3475–6). For Kempe, bursting into tears involved
voice, speech and the entire body. Kempe often fell or lay down to
pray, similar to her description of how the Virgin Mary 'fel down'
at Christ's feet, swooning in grief.[8] Kempe's falling down is also a
moment of prostration, bowing before the presence of God, and
conforms to one recommended manner, prostrate and weeping, of
entering a church. Christian asceticism particularly valued prostration as it placed pressure on the lungs and the stomach, in order
better to induce gut-wrenching crying.[9]

After falling down in the churchyard, Kempe gets up and 'went forth wepyng into the chirche to the hy awter [high altar], and ther sche fel down with boistows sobbyngys, wepyngys, and lowde cryes besyden the grave of the good vicary' (the good vicar, Richard Caister; 1.3471–2). Kempe's violent crying is not static but engages with the site, starting in the churchyard and 'ascending' to the high altar. For Kempe, tearfulness is a way of moving through, and claiming, space. Kempe's devotions do not occur in isolation, but are socially observed:

> the pepil had gret merveyl of hir, supposyng that sche had wept for sum fleschly er erdly affeccyon, and seyd unto hir, 'What eylith the, woman? Why faryst thus wyth thiself? We knew hym as wel as thu.' (1.3485–8)

> therefore the people were greatly astonished at her, supposing that she wept out of some physical or earthly affection, and said to her, 'What's wrong with you, woman? Why are you conducting yourself like this? We knew him as well as you did.'

This is not a moment of private withdrawal, but profoundly public, and Kempe's crying often becomes meaningful when other people see it. The people suppose that she has wept for a physical affection; to them, Kempe's tears are a ridiculous sham, a kind of malady, and suggest her misunderstanding of her relationship with Caister. The bystander's question – 'What eylith thee, woman?' – signals the gap between Kempe's own crying and the view of those around her. This is symptomatic of the charge of insincerity which repeatedly attends Kempe's crying and that of other holy weepers.[10] Is Kempe moved by God or the Devil?

Despite this uncomprehending reaction to her, Kempe's Norwich is a place of friendly supporters and trusted confessors.

At Norwich, Kempe visits William Southfield (d. 1414), a Carmelite friar and native of the city. On the same trip, she enjoys 'holy dalyawns' (1.958) with the anchoress Julian of Norwich (1342–c. 1416) in her cell in the city. Later, Kempe passes through Norwich to make an offering at the cathedral. It was at Norwich that an unnamed 'good man' pays for Kempe's controversial white clothes to be made and, one Saturday evening, presents her with them (1.2449) and where, in May 1415, she receives communion in white (1.2453). Much later, in the early 1430s, Kempe visits Norwich, as she sought permission to make a difficult journey to Prussia (2.168). In Anthony Goodman's words, Norwich seems to have been the place where Kempe was most 'comfortable'.[11] The city was central to Kempe's religious topography, it provided a congenial space for religious expression and, for Kempe, was a place to which she repeatedly returned for recognition. It is then fitting that the unique surviving manuscript of *The Book of Margery Kempe* was copied by one Richard Salthouse (d. before 1487), a monk at the Benedictine cathedral priory at Norwich.[12] Thus it was in Norwich that Kempe's life was preserved and communicated.

'Lambhyth': Lambeth

London, England's capital, does not feature prominently in Kempe's *Book*, although she seems to have spent several significant periods there, including perhaps almost a year in 1433–4. London in the early fifteenth century was a rapidly growing city of about 50,000 people, by far the largest city in England; Westminster, a short distance west of the medieval city walls of London, was the seat of national government.[13] For Kempe, London and its environs were an important staging post in her quest for validation. Two important incidents in the vicinity of London bookend Kempe's story. Early in her spiritual development she is violently traduced at Lambeth Palace, a humiliating incident and an important fulcrum in her conversion narrative. Much later in life, she is the subject of spiteful gossip at an embarrassing dinner in the city.

Around 1411–12 Kempe had conceived a desire to see the places of Christ's life and death, and Christ had put into her mind that she should visit Rome, Jerusalem and Santiago de Compostela, the three 'great pilgrimages' for European Christians. At the same time, she was divinely instructed to wear the white clothes that caused much controversy. In the first half of 1413, Kempe visited the Bishop of Lincoln, Philip Repingdon (c. 1345–1424), in order to make a vow of chastity and gain permission to undertake an international pilgrimage. Her pilgrimage is framed by her desire to become a vowess (a chaste bride of Christ) and to wear white. Bishop Repingdon tells Kempe that he cannot accept her profession of celibacy 'in so synguler a clothyng' without further consideration (1.798–9). Repingdon is cautious; he had himself, until he recanted in 1382, been a Wycliffite, and at the time of Kempe's visit was actively developing an anti-heresy policy that moved from the reactive to the proactive investigation of those suspected of heresy.[14] Giving her a gift of 26 shillings and 8 pence to buy clothes (1.816–17), Repingdon sends Kempe and her husband to his superior, the Archbishop of Canterbury, Thomas Arundel (1353–1414), at his palace at Lambeth near London.

The Kempes duly make their way to Lambeth. Even at this relatively early stage in her journey towards public pious authority, Margery Kempe enters Lambeth Palace with great confidence. She reproves the people there for swearing (especially swearing on Christ or God), something she found shockingly offensive throughout her life.[15] Kempe chastises them, telling them that they will be damned for such conduct. This causes one of them to attack back:

And wyth that cam forth a woman of the same town in
a pylche and al forschod this creatur, bannyd hir, and
seyd ful cursydly to hir in this maner, 'I wold thu wer in
Smythfeld, and I wold beryn a fagot to bren the wyth; it is
pety that thow levyst' (1.823–6).

With that a local woman came forward who was dressed
in a pelisse and who utterly loathed this creature, cursed
her, and said most horribly to her, 'I wish you were at
Smithfield, and I would carry a faggot to burn you with;
it's a pity that you're alive.'

This reaction comes from a 'local woman' dressed in a
'pylche' (a fur gown), a detail that suggests that Kempe had
not put aside her competitive eye for others' finery. The social
competition, particularly with other women, started at Lynn,
continues to dog Kempe.

Kempe stands still and does not answer the woman, and the
Book notes how her husband 'suffred with gret peyn and was ful
sory to heryn hys wyfe so rebukyd' (1.826–7). The archbishop
asks Kempe to join him in his garden, away from the hostile
crowd.

The hall in which Kempe had this humiliating reception was
destroyed in the seventeenth century, but the gardens in which
Kempe walked with the archbishop partly survive (illus. 10), a
beautiful open space, with views across the river to Westminster,
the seat of royal power and government.[16] Archbishop Arundel
himself is scarcely described by Kempe. In her account, he comes
across as a rather bland, unquestioning supporter. This is at odds
with what is known of Arundel historically, an adept politician,
a volatile churchman, and an energetic, dogged persecutor of
heretics. During his period as archbishop, Arundel struggled
to keep religious expression within the bounds of doctrinal

10 The view from Lambeth Palace across the River Thames
to Westminster.

and social orthodoxy. In 1407 Arundel had drafted a set of
'constitutions', decrees against 'Lollard' heretics which were
promulgated in 1409. Arundel's constitutions were designed to
suppress the Wycliffite movement through regulating preaching and the prohibition of translation of the Bible into English.
The constitutions themselves stipulated that there could be no
preaching without a licence; that there would be severe penalties
for preaching about the Eucharist against the orthodox teaching;
that only preachers with a university degree could instruct children in the sacraments; that any book by the theologian John
Wycliffe be examined before it could be read; that translation of
the Bible into English be forbidden; and that a monthly inquisition would take place at the University of Oxford into what
scholars were teaching (an inquisition that came to pass under
Arundel's own energies).[17]

The hostile woman at Lambeth threatens Kempe with burning at Smithfield, which was, and remains, London's meat
market. Beside the meat market was the area known as The

Elms, where, since the twelfth century the capital punishment
of heretics, criminals and dissidents was carried out. The first
such heretic burned to death was William Sawtry (alias Chatrys/
Chatteris), burned at Smithfield in March 1401. Not only had
Sawtry been tried and condemned by Archbishop Arundel, but
he was from Lynn and would have been known to Kempe, for
in the late 1390s he had been parish priest at her church in
Lynn, St Margaret's. In 1399 Sawtry was tried for heresy at Lynn
and at the Suffolk village of South Elmham (the country resi-
dence of the Bishops of Norwich); on this occasion, Sawtry was
persuaded by Henry Despenser, Bishop of Norwich, to abjure.
Subsequently, Sawtry became rector of St Benet Sherehog in the
centre of London. In 1400 and 1401 Sawtry was tried again, and
was evidently a troublesome and unrepentant figure who refused
to go into hiding and, adopting a powerful mode of resistance to
inquisition, maintained a cheerful disposition throughout the
proceedings.[18] According to Archbishop Arundel's register of
the trial, Sawtry had declared several 'Lollard' positions, including that he worshipped Christ's suffering rather than the wooden
cross on which Christ suffered; that one should distribute alms
to the poor rather than to go on pilgrimages to the saints' tombs;
and that the bread in the sacrament of the mass remains bread,
rather than transubstantiating into Christ's body.[19]

   Contrary to popular misconceptions of the barbarous Middle
Ages, punishment by burning was unusual at this time. Even
as it could be used as a punishment for arson or petty treason,
death by fire was very rarely carried out. In 1401, in the wake
of Sawtry's burning, the royal statute *De heretico comburendo*
(On Burning a Heretic) was presented to Parliament, instituting
burning as an appropriate punishment for heretics. This came
about only eighteen months into Henry IV's fragile reign, and
characterizes the emerging climate of surveillance and punishment under the Lancastrian monarchy.

Sawtry was burned at the stake at The Elms in March 1401. Kempe's vicious reception at Lambeth was some twelve or thirteen years later, but Archbishop Arundel, who had overseen Sawtry's execution, remained the incumbent at Lambeth and the threat of death by burning recurs throughout *The Book of Margery Kempe*. At Canterbury, people follow Kempe out of the cathedral shouting:

> Thow schalt be brent, fals lollare. Her is a cartful of thornys redy for the and a tonne to bren the wyth (1.649–50).

> You shall be burned, false Lollard! Here's a cartful of thorns ready for you, and a barrel to burn you with!

At Canterbury, as at Lambeth, the insult 'Lollard' is seamlessly connected with the vocabulary of death by fire and strangers' willingness to commit Kempe to flames. At Cawood, in the Archbishop of York's palace, men call for her to be burned (1.2915). At Hessle, women run out of their houses crying 'Brennyth this fals heretyk' (burn this false heretic; 1.3055). In the Chapter House at Beverley, a hostile Dominican friar tells the Archbishop of York that Kempe was nearly burned at Lynn, saved only on account of his orders (1.3114). In the same difficult interview, Kempe is told that she 'hast seyd inow to be brent for' (1.3151), that she's said enough to be get herself burned to death. She is told that if she returns, the archbishop's men will burn her themselves (1.3167). The imagery and violent present-tense threat of burning runs throughout *The Book of Margery Kempe*, complementing, and contrasting with, the pious 'fire of love' aflame in Kempe's heart.

Despite her hostile reception at Lambeth, Kempe found favour in Archbishop Arundel's eyes, himself an enthusiastic supporter of the 'mixed life'. In 1411 the Carthusian Nicholas Love (d. c. 1424) had presented to Arundel his *Mirrour of the Blessed Life of Jesu Christ*, a work which heavily influenced Kempe's manner of biblical visions-cum-conversations in her 'mind's eye'. Love's *Mirrour* also recommended Hilton's 'Epistle on the Mixed Life'. Arundel licensed the *Mirrour* 'for the edification of the people and for the confutation of heretics or 'Lollards'.[20] Arundel's ideas are reflected at various points in *The Book of Margery Kempe*, including Kempe's insistence on the difference between preaching and teaching (1.2976), her highly personal yet consistently orthodox interpretations of religion, her love of the saints, and her emphasis on, and respect for, local anchorites, vicars and confessors who show 'diligence in prechyng & techyng' with 'no defawte' (1.1212). In February 1414, within a year of Kempe's interview at Lambeth, Arundel died; however, his decrees had a profound effect on the subsequent generation, fostering a religious climate of doctrinal suspicion and a cultural mood of nervous conformity.[21]

'Constawns': Constance

According to John Mirk's guide for parish priests, husbands and wives were not to make vows either of chastity or pilgrimage without each other's consent.[22] For much of the period around 1412–13 Kempe tried to convince her husband to allow her to do both. John Kempe assents to the vow of chastity in Lincoln, in front of Bishop Repingdon, saying:

> 'Ya, my Lord . . . and in tokyn that we bothen vowyn to leve chast her I offyr myn handys into yowyr,' and he put hys handys betwen the Bysshoppys handys (1.781–3).

> 'Yes, my Lord . . . and as a token that we both vow to live in chastity, I hereby offer my hands into yours.' And he put his hands between the Bishop's hands.

At this interview Kempe also announces her imminent departure for Jerusalem (1.799) and, according to Mirk, the only vow that could be made without the spouse's consent was 'the vow to Iherusalem', to undertake this pilgrimage.[23] Part of the 26s 8d received from Bishop Repingdon 'to prey for hym' may well have been used for Kempe's sacred voyage, as she would have offered prayers for others at Jerusalem.

Kempe leaves England in late 1413, sailing from Yarmouth to the Flemish port of Zierikzee. Travelling south towards Venice, Kempe reaches the southern German town of Constance (Konstanz), on the shores of the Bodensee. Constance was an established pilgrims' way station at the head of the Brenner Pass, the most popular way for northern European pilgrims to Italy and thence to the Holy Land. Kempe offers almost no description of Constance but memorably evokes the friction she experienced with her companions. Near Constance she is bullied by the other pilgrims, who cut her gown short to the knees and force her to wear a sacklike 'whyte canwas' (white canvas) so she looks a 'fool' (1.1429–32);[24] they make her sit at the end of their table when dining, refusing to speak to her.

During Kempe's visit to Constance, preparations were being made for the Council of Constance, an international ecumenical meeting which officially opened on 5 November 1414, and turned out to be hugely significant. Christendom in the west was deeply fractured, with popes sitting in both Rome (Gregory XII) and Avignon (Benedict XIII), as well as a third 'antipope' in Pisa (John XXIII). In England and Bohemia the Wycliffite and Hussite heresies had proved popular and enduring, and the English church was under great pressure to show its orthodoxy at Constance. The Council comprised 'all Christendom' (Christians who confessed to the Pope), divided into five *naciones* (national territories): Lombards, Germans, French, Spanish and English. The English were defined by the Council as encompassing Scotland, Arabia,

Persia, India ('ruled by Prester John'), Ethiopia ('where the Moors live'), Egypt, Nineveh and Christians living in these territories.[25] At the time Kempe was there, Constance was, by all accounts, full of some of the most important churchmen in England, as glimpsed in Kempe's encounter with a certain English friar, 'a maystyr of divinité and the Popys legat' (1.1446), who heard Kempe's confession, endorsed her visions and defended her at dinner against her companions. The identity of this 'worshepful legat and doctowr' (1.1463) is not known but he is likely to have been part of the large English delegation for the gathering Council.[26]

Dignity, erudition, subtlety, statecraft and spite were afoot in the small town. The contemporary German chronicle of Ulrich Richental provides a captivating report, with remarkable illustrations, of the Council. Richental vividly describes the churchmen coming from all over Europe, from Riga to Rhodes, the bakers who set up little ovens in the city 'in which they baked pasties, rings, and pretzels', the provisioning of huge quantities of game and fish (a pound of badger, otter or beaver meat cost 8d, a pound of pike 17d), and the regulation of the visitors' lodgings (bedsheets were to be changed every fourteen days).[27] The splendid manuscript containing Richental's chronicles (New York, New York Public Library Spencer MS 32) shows vibrant portraits of the Council alongside city scenes of Constance in the year Kempe visited.

The Bohemian reformist Jan Hus lodged in the Dominican convent on one side of the town, only a few minutes' walk away from where the Pope and his court lodged. The main Wycliffite and Hussite heresies were condemned by the Council in May 1415 (long after Kempe had left town) and Hus was burned in Constance on 6 July 1415. Richental describes how a thousand soldiers led Hus out of the town. Hus fell to his knees three times and prayed. When offered the chance to confess and recant, he instead began to preach in German.[28] Richental's manuscript includes a grimly expressive illustration showing Hus's burning at the stake (illus. 11). On the left, Hus undergoes a kind of *passio* – a Christlike or saintly martyrdom – as reflected in his beatific expression as he burns. On the right, his ashes are thrown into the Rhine, but the blank half of the page expresses the hope of Hus's elimination. Hus's execution/martyrdom rapidly led to a cult growing up in his memory and Richental's image eloquently shows the violent tensions at the heart of western, 'Latin' Christendom at this moment.

Kempe's favourite saint, Bridget of Sweden was also closely scrutinized at Constance. Bridget's visions had, since before her death in 1373, been assembled into a written corpus, designed to support her canonization. This was led by Bridget's friend and supporter Alfonso of Jaén (d. 1389), who applied his own method of *discretio* to Bridget's visions.[29] At Constance, 'growing

11 Jan Hus is burned at the stake on 6 July 1415, and his ashes are cast into the Rhine. From Ulrich Richental, *Chronicles* (c. 1460), New York Public Library.

churchwide concern over the authenticity of holy women's revelations came to a head'.[30] During the considerations of Bridget
of Sweden's sanctity, many churchmen cautioned against
believing in the holiness of 'exceptional' women. Richental
describes how on Candlemas 1415 (2 February), the Feast of
the Virgin's Purification, scholars from Scandinavia submitted
to the Council Bridget's miracles and revelations, requesting
that she be exalted and canonized as a saint. Nine doctors came
forward and confirmed Bridget's miracles and she was sainted.
A Danish archbishop celebrated Mass with a figure of Bridget,
'like a doll', set on the altar. This was followed by a Candlemas
ritual in which the Pope went to a balcony and threw candles
down into the crowd.[31] Bridget's affirmation at Constance took
place at the time that Kempe was travelling in the Holy Land
and in Italy, but it was a loud endorsement for Kempe's role
model, and for Birgittine spirituality.

Kempe passed through Constance only briefly in 1414, but the
effects of the Council were felt throughout her long life. Also at
Constance, from early 1415, was the English Carmelite Thomas
Netter (d. 1430), mentioned in Kempe's *Book* as having crossed
paths with her in the early 1420s.[32] Netter wrote one of the most
important orthodox responses to the Wycliffite controversies, the
Doctrinale, a text with which Kempe's Carmelite confessor Alan of
Lynn would certainly have been familiar.[33] Netter was a resolute
anti-Lollard and returned from Constance determined to rein
in spiritually gifted laypeople.[34] Someone complained to Netter
that Kempe had become 'to conversawnt' (too intimate; 1.3979)
with her long-time supporter Alan of Lynn, whom Netter forbids
from speaking to her or discussing the Bible. Alan, Kempe's *Book*
reports, finds this 'ful peynful'; he is said to have commented that
'he had levar a lost an hundryd pownd . . . than hir communica-
cyon' (1.3983), another characteristically Kempeian valuation
of spiritual virtue in financial terms.

'Venyce': Venice

Upon leaving Constance in early 1414, and after visiting
Bologna, Kempe arrived in Venice, the most cosmopolitan city
of Europe at this time and the epicentre of the pilgrimage industry for those travelling to the Holy Land. Venice might have
seemed familiar to Kempe; Venice, like Lynn, was an entrepot
in which dockside warehouses doubled as living spaces in single
buildings, and where the management of water as the route
to trade and wealth dominated the residents' lives. Kempe's
account of Venice is tantalizingly spare: she merely says she
spent thirteen weeks there and every Sunday she received communion in 'a gret hows of nunnys and had gret cher among
hem' (a large nunnery, and she was warmly welcomed among
them; 1.1518–19). Here, she amazed the resident nuns with her
plentiful tears. There were about forty convents in and around
Venice and its lagoon, but it is likely that the 'gret hows of
nunnys' visited by Kempe was the Benedictine nunnery of San
Zaccaria (St Zacharias) in Castello, moments from the Doge's
Palace and St Mark's; many of San Zaccaria's nuns came from
the city's nobility and it was well known for its splendour.[35] The
convent held more relics than any Venetian church except St
Mark's, and had become a pilgrimage site in its own right on
account of the body of St Zacharias and a piece of the True
Cross. It was an extremely powerful institution, with close links
to the Doges, who made an annual ceremonial visit at Easter, a
ceremony Kempe possibly witnessed. The church Kempe would
have seen has since been rebuilt, but the Romanesque crypt,
containing the body of St Zacharias, survives, albeit in a perma-
nently flooded state (see illus. 12). The beautiful golden Chapel
of St Tarasio (the former chancel of the nuns' church) contains
objects Kempe herself might have seen, including the wooden
statues of St Zacharias and St Proculus and the panels by Stefano

di Sant'Agnese showing the Virgin and Child, now set in the fifteenth-century altarpiece (illus. 13).

Kempe reached Venice in February or March 1414, thirteen weeks before the spring voyages set sail from Venice to Jaffa (galleys left shortly after the feast of Corpus Christi in late May or early June). Kempe's time in Venice is also important for what it does not say: at the time she was in northern Italy, in England the 'Oldcastle Revolt' was taking place, a 'Lollard' rebellion against the king led by Lord Cobham, Sir John Oldcastle (d. 1417). Early 1414 was certainly a propitious time for someone as liable to religious controversy as Kempe to be away from England.[36]

Kempe's long stay in Venice was not unusual for European pilgrims to the Holy Land, although she records how for six of

13 Altarpiece including central panels by Stefano di Sant'Agnese (1385) with wooden statues of St Zacharias and St Proculus (14th century), Chapel of San Tarasio, Convent of San Zaccaria, Venice.

Opposite: 12 The flooded crypt and burial site of St Zacharias, Convent of San Zaccaria, Venice.

the weeks she spent in Venice she was so ill that she thought she would die (1.1526). A mid-fifteenth-century English guide-book, 'Travel Instructions for a Journey to the East', advises the Jerusalem-bound pilgrim that 'the abiding atte Venyse in winter is goodly' (the conditions for wintering at Venice are good) as one can stay either at the 'ostries' (pilgrim hostels) 'or atte sum other Religeous hous'.[37] The author urges pilgrims to equip themselves at Venice for the voyage ahead ('ther men may geder suche stuffe togeder as nedeth for the passage . . .'). He warns against taking the spring voyage (leaving in May/June), because of the hot weather in the Holy Land, a point that Kempe herself laments later in her journey (1.1714). The guidebook also warns pilgrims to be careful at Venice of 'slye' men who will try to deceive with precious stones, jewels and relics; pilgrims are advised to find a patron of a boat who speaks good 'Lumbard, Greke, Sarasyne and Turkesse' (Italian, Greek, Arabic and Turkish); and, at Venice, to purchase 'a pailet of esement covered' (a covered chamber pot) as well as 'urinalles' (urine bottles), 'barelles for water and such wyne as shall like you best', 'fressh brede and erbage' (bread and vegetables), 'pulleyne and fressh egges' (fowl and fresh eggs).

During Kempe's stay in Venice, the canonization process of the mystic St Catherine of Siena (1347–1380) was taking place. Catherine's reputation was being built and examined in Venice, like Bridget of Sweden's was in Constance, and both women would have been hot topics during Kempe's journey. This is a plausible context for Kempe's learning about St Catherine and her remarkable life.[38]

At Venice Kempe records another notable instance of social friction with her pilgrim company. Kempe has been ordered by her travelling companions to remain silent at mealtimes, as they have grown tired of her talking about God. Kempe, ever resistant to being cowed, cannot keep silent as she 'sat at mete wyth hir felawshep.' Instead, 'sche rehersyd a text of a Gospel lych as sche had leryd befortyme' (she repeated a text of the Gospel that she had learned beforehand; 1.1523). Kempe says, 'I must nedys speke of my Lord Jhesu Crist thow al this world had forbodyn it me' (I really must speak of my Lord Jesus Christ, though the whole world has forbidden me to do so; 1.1525). Refusing to keep quiet is one of Kempe's hallmarks and this incident

shows how Kempe was aware of the ire caused by her godly talk.
The conflict with her companions leads to Kempe eating alone
in her room for six weeks (1.1526), an isolated outsider. The
other pilgrims organize a boat for themselves without her, but
she receives a communication from God not to sail with them
(1.1536). Kempe spreads the word that the pilgrims should sail in
a 'galey' (galley) that she has arranged, until 'thei durst not' (they
dare not) sail in the other boat they had organized (1.1538–9).
Similarly, they eventually let Kempe travel with them, as 'thei
durst non otherwise don' (they dare not do otherwise; 1.1542).
The pilgrims are constantly hostile to her, but Kempe suggests
that they are afraid of her implicit prophecies and dare not dis-
believe her entirely. They continue to bully her (a priest steals
her bedsheet), and she piously forgives them for it while also
saying that God forgives them, too (1.1551). At Venice, Kempe
displays her careful management of her companions' ire in the
service of God, and her self-construction as an outsider finding
a voice on her way to the Holy Land.

'Jherusalem': Jerusalem

Kempe records nothing of her sea voyage between Venice and
the Holy Land, other than that she continued to have 'evyr
mech tribulacyon' (1.1547). Given that she was travelling on a
Venetian galley, she would have sailed via the Dalmatian coast,
through Venetian ports such as Pola (Pula) and Zara (Zadar),
and via Greek islands and ports, most of them under Venetian
control, such as Corfu, Modon (Methoni) and Cyprus. Her boat
landed at Jaffa, sometimes known as Port of Jerusalem, the only
disembarkation point for Latin pilgrims allowed by the Mamluk
authorities. Kempe's party would have been met by Franciscan
'greyfriars', the only western European 'Latin' Christian order
permitted to operate in the Holy Land. Travelling east, the

pilgrims would have sustained themselves on a diet of weak beer, Greek wine, boiled eggs, hard cheese, grapes, raisins, bread and whatever they had brought from Venice, including medicinal spices. They would have been guided by local cameleers and ass-men, at once wranglers for the pilgrims' beasts and professional tour guides. Medieval pilgrims usually refer to these guides as 'Saracens', an often derogatory term for local non-Christians (many of whom would have been Palestinian Christians, Jews and Muslims, all of whom were involved in the pilgrimage industry).[39] The friars would have narrated the pilgrimage as they went, explaining holy sites, preaching about the miracles of the Holy Land, emulating their founder St Francis of Assisi, who had visited the Holy Land in 1219–20. Francis's medieval biographer, Ugolino Boniscambi (*fl.* 1319–42), describes how Francis had travelled to the 'holy places where the human God had walked, and touched them with his own feet . . . [and] embraced those most holy places with the arms of faith, kissed them with his lips of love, and watered them with his tears of devotion, so that he moved all who saw him to the greatest devotion'.[40] Such an approach had a profound influence on the entire business of western pilgrimage in the Holy Land and is reflected in Kempe's experiences there.

The pilgrims would have spent their first nights either in dank caves in Jaffa port or, if they made good progress, at a spartan Franciscan pilgrim-hostel in the town of Ramla, about 19 km (12 mi.) to the southeast. Upon leaving Ramla in the direction of Jerusalem, the flat coastal plain starts to rise. After a few more hours, the landscape becomes severe, contrasting rocky peaks with valleys of scrub. The pilgrims pass villages but do not stop at them; they will be full, they believe, of threatening locals, and hold no holy sites to see and therefore no spiritual benefit is to be gained. They pass many other travellers, pilgrims, merchants, children and holy men. Kempe is riding on a hired donkey, a tamed beast that has many times made this journey. The pilgrims' route climbs precipitously, and the pilgrims ascend a high peak, with views commanding the entire land. On first seeing the holy city of Jerusalem, Kempe is so overcome with joy and sweetness that she nearly falls from her donkey, and some German pilgrims have to help her.

Eventually the pilgrims reach Jerusalem. Here, Kempe would have slept in the women-only dormitories, established by the Knights Hospitaller, at the Muristan near the Church of the Holy Sepulchre (she records that she was invited to lodge with the

14 Hospital of the Knights of St John (Knights Hospitaller), Rhodes (built 1440–89).

Franciscan brothers at Mount Zion but, wary of gossip, declined;
1.1740). The Muristan no longer survives but the Hospitallers'
pilgrim hospice in Rhodes gives us some idea of the environment in which Kempe might have stayed (illus. 14), an austere
but imposing shared dormitory in a quasi-monastic complex.

The main site Kempe visits in Jerusalem is the Church of the
Holy Sepulchre, understood as the world's centre and summit
(illus. 15). Christ tells Bridget of Sweden, in whose footsteps
Kempe was following, that when one enters the Church 'ye are
. . . clene of all your sinne als if ye ware now lift oute of the fonte-
stone, and for youre travaile and your devocion, some saules
of your frendes that ware in puragtori are deleverd and went
to blis':[41] the pilgrim is made as innocent as a newly baptized
child, and their friends' souls are sent from Purgatory to Heaven.
The church visited by Kempe had been rebuilt in the eleventh
century, and comprised the huge and rambling Romanesque

15 Pilgrims (left) arrive at the Church of the Holy Sepulchre and pay
local men for entry, with angels (right) at Christ's tomb, from *Book of
Marvels* (15th century), Bibliothèque nationale de France, Paris.

complex of pilgrimage sites encompassing the Holy Sepulchre, Calvary and a galaxy of other shrines and chapels.[42] The church offered the pilgrim a kind of wonderland of ancient and more recent traditions, busy with ancient rock-hewn vaults, crusader-era 'new' altars, late medieval chapels, with traders selling candles and souvenirs throughout.

Kempe's tour of the Church of the Holy Sepulchre is entirely in keeping with those of other medieval Jerusalem pilgrims. She spends a night locked in the church in vigil, from evensong one day to evensong on the next (1.1564). She receives a candlelit tour led by Franciscans of the holy places (1.1568). She visits Calvary, then the Sepulchre itself, the Franciscan Chapel of the Nailing of the Cross, the Stone of Unction (where Christ's body was said to have been prepared for burial), the Chapel of St Helena (where the Cross was said to have been buried), the Franciscan Chapel of the Apparition, where Jesus was said to have appeared to his mother after the Crucifixion, and the Chapel of Mary Magdalene, where Christ said to the Magdalene 'Mary, why weepest thou?' (John 20:15).

The Zürich-born pilgrim Felix Fabri, visiting Jerusalem in the 1480s, describes his pilgrimage to the Holy Sepulchre in ways that help us flesh out Kempe's account. Fabri describes how the keys to the church were held by a local Muslim family, who counted the pilgrims into the church two by two and then locked them inside. For Fabri this was a kind of joyful imprisonment, 'in the most delightful, lightsome, and roomy of prisons, in the garden of the most precious sepulchre of Christ, at the foot of the mount of Calvary, in the middle of the world!'[43] Fabri explains how his Franciscan guide laid out rules of the pilgrimage in the Holy Sepulchre: first, each pilgrim was required to buy a wax taper to carry in procession. The Father Guardian also picked out four altars in the church – the Holy Sepulchre, Mount Calvary, the Stone of Unction, and the Chapel of the

Apparition – at which the Latin Christians should celebrate Mass. These altars map onto those visited by Kempe, and are all Franciscan altars, thereby avoiding friction or contact with the other denominations within the church. Pilgrims' processions through the church combined liturgical chanting, biblical exegesis of the holy sites, powerful emotions (joy, sighs and groans feature strongly in Fabri's account), and the touching of stones and pillars.

Kempe's time in Jerusalem attested to her dedicated devotion and gave her an intimacy with Christ that those at home lacked, a successful reconciliation in body and soul of the 'erdly cyté Jerusalem' with the 'blysful cité of Jerusalem abovyn, the cyté of hevyn' (1.1554–5). Kempe could carry this experience wherever she went, not just through the souvenirs she purchased and through the 'wondyrful' tears that had been granted to her at Calvary. At Ramla, to which she returned after visiting Jerusalem, Kempe received a travelling indulgence on her way home, being told by God that each time she repeats the formula 'Worshepyd be alle tho holy placys in Jerusalem that Crist suffyrde bittyr peyn and passyon in' (1.1748–9; 1.4166) she would gain the same pardon as if she were physically present there. 'Jerusalem' becomes 'the cite of hir sowle' (1.1574–5), ever-present in Kempe's spiritual being after her defining journey there.

'Flod of Jurdon' and 'Mownt Qwarentyne': River Jordan and Mount Quarantine

Kempe's journey moves to its eastern extremity with her visit to the River Jordan and Mount Quarantine near Jericho, the oldest and lowest city on earth, near the Dead Sea in the Judean Desert. Compared to the damp cool of Norfolk, the heat, the dehydration and the sweating must have astonished Kempe.

After seeing the sights of Jerusalem and Bethlehem (which Kempe also visited; 1.1699), many pilgrims want to see other sites from Christ's life, and Kempe spends three weeks in the Holy Land (1.1738). However, Kempe's path, as ever, is not easy. Her group decides that it wants to see the Jordan, the imputed site of Christ's baptism, but 'wold not letyn hir gon with hem' (1.1710–11). Kempe begs God that she might go, and resolves to do so in any case (1.1712). She sets out and 'askyd hem no leve' (did not ask their permission; 1.1713). To reach the Jordan from Jerusalem, Kempe would have travelled along the river-bed of Wadi Qelt, a narrow ravine that carves its way through the desert east of Jerusalem all the way to Jericho. Upon reaching the Jordan, 'the wedyr was so hoot that she wend hir feet schuld a brent' (the weather was so hot that she believed her feet should burn; 1.1714).

At this point in its course, the River Jordan is a shallow brook and did not, for Kempe, merit a description. The experience is not godly, but it is christomimetic, since Kempe, like Christ, is humiliated and scorned by those around her. The point of the journey is further self-validation, rather than the visit to the religious destination, and the experience is described as being bad for Kempe's body (her burning feet) rather than good for her soul.

Mount Quarantine (Jabal al-Quruntul) was identified in the Middle Ages as the site at which Jesus had spent forty days and nights (the *quarantine* of the name) as referred to in the

16 Mount Quarantine (Jabal al-Quruntul) and Monastery of the
Temptation, Palestine.

Gospels.[44] In the twelfth century, a Crusader community of Latin
monks was established there but, by the time Kempe visited,
this had become a small Greek or Georgian monastery. The
monastery (illus. 16) is cut into the rock like a tiny street with
a little cave-chapel; visitors can today reach it by cable car or,
as Kempe would have done, on the steep, dusty path. It is a hard
walk, and Kempe finds herself in distress:

> sche preyd hir felawshep to helpyn hir up onto the Mownt.
> And thei seyd nay, for thei cowd not wel helpyn hemself . . .
> And anon happyd a Sarazyn, a welfaryng man, to comyn
> by hir, and sche put a grote in hys hand, makyng to hym

a token for to bryng hir onto the Mownt. And as swythe
the Sarazyn toke hir undyr hys arme and led hir up onto
the hey Mownt wher owyr Lord fastyd fowrty days. Than
was sche sor athryste and had no comfort of hir felashyp.
Than God of hys hey goodness mevyd the Grey Frerys wyth
compassyon and thei comfortyd hir whan hir cuntremen
wolde not knowyn hir (1.1716–24).

she asked her companions to help her up the mountain.
And they said 'no', because they could barely help themselves up . . . And then a Saracen, a good-looking man,
chanced to come upon her, and she put a groat into his
hand, making signs to him to take her up the mountain.
And swiftly the Saracen took her under his arm and led her
up the high mountain where our Lord fasted for forty days.
Then she was terribly thirsty and had no sympathy from
her party. Then God, in His high goodness, moved the
Grey Friars with compassion and they comforted her when
her own compatriots would not even acknowledge her.

In this moment of spiritual ascent and ascetic emulation,
Kempe continues to be wedded to the physical: her difficulty in
climbing the mountain, her discomfort in dehydration, and the
reference to the good-looking local man. She pays the 'Sarazyn'
a groat, relying on money rather than on God's grace to ame-
liorate the situation. It is hard to read Kempe's experience of
Quarantine as an edifying one, but it shows her dedication and
seriousness as a pilgrim and provides another opportunity to
reveal the lack of assistance she receives from her companions.
Kempe's thirst parallels Christ's suffering in the wilderness, and
her entire experience of the Holy Land allows her to show how
everyone is 'good' and 'gentyl' towards her, except 'hir owyn
cuntremen' (1.1743). Kempe's time in the Holy Land seems

to confirm that, like Christ, she is a holy outsider, but this, she says, makes her able to receive God's communication and able 'mor boldly' (1.1730) to act on it.

Rome

The fourteenth-century poem 'The Stations of Rome' exhorted every person to visit the city of Rome to gain a pardon, 'thi soule bote' (the soul's remedy). The poem describes how pardons are available at Rome's churches, from seven years of pardon at each of the 29 steps at St Peter's in the Vatican to 12,000 years of pardon for visiting the same church during the showing of the holy kerchief (the 'vernicle') of St Veronica.[45] Rome, then a city of about 34,000 people and therefore significantly smaller than London, was thought of as a kind of 'medicin' for the soul, a place saturated with spiritual benefits.[46] Kempe's fellow resident of Lynn, the Augustinian prior and poet John Capgrave (1393–1464), wrote a compendious guide to Rome, *The Solace of Pilgrims*, which details churches and shrines alongside classical wonders, 'dyvers templis of fals goddis turnyd to servyse of seyntis' like 'Sancta Maria Rotunda', the Pantheon, rededicated to the Virgin Mary.[47] After Jerusalem, Rome was the most insistently mediated and over-determined location in the medieval western Christian imagination, vividly evoked in pilgrims' guides, maps and paintings, and connected to every town in England through the papacy. Rome was also, in the fifteenth century, well geared towards pilgrims and other travellers and an Englishwoman like Kempe would have found a significant expatriate community there.

Kempe's time in Rome – from summer 1414 to spring 1415 – was a formative crucible of her devotional authority. Kempe's Rome is a 'magical space' with a 'fairy-tale-like quality'.[48] Coincidences and miracles happen, strangers suddenly become friends, and charity appears when needed. In this section, I consider two key sites in Kempe's Rome: the English Hospice where Kempe stayed for part of her time in Rome and the 'holy' house of a poor Roman woman whom Kempe visited.

In Rome, Kempe's first stop is at what she calls 'the Hospital of Seynt Thomas of Cawntyrbery in Rome' (1.1855), the English Hospice, dedicated to the Most Holy Trinity and St Thomas of Canterbury. The hospice, on the Via di Monserrato, had been founded in 1362, and grew quickly; a chapel was built there in 1376 and the complex, akin to a monastery, became the focal point for visiting English pilgrims, male and female, and of all classes (the institution assumed a charitable role, housing those who could not afford to pay).[49]

Kempe describes how she had been 'hyly belovyd' of the 'Maystyr of the Hospital and wyth alle hys brethryr' (the warden, *custos*, of the Hospital and all his brethren; 1.1857–8). The master at this time was John Thomasson, who held this position from 1406 until at least 1428.[50] Subsequently, due to the arrival of an enemy priest, also an Englishman, Kempe is ejected, 'thorw hys evyl langage' (through the wicked things he has said about her; 1.1862). Kempe's short stay at the English Hospice nonetheless provides the coordinates for her subsequent experiences in the city. First, the hospice is adjacent to the Casa di Santa Brigida, the place where St Bridget of Sweden lived and died on earth. Second, Kempe's expulsion from the English Hospice constitutes her as an 'alien'. Shunned by her own countrymen, despised by the English, through providence Kempe gains a community of others, including 'Margaret Florentyne', an Italian woman who speaks no English; 'Richard with the broke bak', an incapacitated Irishman; Wenceslas, a German or Bohemian confessor, who also speaks no English; Marcello, a Roman man on whose charity Kempe relies; and an Italian 'jentyl-woman' who asks Kempe to be her child's godmother. Kempe therefore starts to define herself as a kind of holy cosmopolitan, mixing with the variety of people Rome offers, rather than as the 'package tour' English pilgrim. Her expulsion from the English Hospice encourages Kempe to rely on the charity of strangers, and in doing so she shows how God provides for her.

Kempe's Roman poverty contrasts with the good fortunes of her maidservant. Kempe leaves England with her 'mayden' (1.748) but by the time they reach Constance the other pilgrims won't let the servant attend to her mistress (1.1481). By Venice, the maidservant abandons Kempe altogether, including during Kempe's illness there (1.1528). In one of several providential encounters that happen to Kempe on her travels, in Rome she re-encounters the maidservant, now 'dwellyng in the hospital in meche welth and prosperyté', having become the wine keeper (1.2216–22). The disloyal maidservant is implicitly contrasted with 'Seynt Brydys mayden' (St Bridget's maidservant) who, through a translator, loyally tells Kempe how the Swedish saint 'was goodly and meke to every creatur and that sche had a lawhyng cher' (a cheerful disposition; 1.2223–8). Kempe's maidservant's success is a counterweight to Kempe's eager embrace of poverty and lowliness in Rome, as she seeks to emulate Bridget through compassion and through spiritual relationships, rather than seeking worldly 'prosperyté'.

The master of the hospice, hearing about the 'lofe' and 'favowr' (love and affection) Kempe has garnered in the city, apologizes for his rough treatment of her, and invites her to return (1.2212). It is representative of a pattern in *The Book of Margery Kempe* that the hospice's rejection of Kempe leads to her being invited back, as she converts her abjection to glory. Repeatedly, Kempe trumps her compatriots, arrives at destinations before them, and makes choices that turn out to be advantageous. In Rome, Kempe shows how a 'holy' reputation

can sustain her, and offers a 'felawschep' far beyond family and
parish, and the hateful pilgrimage group.

In Jerusalem, Kempe is sacralized by visiting the Holy Places
whereas in Rome, her presence sacralizes the places she visits. At
one point, Kempe is invited into a poor Roman woman's house.
The woman sits 'by hir lytyl fyer', offers wine to Kempe 'in a
cuppe of ston' (stone), and has 'a lytel manchylde sowkyng on
hir brest' (a little boy sucking at her breast; 1.2195–7). Kempe's
entry into the poor woman's house suggests a distinctly female
shared space, a domestic arena of childcare and household management, echoing Kempe's earlier description of her own home
as a place of post-natal suffering.[51] The poor Roman mother is
'ful of sorwe and sadnes' (overcome with sorrow and sadness),
but it is Kempe who bursts 'al into wepyng' (1.2199). This is not
through Kempe's sympathy for the poor woman's plight. Rather,
Kempe's view of the poor family transforms into a vision of the
Holy Family, 'owr Lady and hir sone in tyme of hys Passyon'
(Our Lady and her son at the time of His Passion; 1.2200). The
poor woman asks Kempe to desist from crying, 'not knowing why
sche wept', but Kempe's Christ intervenes:

> Than owr Lord Jhesu Crist seyd to the creatur, 'Thys
> place is holy.' And than sche ros up and went forth in
> Rome and sey meche poverté among the pepyl. And than
> sche thankyd God hyly of the poverté that sche was in,
> trostyng therthorw to be partynyr wyth hem in meryte
> (1.2195–206).

> Then our Lord Jesus Christ said to the creature, 'This
> place is holy.' And then she got up and went out in to
> Rome and saw much poverty among the people; and then
> she thanked God highly for the poverty that she was in,
> trusting to partake in merit with them.

Holiness thus follows Kempe. The interaction here is again scripted by predecessors, not only Christ's humble incarnation but Catherine of Siena, who felt 'wonderfully compassionate towards the poor', and Bridget of Sweden, who rejoiced in washing the feet of the destitute. Catherine had a famous vision of Christ as a beggar to whom she gave her tunic; in return he appeared to her in a vision and produced a miraculous garment from his side-wound, that evermore kept her warm. Elsewhere, a leper woman is Catherine's 'Heavenly Bridegroom' (Christ) and Catherine drinks stinking pus from another woman's sores.[52] The interaction with the poor brings rewards, as these women fulfil the command of the corporal Works of Mercy, to feed the hungry, to clothe the naked, to visit the sick and to shelter the homeless. Kempe noticeably does *not* help the poor Roman woman, but rather uses the incident to sanctify her own passage through Rome. Kempe's weeping has consecrated the ground with tears, as she demonstrates how her mind is entirely occupied by the memory or vision of Christ and His family.

Also in Rome, Kempe is commanded by 'Wenslawe' (Václav, Wenzel), a foreign confessor, to serve 'an hold woman that was a poure creatur' (an old woman who was a poor creature; 1.1992), and to live in squalor, begging and lice-ridden, for some six weeks. Kempe transforms from giver of charity to its recipient. Becoming a poor beggar on the streets of Rome is another way for Kempe to ask for God's favour, and further to renounce worldly goods. Kempe's Rome, like Bridget of Sweden's, is conspicuously a city of the poor, where Kempe both views and experiences poverty through radical charity and transformative renunciation.[53]

At precisely the same time that Kempe was in Rome, Francesca (Ponziani) Romana (1384–1440) was building a reputation that would make her a popular saint. Francesca was from a similar elevated social class to Kempe, and in the early fifteenth century she dedicated herself to relieving Rome's poor and sick, begging for charity, and urging wealthy Roman women to give alms. Francesca also received a number of divine revelations, some of which also show the marked influence of Catherine of Siena's spirituality. Francesca made herself voluntarily poor, rejected fine clothing, refused family banquets, insisted on speaking to servants as her equals, and fiercely attacked anyone who swore oaths on God. In 1433 Francesca founded a convent, the Tor de' Specchi, the oblates of which served Rome's poor.[54] As Guy Boanas and Lyndal Roper have noted, 'Francesca's most distinctive characteristic was that, like Margery Kempe, Catherine of Siena and Bridget of Sweden, she was a married woman, offering a model of holy life to those non-virgins who had taken the spiritually lesser path of matrimony.'[55] In one of Francesca's miracles, she gives her remaining wheat to the poor during a famine, only to find that God has rewarded her and her family with eight tons of the best grain, which has miraculously appeared in their granary.[56] There is certainly a shared devotional sensibility between Francesca Romana and Margery Kempe, based on charity, ascetic poverty, mystical communication and civic piety.[57] Francesca's life and cult evoke the city of Rome as a cosmopolitan place teeming with the poor side-by-side with the wealthy, in which public charity, especially for women, was a well-established route to holiness.

INTERLOGE:
'my weddyd wyfe', Rome, 1414

MARGERY BURNHAM HAD married John Kempe in the 1390s, but in 1414 she undertook another kind of marriage: to the Godhead, the triune divinity of Father, Son and Holy Spirit. I take this mystical marriage as the first 'interloge' of three in telling Kempe's life; the episode is ripe for analysis both as an interlude in Kempe's travels and as a distinct and transformative moment that is foregrounded within Kempe's *Book* as different from what comes before and after.

The church of Santi Apostoli, the 'Postelys Cherch' (1.2000), is a minor basilica in Rome, located beneath the Quirinal Hill near Trajan's Forum, less than a mile east of the English Hospice. In Kempe's time, the church would have been in a state of disrepair, having been largely abandoned after an earthquake in 1348 (restoration work did not begin on the church until 1417). This conforms to St Bridget's vision of Rome as a wrecked place of 'desolate' altars, 'sparpled [scattered] aboute bi lust and liking of fleshe'.[1] Santi Apostoli is where Kempe underwent her mystical marriage to the Godhead, becoming a holy 'spouse' akin to Bridget.[2] The church was not one of Rome's major pilgrimage churches; the most celebrated relic shown to pilgrims at Santi Apostoli, according to Kempe's Lynn contemporary, John Capgrave, was St Philip's arm, 'al hool' (entire).[3] The shrines of the apostles James and Philip were in the church, and the tabard of St Thomas the Apostle was another of its storied relics.[4] Kempe's choice of Santi Apostoli explicitly casts her in an imitative apostolic pose, and the 'twelve apostelys' plus saints Katherine, Margaret 'and many other seyntys and holy virgynes' (1.2029–30) are the witnesses to Kempe's mystical marriage. As

elsewhere in her travels, Kempe's description of the physical site
is sparse, because her emphasis is on seeing with the eye of faith.

Before she went to Rome Kempe had a ring that she called
her wedding ring of Christ. This suggests that she already presented as a 'bride of Christ', a vowess, who had made a spiritual
marriage to Christ. Indeed, Kempe recalls how it is in Rome that
the Godhead first speaks to her, 'al hir lofe and al hir affeccyon'
having previously been in the 'manhode' of Christ (1.2018).
In Rome, she moves beyond this to marry the triune Godhead.
Kempe says that the marriage took place on St Lateran's Day
(9 November 1414), the liturgical feast of the dedication of the
'mother' and chief church of all Latin churches in the world,
Rome's basilica of St John Lateran. Therefore, Kempe asserts
her unity with the *global* and cosmological church, like an
apostle, on the date of a feast that celebrates the centrality
of that place – Rome – as she is visiting.

At the same time, Kempe domesticates (or occupies) this
cosmic space by using the language of a late medieval English
wedding ceremony to marry the Godhead. She casts herself
partly as an overawed virgin bride; 'sche is yet but yong and not
fully lernyd' (1.2026–7) says Christ to God, to explain Kempe's
diffident silence. The vows take place 'in her soul', with the
Godhead saying:

'I take the, Margery, for my weddyd wyfe, for fayrar, for
fowelar, for richar, for powerar, so that thu be buxom and
bonyr to do what I byd the do. For, dowtyr, ther was nevyr
childe so buxom to the modyr as I schal be to the bothe in
wel and in wo, to help the and comfort the. And therto I
make the suyrté' (1.2030–34).

I take you, Margery, to be my wedded wife, for better, for
worse, for richer, for poorer, so that you dutifully and

submissively do what I ask you to do. Because, daughter, there was never a child so obedient to its mother as I shall be to you, both in good time and bad, to help you and comfort you. And that is what I pledge to you.

The Godhead's vows are clearly modelled on, but not identical to, familiar English marriage liturgy. The fifteenth-century Sarum *Manuale* (a liturgical manual) gives the wedding vows of a bridegroom thus:

> I, N., take the, N., to my wedded wif, to have and to holde from this day forward, for bettere for wers, for richere for pouerer, in sykenesses and in hele; tyl dethe us departe, if holy churche it woll ordeyne, and thereto y plight the my trouthe.[5]

> I, N., take you N., as my wedded wife, to have and to hold from this day forward, for better for worse, for richer for poorer, in sickness and in health, until death us do part, if Holy Church ordains it, and thereto I plight you my troth.

In one version of this rite, the bride makes a similar set of vows, adding, in an echo of Kempe's Godhead's vows, that she will 'be bonere and boxsom, in bedde and atte bord' (meek and obedient, in bed and at table). Kempe's Godhead's vows are a Kempeian adaptation, the bridegroom's words becoming a pledge of mutual obedience, the Godhead and Kempe being 'buxom' towards each other. Both everyday marriage vows and Kempe's marriage in Rome end with the swearing of a vow, but in Kempe's version it's the Godhead who pledges His fidelity (suyrté) to her. Kempe does not describe her vow to the Godhead, but instead answers His pledge with 'joy', tears and grateful thanks.

The ceremony boldly authorizes Kempe as the heir and imitator of other mystical brides. According to Jacques de

Vitry, Marie d'Oignies (1177–1213) described the 'bridal bed of divine counsel', with God calling her his 'turtle dove', using the marital language of the biblical *Song of Songs*.[6] Mechtilde of Hackeborn (1241–1298) recounted her mystical marriage with Christ, in which Christ wore white and dressed her in white (for innocence) and red (for his Passion).[7] Catherine of Siena (d. 1380) contracted a mystical marriage (an 'espousal in faith' with a diamond ring invisible to the rest of the world) with Christ.[8] Meanwhile, the mystic Doror hea of Montau (1347–1394) described Christ as the 'celestial groom'. In all these cases, the 'marriage' was mystical and resolutely non-physical. Bridget of Sweden's mystical marriage to her 'husband-spouse' Jesus is carefully framed as a marriage to the 'godhede' too: Jesus explains that even in His death in 'manhede' he continues to live in His 'godhede'. As Naoë Yoshikawa has suggested, for both Bridget of Sweden and for Margery Kempe mystical marriage 'is a threshold for their perception of spiritual life, and it empowers them as their awareness of a special mission grows'.[9] Kempe's marriage to the Godhead boldly affirms her special, chosen status and, following the marriage, she experiences divinity everywhere in the form of holy dust motes and indescribable smells and sounds. In Rome, on 9 November 1414, Kempe proclaims her eternal mystical union; this union lives on in the Church of England, which celebrates 9 November as Margery Kempe's commemoration day in its calendar of saints. Thus at Rome in 1414, in her own way, Kempe does enter into the litany of the distinguished faithful.

FOUR

Friends and Enemies

In *The Fire of Love*, the hermit, mystic and writer Richard Rolle (d. 1349) defined friendship as the 'knytynge of two wyllis' (the knitting of two wills), as between God and a person's soul. Rolle encouraged his audience to develop strong friendships with virtuous people, in which one behaves to a friend as if they are 'hym-self in anodyr body' (oneself in another body): friendship should be radically equal, 'betwyx thame that ar lyke in vertewe' (between those who are equal in virtue).[1] Kempe's friendships neither conform to Rolle's model nor meet his standards, but her friends are a source of comfort and solace.[2] Kempe's friendships tend to be highly consequential for her but are transient, hierarchical and contingent on money, patronage or circumstance. Kempe was able to attract followers and helpers, and she modelled her life on figures she regarded as intimate authorities. Her 'frendys' include confessors and patrons, and those who protect and support Kempe on her pilgrimages, and anchoresses and hermits to whom Kempe turns for holy conversation.

Actual supporters encountered within the pages of the *Book* frequently flicker in and out of the narrative: they include people at home, like her confessors Alan of Lynn, Robert Springold and William Sleightholme, the anchorite Julian of Norwich, and people she encounters on her route, like the English friar-legate at Constance (1.1446), William Weaver of Devon (1.1490),

Richard the Irishman (1.1774) and 'Margaret Florentyne' (1.1845). Kempe, by her own account, relied on the support of male clerics and her experiences are repeatedly legitimized through a combination of confession to supportive priests and her successful negotiation of her detractors.[3] A separate category of friends includes the written authorities Kempe and her confessors encountered – and many of these are listed in the *Book* itself – and embraces the English mystics Richard Rolle, Walter Hilton, Nicholas Love and continental sources such as Jacques de Vitry, Bridget of Sweden and Catherine of Siena.

'Robert Spryngolde' and 'Master Alan': Robert Springold and Alan of Lynn

Kempe was supported by a wide range of educated clerical men to whom she confesses and who act as her spiritual counsellors. In Lynn, these men include the Dominican hermit, a visionary and early believer in Kempe's visions (1.393), Alan of Lynn (who judged the episode of the falling beam at Lynn to be Kempe's first 'miracle'), her parish priest Robert Springold, who succeeded the hermit as her principal confessor, and Thomas Hevingham, Lynn's Benedictine prior. An unnamed secular priest, who revised Book I and wrote Book II for Kempe, was also a Lynn cleric. At Norwich, she is supported by Richard Caister, vicar of St Stephen's, William Southfield, Carmelite of Norwich and a visionary (1.927), and Reginald the Hermit (2.187). Many other confessors and clerical supporters appear more fleetingly in the *Book*: Wenzel of Rome (1.2138); William Sleightholme (d. 1420), a confessor (1.3033); a priest who visited Lynn with his mother and read devotional writings to Kempe (1.3370); a chaplain at St James's Church, Lynn (1.3514) who excused Kempe's crying to a visiting friar; Thomas Andrew and John Amy (1.3999); and the chaplain of the Gesine chapel at Lynn

(1.4007). On the whole, Kempe's preference is for educated men. The *Book* often records their university degrees, like 'a worschepful doctowr whech hite Maistyr Custawns' (1.3922, the Norwich Dominican Thomas Constance), many of whom have a local reputation for learning or holiness, 'men whose authoritative stamp would enhance her pious reputation'.[4]

The two most important figures for Kempe are Alan (Warnekyn) of Lynn and Robert Springold. Alan, a Carmelite friar, is also an interesting presence because information exists about him from sources outside the *Book*. Kempe refers to him sometimes by name and sometimes as 'the White Friar', and he appears throughout the *Book* as a confessor, advisor and guide. Born in Lynn, he wrote a large number of theological texts, mostly now lost, although two manuscripts of his theological indices, including his *tabula* of St Bridget's *Revelations*, survive.[5] Recent research has demonstrated that Alan was from the 'esterling' – Flemish or German – Warnekyn family that seems to have assimilated rapidly into Lynn society.[6] In her *Book* Kempe associates herself with most of the monastic orders, but it is perhaps significant that she chose a confessor from the Carmelite order, which was smaller than the Dominican or Franciscan orders, placed great value on asceticism, and had sustained links to the aristocracy. Alan was clearly in Lynn for pivotal moments in Kempe's life. He was the person who weighed the stone that fell from the rafters of St Margaret's, effectively certifying Kempe's first miracle. Later, Alan falls gravely ill and Kempe receives a revelation that he will live and so she can speak with him again; she reminds the Virgin of how Alan spoke about her in his 'sermownys' (1.4022), and he recovers from his illness, confirming Kempe's prophecy. Kempe enjoys 'a dyner of gret joy and gladnes' with Alan and a local vowess (1.4039).

Robert Springold, sometimes referred to in the *Book* as Master Robert Spryngolde, Master Robert, Master R., a bachelor of canon law, a ghostly father and her main confessor, is undoubtedly one of Kempe's most significant supporters. He is not the first key confessor in the *Book* – that is a Dominican anchorite to whom Kempe was directed by Christ (1.393) – but Springold a 'scharp' confessor, validates Kempe early in her *Book* and hears her last confession. He is the priest mentioned most frequently by Kempe. Springold, may have been the parish priest who failed, as a young confessor, to enjoin Kempe to complete her confession of the terrible sin that she never did confess.[7] Many readers feel that Springold's voice and persona profoundly shaped *The Book of Margery Kempe*, and some have asserted that Springold is the main amanuensis to whom Kempe dictated her story, and who shaped the *Book* as it is today.[8]

Springold confessed to Kempe for a period of at least 25 years, from 1413 to 1438. Springold deliberates with the prior of Lynn, Thomas Hevingham, about Kempe and a complaint received from a new monk recently come to Lynn (1.3282–6). This monk refuses to allow Kempe to take communion in his chapel. Springold's stout defence of her allows this complaint to be turned to glory: ejected from the chapel, Kempe takes communion at the high altar at St Margaret's (1.3293) where 'sche cryed so lowde that it myth ben herd al abowte the chirche and owte of the chirche as sche schulde a deyid' (1.3295–6). Through sound, Kempe claims much more space than the chapel alone.

Alan of Lynn and Robert Springold converge in a noteworthy moment, in 1417, when Kempe returns from her ordeals in Leicester and the north (most recently her arrest at Hessle). Kempe's two confessors and her husband leave Lynn together and sail across the River Great Ouse to the village of West Lynn, where Kempe is waiting, reluctant to enter the town without a letter of endorsement from the Archbishop of Canterbury (1.3213–18). West Lynn, which was not part of the borough of Lynn, was connected to Lynn by a ferry (the one named

ferry-boat we know of was called the *Sturdy Cunt*).[9] This moment
at West Lynn draws together Kempe's three most important and
enduring allies: her husband and these two confessors. Kempe
was certainly an indomitable and, in many ways, independent
person, but here we see her dependence on (male) figures of
authority, both spiritual and worldly. Kempe's reliance on clerical amanuenses and scribes to write down her *Book* similarly
shows how independence was brokered through her power to
make helpful allies. Much of the *Book* is highly colloquial, but
men like Alan of Lynn and Robert Springold assuredly had an
impact on the *Book*, not least in the frequent appearance of clerical, Latinate diction. Words like 'compassyf' (compassionate;
1.424), 'cotidianly' (1.1593), 'delectabyl' (1.2061), 'erroneows'
(1.3124), 'expedient' (1.4123) and 'vexacyon' (1.1173) sound
far from everyday speech, suggesting the clerical filter which
authorized Kempe and mediated her life.

'Dame Jelyan': Julian of Norwich

Kempe visited Norwich in the first half of 1413, anxious to know
if her visions were deceitful illusions (1.931). She met first with
the Carmelite friar and visionary William Southfield (d. 1414).
Southfield blesses Kempe's meditation, telling her that the Holy
Ghost is working in her soul (1.927). Southfield cites scripture
in Kempe's support, telling her that the Holy Spirit 'fleth al
fals feynyng and falshede' (flees from all falseness and fakery;
1.945), paraphrasing Wisdom 1:4–5 ('the Holy Spirit of disci-
pline will flee from the deceitful'). Kempe is then commanded
in her soul to visit Julian, at her anchorhold at St Julian's, about
half a mile south of the city. Julian is now celebrated for her lyrical *Revelations of Divine Love*, a supremely eloquent account of
mystical vision. Kempe, however, does not seem aware of Julian
as a writer or 'author', but consults her for meditation and lofty

contemplation, the two women spending 'many days' (1.987) together in holy conversation. Julian is, evidently, an authority for Kempe and, like Southfield, Julian cites scripture in Kempe's support. Notably, Julian quotes 'Seynt Powl' (St Paul; 1.975) to endorse Kempe's prayerful lamentation and weeping: 'For we know not what we should pray for as we ought; but the Spirit himself asketh for us with unspeakable groaning' (Romans 8:26).

Julian was an anchoress, and had therefore committed to living in a 'perpetual prison', a 'living grave', in her small cell beside the church. This was not a rare vocation and Lynn itself had various recluses: in Kempe's lifetime, 'John' and 'Thomas' were recluses at Kempe's church of St Margaret's, Joanna Catfield was the anchoress at the Carmelite priory and there were also anchoresses at All Saints Church in South Lynn, where a putative anchorhold survives.[10] Anchoritic withdrawal did not always mean total isolation, as recluses frequently received visitors, alms and bequests. Indeed four such bequests survive to Julian, two of them funding her servants, Sarah and Alice.[11] Julian was one of several recluses Kempe consulted but is unique as a woman in the *Book* in taking on a quasi-clerical role, of spiritual teaching and opining on the discernment of spirits. A recluse's support could be a powerful endorsement and recluses had been forbidden, since a thirteenth-century statute by the Bishop of Chichester, from receiving visitors who might arouse suspicion.[12]

Early on in her conversion, Kempe receives fulsome backing from the Dominican hermit at Lynn and from Julian at Norwich, but Kempe's later interactions with recluses suggest their wariness at being associated with her, and of the perils of this kind of religious intimacy.[13] Kempe was close to an unnamed anchoress in 1413 but, in York in 1417, this anchoress repudiated Kempe because of what she had heard being said about her.[14] In Norwich, also around 1417, Kempe visits a renowned foreign anchorite at the College of St Mary in the Fields just outside Norwich, who 'befortyme had lovyd this creatur ryth meche' (previously had loved this creature very much; 1.2416); he has, however, turned against her because of what he has heard about her, telling her that her white clothes are an error and quizzing her about her childcare arrangements (1.2420). Later, Reginald, a Norwich hermit, unhappily accompanies Kempe during a pilgrimage to Walsingham and escorts her to Ipswich and then, later, travels back to Lynn with her. Solitaries and anchorites occupied an ambiguous position in medieval life, on the same continuum of the 'mixed life' as Kempe. Their relations with the church were fluid but precarious; they were spiritually empowered and culturally prestigious but relied on charity and reputation. Reginald tells Kempe that he has been blamed for her 'defawte', her disobedience, and wants nothing more to do with her. Kempe 'spak fayr and preyd for Goddys lofe' but only induces Reginald to come back to her when 'sche proferyd hym to aqwityn hys costys be the wey homward' (she offered to pay his costs for the homeward journey; 1.649–53). Her valued, spiritual friendship only survives because of the monetary bond. Such spiritual friendships seem fragile for Kempe, not least because they involve her submission to the direction and instruction of others.

'other frendys': Other friends

Returning from Rome to England after Easter 1415 (1.2338), Kempe is poor and in debt. During the winter she keenly feels the cold (1.2440; 1.2463–4). People scorn her, they say she has 'the fallyng evyl' (epilepsy; 1.2474), and spit at her (1.2476). They tell her that she howls like a dog (1.2477) and mock her white clothes. Some former friends refuse to support her, because she has given away all her money. God tells her not to worry, that He will provide for her. Kempe was able consistently to gain practical and local support, and at this time, an 'honour-able' man in Norwich liked her manner of talking and bought a bolt of white fabric for her; citing God's permission, she had white garments made from it, 'a gowne . . . and an hood, a kyrtyl, and a cloke' (1.2449). Shortly afterwards, Kempe's intent turns towards making her pilgrimage to Santiago de Compostela, a trip partly funded by a friendly woman of Lynn, who gives Kempe the sum of 7 marks to offer prayers for her at the shrine of St James (1.2492).[15] The comfort, solace and protection of friends is a theme that runs throughout Kempe's *Book*.

Kempe encountered some extraordinarily powerful and important figures during her travels: clergy, aristocrats and re-nowned spiritual authorities. Kempe received the support of Joan (Beaufort) Neville, Countess of Westmorland (d. 1440) of Raby Castle (Durham), the daughter of John of Gaunt (by his third wife Katherine Swynford) and half-sister to king Henry IV. It appears from the *Book*'s oblique account that Kempe visited Beaufort's household in 1413–14 (1.3155), probably at Raby, and was accused (1.3150) of advising Beaufort's daughter, Elizabeth Greystoke, to leave her husband (referring to one of the per-ceived dangers of women allying with each other, mentioned several times in the *Book*).[16] Yet Kempe also stirred sympathy and care: later in her life, a ship's captain is 'as tendyr to hir' as if she were his mother, between Norway and Gdańsk (2.254); the 'good wife' of the hostel near Aachen assigns two maidens to protect Kempe from sexual assault (2.391); a 'good powr man', a stranger, helps her to Canterbury (2.539–40).

In the summer of 1417 Kempe was detained in Bristol for six weeks, waiting for a boat to Spain in order to undertake her pilgrimage to Santiago de Compostela. In Bristol is also her friend Thomas Marshall, who appears suddenly, introduced as being from 'Newe Castel' (1.2534), probably the market town of Newcastle-under-Lyme (Staffordshire), about 200 km (125 mi.)

north of Bristol. Marshall, we are told, had undergone a spiritual transformation thanks to Kempe; he often invited her to dine with him and hear her conversation and, thanks to Kempe, 'he was al mevyd as he had ben a newe man' (he was all altered as if he were a new man; 1.2537–8). Marshall's evident closeness to Kempe is demonstrated when he addresses her as 'Modyr' (mother; 1.2544), casting himself as her spiritual son; she later refers to him as her 'sone' (1.2766). As with many of Kempe's peripatetic friendships, there is a vertical relationship here too of charity and patronage: Marshall provides Kempe with food and the sum of 10 marks to pay for her passage to Santiago. In return, she provides him with devout conversation. Such friendships empower Kempe's holiness, but we should not forget that this was a precarious dependence.

Marshall travels with Kempe to Santiago, although Kempe's *Book* records almost nothing about the trip. The voyage out takes seven days and the pair stay in Santiago for fourteen days. Kempe's party would have landed at the port of A Coruña (known to English travellers as 'The Groyne') and in Santiago would have visited the magnificent cathedral shrine of St James.[17]

On returning to England, Kempe and Marshall travel to the Cistercian abbey at Hailes in Gloucestershire together, another prestigious pilgrimage, in order to see the phial of the Holy Blood. Here, Kempe confesses and has 'lowde cryes and boystows wepyngys' (1.2601–2). At Hailes she gains yet more indulgences, as pilgrimage to Hailes could 'clens yowre sawle', according to a fifteenth-century poem written for pilgrims.[18] Kempe and Marshall probably stayed at the pilgrims' hostel there, which was within the abbey and run by the monks, and they would have prayed at the thirteenth-century chevet with radiating chapels, at the centre of which stood the precious blood relic. As with her other pilgrimages Kempe little describes her surroundings, focusing instead on the somatic reaction she experiences in a specific place. The only detail included in *The Book of Margery Kempe* about this excursion is that Kempe is made welcome at Hailes but she reprimands the monks for swearing oaths – a subtle reiteration of Kempe's considerable public spiritual authority at this point, focusing on her right to correct the clerics, rather than on their celebrated and popular relic.[19] From Hailes, the pair travel to Leicester, where they get into a great deal of trouble with the authorities (described in detail in due course), and Marshall is imprisoned and interrogated due to his association with Kempe (1.2671). Marshall evidently waits in the nearby town of Melton Mowbray while Kempe is interrogated in Leicester, to ensure her safety (1.2787).

Kempe repeatedly describes herself as 'modyr' to men and children whom she calls 'son', from Jesus to the young boys of Rome whom Kempe kisses in His stead.[20] Can we understand a man like Marshall then as a kind of disciple, or perhaps a surrogate son, of Kempe's? Marshall certainly seems to have put himself in peril for Kempe, yet he disappears from the pages of *The Book of Margery Kempe* as swiftly as he entered them. Kempe then pays another friend, Patrick, to accompany her to York. Kempe's *Book* shows how she attracted, needed, valued and used friends, and she does not seem to have gained much solace in solitude. The fact that Kempe little mentions her children is often read as evidence that human relationships were unimportant to her. Yet her *Book* discloses her desire for companionship, her valuing of transient fellowship and mutual help, and her understanding of the utility of friendship in building communities of like-minded people.

'Seynt Bryde': St Bridget of Sweden

In almost all cases, in the Middle Ages the building of a textual edifice was a masculine imperative: to turn a life into text,

and to turn oral culture into a book, puts Kempe into a male-authorized and monastic frame, rather than the more informal and various communities, many of which included women, we know she encountered. Kempe's *Book* is pervaded by imitative allusions and other voices, a process that has been called 'public interiority', a distinctive feature of fifteenth-century English culture.[21] 'Public interiority' describes how an 'individual' life is written through other people's stories, as the 'interior' self is also a public persona.

Perhaps Kempe's closest 'friend', on whom her life was modelled, was St Bridget (Birgitta Birgersdotter; 1303–1373) of Sweden. Kempe's *Book* shows the influence of several Continental mystics – including Catherine of Siena, Marie d'Oignies and Elizabeth of Hungary – but Bridget's influence is the most pronounced.[22] Born into the Swedish aristocracy, Bridget had eight children and was widowed around the age of forty; in her widowhood, Bridget held herself to have become a 'sponsa Christi', a bride of Christ. She developed a distinctive and hugely popular mystical voice, as recorded in her *Liber celestis* or *Revelations*.[23] Her degenerate son, Karl, who predeceased her, features as an important character in Bridget's revelations, which were revealed to Bridget by an angel in over seven hundred visions. A devoted pilgrim, Bridget visited Jerusalem and lived in Rome, similarities to Kempe that are explicitly drawn out in *The Book of Margery Kempe*. A monastery at Vadstena in southern Sweden was founded in Bridget's honour, and her canonization as a saint took place in 1391 and was reconfirmed at Constance in 1415. Bridget became famous not only as a holy woman but as a holy *auctrix*, an authority, and her attributes included a pen or quill and an open book, as in a painted glass image of her from Sandringham (Norfolk) near Lynn (illus. 17). We cannot

17 'Sancta Brigina', St Bridget of Sweden, with St Margaret from the Church of St Mary Magdalene, Sandringham, Norfolk, c. 1500.

be certain when Kempe first encountered Bridget's cult, but it was likely in Norfolk in the first decade of the fifteenth century. A Norwich monk, Adam Easton (who was based in Rome for many years and died there in 1397), wrote a *Defensorium Sanctae Birgittae*, supporting Bridget's swift canonization;[24] Kempe's confessor Alan of Lynn wrote indices to Bridget's *Revelations*. Kempe certainly encountered Bridget's cult in several forms: at Rome, where she visited the Casa di Santa Brigida, adjacent to the English Hospice, and she met women who had known Bridget during her lifetime. Kempe's Italian friend, Margaret Florentyne, was likely a member of the wealthy Alberti family of Florence, who had founded the first Birgittine house in Italy (the Paradiso in Florence) and gave the name Brigida to several daughters in their family.[25] Bridget's *Liber celestis* was widely read in England and some of Kempe's most memorable imagery is modelled on Birgittine images.[26] In 1434 Kempe visited the Birgittine monastery at Syon (Middlesex), founded by Henry v in 1415, and received the famous Lammas Indulgence there.[27]

At several points in her *Book*, Kempe records how, during sea voyages, she remains safe where others suffer. For instance, on a journey from Calais to Dover, she is protected from embarrassing seasickness where all her companions vomit, 'voydyng and castyng ful boistowsly and unclenly' (vomiting and throwing up violently and filthily; 2.530–31). This seems to be a knowing parallel to Bridget's account of how she was miraculously kept warm one night while sailing to an island, whereas her servants were so cold that they could hardly bear it.[28] In the morning, Christ tells Bridget that He is the only source of 'kindeli hete' (natural heat), and if people will trust in Him, He shall warm and look after them, body and soul.

Like Kempe, Bridget 'was in dispaire of hir life in travellinge of childe' (during pregnancy). Like Kempe, Bridget enjoyed holy conversation with Christ and the saints. Like Kempe, Bridget was commanded to 'wende' from northern Europe to Jerusalem and Rome, where she loved 'wilfull povert' and gave away everything she had. Like Kempe, Bridget hated cursing and godless talk, was unafraid of counselling bishops, and was famous for her book.[29] Yet the social competition that Kempe discloses about her early life in Lynn continues in her relationship with St Bridget. After a striking and beautiful vision in which the holy sacrament flutters to and fro 'as a dowe flekeryth wyth hir wengys' (like a dove flutters its wings; 1.1080), Kempe wishes to see it again. Jesus tells her that the vision will not be repeated, but that she should thank God for having seen it at all, since 'My dowtyr, Bryde, say me nevyr in this wyse' (my daughter, Bridget, never saw me in this way; 1.1085–6). Even as this incident echoes one of Bridget's own visions, in which she saw a lamb in the Host, Kempe asserts a privileged intimacy with Christ that even St Bridget could not claim.[30]

A different kind of intimacy with St Bridget is glimpsed when Kempe is in Rome, in 1414–15. A Roman gentlewoman asks Kempe to be 'godmodyr of hir childe & namyd it aftyr Seynt Brigypt' (godmother of her child, and named her after St Bridget (of Sweden); 1.2207–8). Kempe explains that the mother had known St Bridget during her lifetime. As godmother, Kempe would have been a sponsor at the child's baptism, and would notionally have been responsible for teaching the child her fundamental prayers, like the *Pater Noster* and the *Ave Maria*, but Kempe was probably asked to be godmother here because she had become known as a holy woman. For Kempe, such surrogate activities are frequently spiritually very rewarding: through God's grace, Kempe then received 'gret lofe [love] in Rome, bothyn of men and of women, and gret favowr among the pepyl' (1.2209–10). The Roman 'jentylwoman' naming this child after St Bridget places Kempe very precisely within the cultural environment of Birgittine-Dominican patronage at this time; Bridget was an especially favoured saint among some of the most wealthy and influential people in Florence and Rome.[31] After the canonization of Bridget in Rome in 1391, the name Brigida became a fashionable forename in Italy, and here Kempe's emulation of and proximity to St Bridget is also proximity to wealth, power, status and fashionable devotion at the heart of what we now call the Italian Renaissance.

'sche herd redyn': She heard through reading

The influence of St Bridget on *The Book of Margery Kempe* is clear and explicit. Kempe was familiar with a range of other later medieval mystical writings, and named texts included those by Walter Hilton, saints' lives, the *Stimulus amoris* attributed to Bonaventure, and Richard Rolle's *Fire of Love*. Rolle's presence is felt throughout Kempe's *Book*, as is another text not named – the *Mirrour of the Blessed Life of Jesu Christ* by the Carthusian writer Nicholas Love. The influence of Rolle and Love on Kempe's *Book* demonstrates the intimacy Kempe and her amanuenses had with these writers.

Richard Rolle (d. 1349) of Hampole (Yorkshire) was a hermit and a prolific author of devotional writings, in Latin and Middle English. His name (given as 'Richard Hampol, hermyte'; 1.3642) is adduced in *The Book of Margery Kempe* as providing material to Kempe's priest-amanuensis 'to gevyn credens' to her visions. Rolle's *Incendio amoris* (*Fire of Love*) is mentioned especially, and the Rolleian 'fire of love' is one of Kempe's favourite idioms for describing the kindling of God in her heart (for example, 1.1624; 1.2060; 1.2067; 1.2313; 1.4682).[32] Rolle was an Oxford student who, at nineteen, underwent a spiritual conversion. His experience of God was described through qualities of heat (*fervor* or *calor*), sweet smell and taste (*dulcor*), and angelic, heavenly song (*canor*) (1.28.36). *Fervor/calor* is Kempe's 'fyer of lofe', while *dulcor* and *canor* appear in Kempe's account of how, for the 25 years after she visited Rome,

> Sumtyme sche felt swet smellys wyth hir nose; it wer swet-tyr, hir thowt, than evyr was ony swet erdly thyng that sche smellyd beforn, ne sche myth nevyr tellyn how swet it wern, for hir thowt sche myth a levyd therby yyf they wolde a lestyd. Sumtyme sche herd wyth hir bodily erys sweche sowndys and melodiis that sche myth not wel heryn what a man seyd to hir in that tyme les he spoke the lowder (1.2039–43).

> Sometimes she felt sweet smells in her nose; it was sweeter, she thought, than any sweet earthly thing she had smelled before, and she could not describe how sweet it was, as she thought she could have lived on those smells if they had lasted. Sometimes she heard with her physical ears such sounds and melodies that she could not hear at that time what people said to her unless they spoke louder.

Kempe's feelings are markedly like Rolle's overlapping, spreading sensations of warmth, sweetness and melodiousness. Likewise, Rolle describes the delightful, pliable condition of 'melting' into soulful experience ('my saule is moltyn'; 1.1.15, 1.18.20), echoed in Kempe's rhyming description of how 'sche gan meltyn and al to relentyn' (she began to melt and utterly dissolve) when gazing on a crucifix at Leicester, due to the kindling of the fire of love in her heart (1.2609–10). Rolle explains how the fire of love is a gift from God, but this fire is tempered by 'fylthis of flesch' (1.1.24), idleness and worldly vanities. Rolle's book is a manual explicitly targeted at 'boystous and untaught' (humble and uneducated) people – like Kempe – to put aside worldly things and strive to kindle this fire of love which purges sin.

Kempe certainly knew of Rolle, but her *Book* does not mention Nicholas Love, who also wrote for the laity. However, Love's
only known work, his *Mirrour of the Blessed Life of Jesu Christ*, had
a profound influence on Kempe. Love was the first prior of the
Charterhouse of Mount Grace in Yorkshire in 1410 (the monastery at which *The Book of Margery Kempe* would be avidly read
about a hundred years later). Love's *Mirrour is* a Middle English
translation of the creative Latin life of Christ, the *Meditationes
vitae Christi* (Meditations on the Life of Christ), then attributed
to St Bonaventure (d. 1274).[33] The explicit aim of Love's translation was to stir every man and woman, of 'every Age & every
dignite' (every age and class), to think about the everlasting
life promised to mankind by Christ, given in the form of His
Passion. In his well-known prologue, Love explains that his book
is translated 'in Englyshe to lewde [uneducated] men & women
& hem [they] that bene [are] of simple undirstondyng', suggesting its universal application and audience.[34] Love states that the
'devoute meditacions of cristes lyfe' in his book are 'more pleyne
in certeyne partyes' than the gospels, offering a more accessible
version of the Bible. Love casts the text's readers as if they are
'childryn', who 'nede to be feede with mylke of lyghte doctrine'
rather than the 'sadde mete' of clerical theology and contemplation.[35] Love's *Mirrour* popularized vivid tableaux of Passion
meditations in which the reader is invited to see in their 'mind's
eye' moments from the Bible as if they were there themselves.

Such visionary tableaux appear frequently in *The Book
of Margery Kempe* and are very similar to Love's elaborated,
sensationalized narrative. For instance, Kempe engages in a pro-
tracted meditation on the Passion, in which she and the Virgin
Mary talk to Christ as He carries the Cross after being violently
scourged. Kempe's vision makes much of the weight of Christ's
'hevy crosse'; 'it was so hevy and so boystows that unethe he
myth bere it' (it was so heavy and so gigantic that He could

hardly bear it; 1.4536). The Virgin then offers to help her son
carry 'that hevy crosse', but she swoons. The immense heaviness
of the Cross is a non-biblical detail that Kempe or her amanuenses are likely to have taken from Love's *Mirrour*. Love richly
describes how Christ carried a 4.5-metre (15-ft) cross 'that was
ful hevye & fulle longe'; when the Virgin met him, and saw him
'overleide with so grete a tree of the cross' she swooned and was
herself 'half dede' out of sorrow.[36] Love's *Mirrour* was one of the
most popular pieces of writing in fifteenth-century England, and
such imagery pervaded the religious consciousness of all kinds
of people, so its presence in Kempe's *Book* is no surprise: indeed,
such saturation of popular and affecting imagery was the purpose
of Love's translation.

Kempe's imaginative inventiveness and her spectacular,
affective intimacy with Christ and the Virgin Mary is profoundly
indebted to Love's *Mirrour*.[37] In her early communication with
the pregnant St Anne and then with her daughter the Virgin,
Kempe acts as a kind of servant and wetnurse (Kempe asks St
Anne if she can be her 'mayden', or lady-in-waiting; 1.407). This
allows her powerfully and intimately to experience the biblical
narrative in the manner extolled by Rolle and Love. The Virgin
becomes a kind of friend and patroness of Kempe's, like a medieval gentlewoman with whom she passes time and for whom
she intimately cares. This is most memorably expressed during
Kempe's vision after Christ's Crucifixion, when she offers the
Virgin a 'cawdel' (1.4031–4), a restorative hot broth.[38] Later on,
Kempe describes Christ's Passion as if she is an eyewitness, listing
the gruelling suffering to which He was subjected at Calvary,
her mode of entering into 'dalyaunce' with biblical figures akin
to that described by Love. Such scenes reflect the emotionally
engaged memory practices that were fundamental to medieval
ideas of the retention of valued knowledge.[39] The art of memory
was concerned with touching the emotions in order to make a

deeply personal 'engagement of the senses', with 'each memory as much as possible [made] into a personal occasion by imprint-ing personal associations like desire and fear'.[40] The scenes of Christ's human life and graphic suffering as described in Love's *Mirrour* were a way for people like Kempe to make an active memory image, one that would be indelibly imprinted in their 'mind's eye' and on their soul.[41]

'Erchebischop of Yorke': The Archbishop of York

At York, in 1417, rumours and evil accusations about Kempe have sprung up, and a preaching monk, a Dominican or Franciscan, having heard these 'slanders', repeats them to a crowd of people. Kempe is all the happier for this, a further public test of her. Kempe had evidently become considerably emboldened as a charismatic controversialist, and this kind of infamy provoked one of her more outrageous challenges to the clergy. In York Minster (1.2886), she is summoned to appear before the arch-bishop (the second most senior bishop in England) and he commands that Kempe be held in prison until she can be examined; she evades imprisonment because some local people – probably her local advocates, the priests John Acomb and John Kendal – speak in support of her (1.2849).

Travelling the short distance from York down the River Ouse, Kempe obeyed the summons to see the archbishop at his magnificent palace in the village of Cawood. The archbishop at this time was Henry Bowet (d. 1423), a Cumberland gentleman who had studied at Cambridge and served at the papal court. He was close to Henry IV and Henry V, a member of the Lancastrian inner circle, and, like these kings, a stern prosecutor of heresy. This makes Kempe's behaviour at Cawood all the more daring.

Led into the archbishop's hall, Kempe receives a hostile reception. The archbishop's retinue sneers at her, and calls her names – 'Lollard', 'heretic' – and threatens to burn her. Kempe does not record fear or terror here but finds an apparently confident voice of pious reproof:

> 'Serys, I drede me ye schul be brent in helle wythowtyn
> ende les than ye amende yow of yowr othys sweryng,
> for ye kepe not the comawndementys of God. I wolde
> not sweryn as ye don for al the good of this worlde'
> (1.2916–18).

> 'Gentleman, I'm afraid that you shall be burned in eternal
> Hell unless you correct yourselves for swearing oaths, as
> you do not keep God's commandments. I would not swear
> as you do for all the money in the world.'

Her censure has its effect. The men fall silent, turning away ashamed. Here, Kempe was co-opting the well-established pose of fraternal correction, the lay admonition of one's clerical superiors. Kempe strategically constructs herself as an 'impeccable corrector', an 'institutionally sanctioned critic of institutionally proscribed speech': that is, a kind of ethical watchdog for the clergy.[42]

Archbishop Bowet does not respond happily. Accompanied by some of his clerics, he then questions Kempe, rudely, intrusively, while she kneels in front of him in a gesture of both supplication and devotion. 'Why gost thu in white? Art thu a mayden?' (1.2923) he asks, enquiring about her clothing and her virginity. He articulates the hierarchical relation between them by addressing her with the familiar 'thu' where she answers respectfully with 'ye' (1.2926). This is a dramatic portrait of a less powerful woman against a hostile man, but it is also a description of Kempe as individual layperson against Bowet as institution. There is also a rare moment of dissimulation, as Kempe records how she was trembling and shaking so much that she had to hide her hands under her clothes, even as she spoke and prayed with composure, and answered doctrinal questions carefully without straying into heresy.

Kempe's interview with Bowet was a high-stakes encounter, and she did little to calm things. It is also an excellent description of the workings of gossip and shame, as Archbishop Bowet says to Kempe, 'I am evyl enformyd of the; I her seyn thu art a ryth wikked woman' (I have been told very evil things about you; I have heard tell that you're an utterly wicked woman; 1.2950–51). Infamy and celebrity are the cousins of sanctity, but this cannot have been the reception Kempe wanted. She seems to have decided that speaking truth to power was the most effective stratagem, and she replies to Bowet's assertion of her wickedness:

> 'Ser, so I her seyn that ye arn a wikkyd man. And, yyf ye ben as wikkyd as men seyn, ye schal nevyr come in hevyn les than ye amende yow whil ye ben her' (1.2952–3).

> Sir, likewise, I hear tell that you are a wicked man. And if you are as wicked as people say, then you will never get to Heaven unless you mend your way while you are here [on Earth].

Kempe takes a risk, and is able to seize the spiritual initiative, even in – especially in – a context as exalted as an archbishop's palace. The archbishop moves to get rid of Kempe by asking her to leave his diocese – a massive area from Derbyshire to Westmorland – as soon as possible, and to promise that she will neither teach nor censure (that is, act as a preacher) there. Kempe must refuse, because of her stated reason that she wishes to go to Bridlington to speak to her confessor Sleightholme (who had also been the confessor of the recently sainted John of Bridlington), but clearly she does not wish to back down in the face of her exalted opponent. By this point, well into her spiritual conversion, she saw herself as a charismatic speaker, skilled in 'dalyawns', although not a public preacher.[43] Thus one of the archbishop's men produces 'a book' and quotes St Paul, that no woman should preach (1 Corinthians 1:34).

Kempe responds to this enmity by telling the archbishop and his men a startling parable of a priest, a pear tree and a shitting bear. Kempe describes how a priest got lost in a wood and, at night-time, found a 'fayr erber' (pretty garden; 1.2982) with a blossoming 'pertre' (pear tree) in the middle of it. Suddenly a vicious bear, 'gret and boistows' (1.2984), appeared, and shook the tree causing its blossoms to fall. The bear 'devowryd' all the blossoms and then turned his 'tayl-ende' towards the priest and 'voyded hem owt ageyn at the hymyr party' (excreted them out of his nether regions; 1.2986–7). The priest felt great anxiety at this sight.

The next day the priest came across an old man, dressed like a pilgrim, and asked him what the sight of the bear meant. The old man reveals himself to be God's messenger. He says that the priest is the pear tree, 'florischyng and floweryng' through his services and administering the sacraments; the priest receives 'the frute of evyrlestyng lyfe', the eucharist, but he does so 'unde-vowtly', not being careful about how he says his prayers and by wasting his time, 'bying and sellyng, choppyng and chongyng'. The priest, the old man says, is a lustful glutton, a letch, a swearer, a liar, and so he is also like the horrible bear: 'thu devowryst and destroist the flowerys and blomys of vertuows levyng' (blooms of virtuous living; 1.2996–3007). Kempe's bravura performance here is a direct attack on clerical hypocrisy. Her description of the beautiful garden and the pear tree may have been suggested to her by the magnificent and unusual grounds at Cawood which had, since the thirteenth century, boasted elaborate gardens with their own canals, reflecting pools and orchards next to the hall and chapel where her interview took place.

Kempe's tale of the shitting bear has the ring of a preacher's *exemplum*: a pithy story used to illustrate a larger moral point. The inspiration for the story may lie in Bridget of Sweden's vision of the Son of God describing a gluttonous, defecating abbess, a 'fatt kye' (fat cow) that 'gone in the filth, and with hir taile files other aboute hir' (wades in mire and splatters bystanders with the dung from her tail). Thus she splatters the convent with her immoral example.[44] Similarly, medieval preachers' tales feature multiple related stories: for instance, the northern European story of the priest who, having led an evil life, is tormented by a vision of a bear eating him; or the widely repeated story of the monk who decides to leave his monastery but finds himself tormented by nocturnal visions of a bear.[45]

Kempe's story also seems indebted to the writings of St Catherine of Siena, for whom the blossoming tree was a fundamental image and whose cult had spread in England via William Bakthorpe, a Dominican prior of Lynn.[46] In her *Dialogue*, Catherine describes how 'the soul is a tree', which should produce 'fragrant flowers of virtue', fed by love, but often produces 'stinking flowers', a tree of corruption. Similarly, Catherine describes the 'tree of death', 'nourished by sensitive self-love', producing mortal fruits which draw their nourishment from 'the roots of pride'.[47]

Kempe's 'good' tale (1.3009) has the desired effect: Archbishop Bowet greatly enjoys the story, and one of the clerics who had previously questioned her says 'this tale smytyth me to the hert' (1.3010–11), showing how Kempe has compassionately touched him. Without preaching or straying into heresy, Kempe establishes her moral authority in a hostile and dangerous arena; she is given 5 shillings, and conducted out of the region by a member of the archbishop's household, heading for Bridlington

on the coast to speak with her confessor, Sleightholme. As well
as seeing Sleightholme, it is likely that she visited the shrine of
St John of Bridlington (d. 1379) at the wealthy Augustinian
priory there. John, who had received the gift of tears and practised fervent prayerfulness, had been made a saint in 1401 and
his cult was endorsed by Henry v, who was one of the early pilgrims to his shrine. Sleightholme himself had been St John's
confessor, a direct link for Kempe to prestige and divinity. Kempe
does not linger at Bridlington, but travels south to Hull and
onwards to Hessle. 'Malicyows pepil' (1.3042) are everywhere.
At Hull, a 'gret woman' (1.3039) 'despysed' her, and other people
threaten her with prison and other punishments. At Beverley,
Archbishop Bowet meets her again: 'What, woman, art thu come
agen?' (1.3102) he asks, astounded. He publicly states that he
'fond no defawte in hir' (found no error in her; 1.3105) but by
this point Kempe had encountered another enemy, in the form
of the retinue of the Duke of Bedford.

'the Duke of Bedforth': The Duke of Bedford

Kempe was never formally tried for heresy, but her arraignment,
in 1417, by the officers of John, Duke of Bedford, was one of her
most challenging encounters. It brought her into the orbit of
the most powerful person in England, a man who was assuredly
an enemy of Kempe's.

At the small port of Hessle, a crossing point of the River
Humber, Kempe happened upon 'too Frer Prechowrys and two
yemen of the Duke of Bedforthys' (two Preaching Friars and two
of the Duke of Bedford's yeomen; 1.3046–7). The yeomen arrest
her as she's about to board her boat, and they tell her

> 'For owr Lord,' thei seyd, 'the Duke of Bedforth hath sent
> for the. And thu art holdyn the grettest loller in al this

cuntré er abowte London eythyr. And we han sowt the in
many a cuntré, and we schal han an hundryd pownde for
to bryng the beforn owr Lord' (1.3049–52).

'Our lord, the Duke of Bedford, has sent for you,' they said,
'and you are held to be the greatest Lollard in this whole
region, and around London too. And we've been looking
for you in many regions, and we'll get a hundred pounds
for bringing you before our lord.'

Kempe is, by her own account, nationally notorious. According to his yeomen (attendants in his household), John of
Lancaster, Duke of Bedford (1389–1435) had personally organized Kempe's arrest on charges of heresy. John, created Duke
of Bedford in 1414, was the third son of Henry IV and he was, in
1417, Lieutenant of England, effectively governing England while
his brother, Henry V, was occupied with the invasion of France,
the battle of Agincourt and siege of Harfleur (1415), and the
conquest of Normandy (1416–24).[48] Bedford was also a cousin
of the Beauforts, with whom we know Kempe was familiar.

This begins perhaps the most dangerous moment for
Kempe in her *Book*, as Bedford was at this time pursuing the
Lancastrians' stringent anti-'Lollard' policies, of inquisition and
violent penalties. Around the very time that Kempe was arrested
at Hessle, Bedford presided over the pursuit of the prominent
'Lollard' Sir John Oldcastle (whose revolt, in 1414, had taken
place while Kempe was in Italy). In July 1417 Bedford's men
were looking for Oldcastle in Northamptonshire following his
escape from the Tower of London, and from August to October
that year Oldcastle went into hiding in Herefordshire, during
which time Bedford searched for him doggedly. During this
period, Bedford had himself been at Bridlington, with his cousin
Thomas Beaufort, who was very much involved in commercial

life in Lynn, and this is plausibly how Bedford might have heard about Kempe.[49] Oldcastle seems to have been heading north when he was arrested near Welshpool on the Welsh border in late October 1417, and this could account for the apparently feverish atmosphere in Yorkshire surrounding Kempe's arrest. Oldcastle was hanged and burned in London in December 1417.

The Duke of Bedford was an immensely powerful and accomplished man. The context of worries about heresy informs most of Bedford's career from about 1415 until the 1430s. Bedford's patronage, like his politics, was in step with that of Henry V: that is to say, both brothers were devout and strictly orthodox, and dedicatedly anti-Lollard. The Duke of Bedford made significant donations to St George's Chapel at Windsor Castle, the chapel at which the Order of the Garter was based, and in 1427 Bedford would lay the foundation stone of the new Birgittine monastery at Syon (as visited by Kempe seven years later).[50] Later, in 1431, Bedford would achieve fame, or notoriety, for his pursuit of Joan of Arc. While Bedford did not personally preside over Joan of Arc's trial, his strict orthodoxy and his fear of dissent, alongside his commitment to the English claim on France, meant that Joan was subjected to a gruelling heresy trial and it was as a relapsed heretic that she was burned. In particular, the bishops questioned her about the validity of her holy conversations with St Margaret and St Katherine and the source of her revelations. The Bishop of Norwich, William Alnwick, briefly glimpsed in *The Book of Margery Kempe* (1.1360), was also present at one of Joan's trials, which he attended while conducting a frenzied campaign against heretics in his own diocese.[51] A heightened fear of heterodoxy and a belief in the Devil's ability to work through a woman like Joan can be seen in the relentless theological interrogation of her. Bedford's own zeal is glimpsed in his suspicion of Margery Kempe some fourteen years earlier in Yorkshire.

At Hessle in 1417, local men shout out at Kempe, calling her 'Lollard', and the *Book* provides the memorable detail that 'women cam rennyng owt of her howsys wyth her rokkys' (women came running out of their houses with their distaffs; 1.3054), demanding that Kempe be burnt as a heretic. The women's distaffs, their spindles, suggest their womanly industry as opposed to Kempe's contemplation, and their noisy rage as opposed to Kempe's quiet patience. Kempe's *Book* records that, subsequently, during the 14-kilometre (9 mi.) journey from Hessle to the town of Beverley, local people tell her to abandon her way of life, 'go spynne and carde as other women don' (go and spin and card wool as other women do; 1.3057–8). The people of Yorkshire in 1417 and/or Kempe's scribe invoked Kempe's gender here as a way of understanding her perceived heresy; to them, she should be safely spinning wool rather than perverting her gender and religion.

At Beverley she is accused by Bedford's men of being 'Combomis dowtyr' (Cobham's daughter, that is, a disciple of John Oldcastle, Lord Cobham; 1.3116) and of having lied about her pilgrimage to Jerusalem (1.3118). 'Lollards' were opposed to pilgrimage, and so the charge of Kempe's deceit is to make her guilty by association in order to present her as a 'Lollard'. Archbishop Bowet comments that he wouldn't want the Duke of Bedford to be angry with him (1.3128), as if to show under whose orders the interrogation of Kempe was taking place. At Beverley, Kempe is humiliated, insulted, threatened with forty days' imprisonment, but receives a testimonial in the form of a letter from Bowet with his seal. Similar incidents of persecution and interrogation follow quickly at Lincoln (1.3195) and Ely (1.3226), even as Kempe received a similar letter shortly afterwards, vouching for her, from Henry Chichele, Archbishop of Canterbury, at Lambeth.

By 1417, Kempe's notoriety drew her to the attention of formidable enemies. During these tribulations, Kempe has few

friends. However, she shows how she can find allies. The Duke
of Bedford is a powerful adversary, but Kempe charms his yeomen
by telling 'good tales'. At Beverley, she is locked up and put
under house arrest. Her purse and her ring are confiscated, denying her two of her most important tools – her financial means
and her proximity to her spiritual husband, Jesus. She stands
at the window and tells religious stories to local women. She
grows terribly thirsty, and asks her jailer's wife for a drink. The
wife doesn't have a key, but sets a ladder to the wall and brings
Kempe a pint of wine, and tells Kempe to hide the pot and cup
somewhere in case her husband should see it. This is a memorable moment, but it also encapsulates Kempe's bind: by seeming
to preach and by making alliances with wives, she is both disruptive and superficially 'Lollard' – as one of the accusations
made against those labelled 'Lollard' was the inappropriate role
they allowed women to play in religious life.[52] Even though
there is no evidence of Kempe being a heretic, it was the readily
available insult and accusation to make against a spiritual but
unenclosed woman, a hazard of Kempe's independence and her
determination to live a mixed life.

'hir gostly enmy': Her spiritual enemy

Kempe's encounters oscillate between favour and disfavour,
praise and blame, love and hate. One day, a Lynn neighbour
casually and spitefully throws a bowl of water over her in the
street (1.3235). Another time, Kempe's confessor tells her, in
a poetic turn of phrase, that everyone but 'the mone and the
seven sterrys' (stars; 1.3667) has turned against her. Mostly, her
detractors are less clearly delineated than her supporters but
they play an equally important part in her story. Kempe is beset
by gossips, churchmen and others who accuse her of heresy but
throughout her story, her main enemy is the Devil.

In late medieval Christianity, the Devil was not the all-powerful presence, an anti-god, that he is in Protestantism, but diabolical forces do play a significant role in *The Book of Margery Kempe*.[53] It is the Devil who, at the opening of Kempe's account of her life (1.137), hindered her from going to confession (and hence she never confessed that mysterious, heinous sin). Around the same time, Kempe's lack of dread of the Devil ('sche dred no devylle in helle, for sche dede so gret bodyly penawnce'; 1.303) reveals the flimsiness of her early attempts at penitence. Diabolical agency in the *Book* is hard to define as Kempe's Devil and his demons have the potential to be everywhere. Yet Kempe is repeatedly told that the Devil cannot work grace of the kind experienced by Kempe; as the English friar at Constance assures her, 'the devyl hath no powyr to werkyn swech grace in a sowle' (1.1457). Her Devil can be the Satanic arch enemy but can also be a devil inside her, a familiar: the late medieval Devil is a fiend who can take many forms – a heathen god, a fallen angel, Antichrist, Satan himself, 'mannes disceyvour'. This range of devilish forms is manifested in the Middle English vocabulary of devils: from the 'gobelin', 'mare', 'pouk', 'ragge-man', 'shucke', 'skulke' and 'spratte' (all words for devilish spirits), to the more calculating 'gilour' (beguiler), 'preiour' (predator), 'temptator' and 'unwine' (adversary) to the yet more powerful and person-alized Lucifer (the chief of the fallen angels), 'Mahoun' (the false god, a corruption of the name Mohammed) and 'Sathanas' (Satan, the embodiment of evil).

One definition of the Devil offered by *The Book of Margery Kempe* follows the Bible: the Devil is the 'fadyr of lesyngys' (father of lies; 2.337), quoting John 8:44, the Devil as a dishon-est man made indignant by Kempe's virtuous living. Another definition is that offered by Julian of Norwich during her con-versation with Kempe, that 'God and the devyl ben evyrmor contraryows, and thei schal nevyr dwellyn togedyr in on place'

(God and the Devil are always contrary to each other, and they shall never live together in one place; 1.980–81). Julian's strict delineation of the opposition of God and the Devil responds to the way in which the Middle English lexicon of diabolical evil often emerges in moments of 'misleading ambiguity'[54] – around falseness, hypocrisy and inconstancy, those very accusations with which Kempe repeatedly finds herself wrangling. Kempe's Devil is responsible for many moments in which her godliness is in doubt, but the Devil is also allied to the disbelievers who doubt Kempe's holiness: the Devil is a 'gostly enmy' (spiritual enemy; 1.4200), like the people who gossip spitefully about her are her worldly enemies.

Women were thought to be, like Eve, particularly suscep-tible to the Devil and his demons. In the York mystery plays, which Kempe may well have seen during the summer of 1413 (1.520), the Devil, 'Satanas', appears in a 'wormes likenes' in the Coopers' (cask-makers') Play of the Fall of Man. His role is to deceive Eve into eating the forbidden fruit. He promises her that 'to gretter state ye may be broughte', appealing to her ambition and pride as well as her disobedience. Satan promises Eve that she will be 'wise' as God. With Satan's coaxing, Eve takes the fruit, with Satan lustily egging her on: 'Byte on boldly, be nought abashed.'[55] Like Eve in the York Plays, Kempe her-self says that she was motivated by pride and that early on in her spiritual journey 'she levyd the develys suasyons and gan to consentyn for because sche cowde thynkyn no good thowt' (1.331), and believed the Devil's lie that God had forsaken her.

In later medieval iconography, the serpent often appeared at the Temptation of Adam and Eve in the guise of a woman, as a more explicitly anti-feminist moral was taken from the story of the Fall (illus. 18).[56] The York Plays help us understand how Margery Kempe's gender, as kin of Eve and Satan, may have informed the repeated assertion that she has a devil inside her.

18 Adam (left) and Eve (right), with Satan in the form of a wimpled woman, from James le Palmer, *Omne Bonum* (England, *c.* 1370), British Library, London.

The gendered aspect of such allegations would have been known to Kempe from a spectacular allegation that gripped the country in the autumn of 1419, as Joan of Navarre (1368–1437), Henry iv's widow and Henry v's stepmother, was accused of, and imprisoned for, attempting to kill her stepson, the king, through necromancy and poisoning. Joan was said to have collaborated with her confessor, a Franciscan friar named John Randolf; women of all social classes were thought to be particularly open to Satan's work, as conducted through fallen churchmen.[57]

At least seven times in her life, Kempe is accused, usually by religious men, of having a devil within her. They use strikingly similar language: 'thow hast a devyl wythin the' she is told at Canterbury (1.631); a priest says to her 'thu hast a devyl wythinne the' (1.1977); elsewhere 'sche had a devyl wythinne hir' (1.2470); 'sche hath a devyl wythinne hir' (1.2973); 'seyd summe men that sche had a devyl wythinne hir' (1.3537); 'summe seyd that sche had a devyl wythinne hir' (1.3649); another friar says 'sche hath a devyl wythinne hir' (1.3917). That the people around her think and say that she has a devil inside her shows the social construction of Kempe's reputation and that demonic inspiration is a part of her *inner* life, 'a devyl wythinne hir', not just her outward actions. The repeated form of words acknowledges widespread worry about diabolical, rather than divine, inspiration. Satanically inspired necromancy was especially associated with the 'Lollard' heresy at this time; an anti-Lollard poem, 'Friar Daw's Reply', written in Norfolk or London around 1420, complained that 'Sathanis pistile' (Satan's epistle) had supplanted 'Goddis gospel' (God's gospel) with 'sorowe' and 'sorcerie' and 'al maner of dolosite' (all kinds of deceitfulness).[58]

Any kind of mystical vision could be ascribed to the Devil, and a lively body of theological literature had developed, concerned with the discernment of spirits.[59] At the time *The Book of Margery Kempe* was being written, these were the grounds on which Bridget of Sweden's sanctity was interrogated and on which Joan of Arc was both tried and defended. At the Council of Constance in 1414–15 and in the following decade, the French theologian Jean Gerson (d. 1429) strenuously defended the divine inspiration of Joan's personal revelations but, in seeking to supervise and codify such revelations, the literature of spiritual discernment became deeply ambiguous and confused.[60] Central to these discussions was the notion that holy women, especially, might be mouthpieces for the Devil, rather than for God.

Gerson addressed this issue in a number of treatises, including *On Distinguishing True from False Revelations* (1401–2), *On the Proving of Spirits* (1415) and *On the Examination of Doctrine* (1423). Gerson was repeatedly very cautious about mystical experience. In *On Distinguishing True from False Revelations* he used the imagery of the moneychanger and the coin as a motif for the proper discernment of spirits; the changer has to examine the coin to ensure its authenticity and thus gauge its proper worth. A central tenet of Gerson's thought was that moderation in devotion was needed for correct discernment – he inveighed against the extreme asceticism and emotional indiscipline because they showed a failure of discernment. Gerson was particularly concerned about women's visions, because women, according to Gerson, are 'too easily seduced' and 'too obstinately seducers'.[61]

Demonic activities in the lives of other medieval female mystics frequently included terrifying animals and beasts, physical abduction with unwelcome journeys, sexual harassment and frightening scenes of erotic possession.[62] One of Kempe's most memorable visions is 'sent from the devyl' and consists of 'horybyl syghtys' of men's penises:

Sche sey as hir thowt veryly dyvers men of religyon, preystys, and many other, bothyn hethyn and Cristen comyn

befor hir syght that sche myth not enchewyn hem ne
puttyn hem owt of hir syght, schewyng her bar membrys
[their bare genitals] unto hir. And therwyth the devyl bad
hir in hir mende chesyn [the Devil commanded her in
her mind to choose] whom sche wolde han fyrst of hem
alle and sche must be comown to hem alle. And he seyd
sche lykyd bettyr summe on of hem than alle the other
(1.3427–32).

Different clerics, and many others, Christian and non-
Christian, display their bare penises in front of her, and she agrees
to be held 'in common' by them. This account explicitly juxtaposes Kempe's vision with her sometimes erotic devotion to
the incarnate 'manhod' of Christ (1.3424). Her vision is related
to stories of incubi, male demons who sexually tempt, cajole
and harass women. The demonic possession of Alice Kyteler of
Kilkenny, the first trial in the British Isles of a woman for hosting
an incubus, had taken place in 1324; Kyteler, a wealthy merchant's wife of Flemish origins, was said, among other things, to
have received an incubus and allowed him to copulate with her.[63]
St Francesca Romana, whom Kempe would almost certainly have
heard about in Rome, had similar visions of men, women and
children having sodomitical sex with each other.[64] Sexually
harassing demons and the *spiritus fornicationis* were particularly
common in people who sought Bridget of Sweden's help.[65]

Kempe was never accused of witchcraft or sorcery, and indeed
witchcraft was only just becoming codified and prosecuted at
this time.[66] Kempe's visions of priestly genitalia are described as
coming not from the Devil but authorized by God, as a punishment for Kempe's prior refusal to believe God's judgements of
who will count among 'the dampnyd as of the savyd'. God *allows*
the Devil to give Kempe the genital visions, so the incident functions as a vignette of *discretio*, of Kempe learning to differentiate

kinds of spiritual vision. This happens to her at several points, as she later discloses: 'whan sche dowtyd er mistrostyd the goodnes of God, supposyng er dredyng that it was the wyle of hir gostly enmy to enformyn hir er techyn hir otherwyse than wer to hir gostly hele' (1.4775–9). Kempe's sins are forgiven, but the Devil and his demons are never far, and the *Book* shows how one must constantly be vigilant of misreading spiritual vision. The inclusion of diabolical incidents are important ways of signalling Kempe and her confessors' awareness of visionary carefulness, and the dangers of mystical vision. Kempe's ambitions for holiness would easily have been interpreted as Eve-like disobedience, diabolically inspired, and if she has a Devil inside her it is, like her Christ, a personal one.

'fals strumpet', Leicester, 1417

BETWEEN 1414 AND 1417 Kempe had completed the three 'Great Pilgrimages' available to medieval Latin Christians, to Jerusalem, Rome and Santiago. Such journeys were expensive and risky, but Kempe had survived them, and proved herself as a pilgrim. After returning from Santiago and visiting Hailes in 1417, Kempe travelled to Leicester, a journey of about 100 km (62 mi.). Leicester is unusual in Kempe's topography for not being a significant pilgrimage site, and it marks another interlude, in which she is arrested, detained and subjected to a sustained interrogation.

At a church (possibly the magnificent Augustinian abbey of St Mary, almost nothing of which survives) Kempe regards a crucifix, dissolving in tears of pity and compassion (1.2610). This establishes her orthodox religiosity (banishing the worry that she may have a 'Lollard' antipathy to images) in a public setting. However, the next step is also characteristically Kempeian: the 'fire of love' is kindled so smartly in her that she cannot hold it in, she cannot keep it private, and she cries out, weeping and sobbing so loudly that people gawp at her. The transfer from internal spiritual excitement to external social controversy is one of Kempe's most established moves, but at Leicester it seems to have led swiftly to her arrest.

Leaving the church, a man, a stranger, grabs Kempe by the sleeve. "'Damsel, why wepist thu so sor?'", he asks. She replies to him with a polite but cryptic rebuttal: "'it is not yow to telle'" (you are not to be told; 1.2615–16).

Kempe describes how she and her friend Thomas Marshall secure lodgings in an inn in Leicester and have dinner there;

then she asks that Marshall write a letter to John Kempe, so he can bring her home. In the light of her subsequent arrest, this detail invokes John Kempe to show his jurisdiction over his wife as she places of herself under male authorities – Christ, Thomas Marshall and John Kempe – that she has chosen, rather than those who seek to impose themselves on her.

Kempe – now a woman in her mid-forties, a mother and mystic who has been away from home for many months – is sitting in her room when the innkeeper suddenly bursts in, takes her purse and tells her that she must come and speak to the mayor. By taking the purse the innkeeper effectively stops Kempe from fleeing the town: she is being treated as a suspected criminal.

At this time the mayor was a Leicestershire man named John Arnesby. In Leicester, the mayor was chosen from among the city's leading burgesses and acted as the figurehead '*de communitate Leycestrie*', that is, the head of the city as community. Arnesby is brusque with Kempe, and demands to know what region she is from and whose daughter she is. Arnesby asks Kempe about her father because he is trying to put her, a roving outsider, into a social frame. Kempe, the mayor of Lynn's daughter and from a milieu very similar to Arnesby's, answers as clearly and tersely as the mayor's question:

'Syr,' sche seyd, 'I am of Lynne in Norfolke, a good mannys dowtyr of the same Lynne, whech hath ben meyr [mayor] fyve tymes of that worshepful burwgh [borough] and aldyrman also many yerys, and I have a good man, also a burgeys of the seyd town, Lynne, to [for] myn husbond' (1.2621–4).

Early on in *The Book of Margery Kempe* the scribe/amanuensis had tried to obscure the specific geography and origins of its protagonist ('the town N'; 1.205). By the time Kempe reaches

Leicester, it is crucial to disclose her family background to assert
her social and familial pedigree, her right to be respected. This
allows her later to tell Arnesby boldly, 'ye arn not worthy to ben a
meyr' (1. 2720). Arnesby repeatedly accuses Kempe of 'falsness':

> 'A,' seyd the meyr, 'Seynt Kateryn telde what kynred sche
> cam of and yet ar ye not lyche, for thu art a fals strumpet, a
> fals loller, and a fals deceyver of the pepyl, and therfor I schal
> have the in preson' (1.2625–7).

> 'Ah', said the mayor, 'St Katherine described what kin she
> came of, and yet you're not like her, because you're a false
> strumpet, a false Lollard, and a false deceiver of the people,
> and therefore I shall have you imprisoned.'

Arnesby cleverly uses the popular figure of St Katherine
of Alexandria (illus. 19), a role model of female authority and
martyrdom, to show how, to his mind, Kempe *lacks* authority,
like a false saint. Arnesby allies himself with the cult of saints
(one of the aspects of religion the Wycliffites and 'Lollards' most
decried) and judges St Katherine to have been honest where
Kempe is deceitful.[1] St Katherine, a well-born woman preacher,
also presages and parallels Kempe's longer ordeal in Leicester,
because St Katherine was a famous prisoner: in her legend,
Katherine was tried by a tyrant emperor named Maxentius,
stripped naked, beaten with scourges and placed in a dark prison,
tormented with hunger for twelve days. The fifteenth-century
East Anglian version of Katherine's legend by Osbern Bokenham
describes how Katherine, educated and eloquent, reasoned with
Maxentius to convert him to Christianity. In reply, Maxentius
accuses Katherine of trying to ensnare him through 'treccherous
sotylte' (treacherous subtlety) and philosophical discussion; in
response, 'to presoun he hyr sent'.[2]

De sancte katherine. a

ndens et migilans
migo qualis es aun hpū
so illo qui te elegit de mūe

Kempe's reply to Arnesby subtly and wittily turns his words on him: 'I am as redy, ser, to gon to preson for Goddys lofe as ye arn redy to gon to chirche' ('I am as ready, sir, to go to prison for God's love as you are ready to go to church'; 1.2627–8). With great effect, Kempe rebukes the mayor. She reveals a common medieval understanding of the prison cell as the exemplary place for the reception of self-growth and God's grace.[3] She also reclaims St Katherine: she will emulate Katherine by turning imprisonment into a moment of glory, a willing suffering that proves her devotion. This echoes St Katherine's experience of imprisonment, as her 'dyrk prysoun' cell shone with light and in it she was visited first by 'an aungel bryht', a 'whyht dowe' (white dove) who brought food for her from Christ, and then by Christ Himself.[4] It is thanks to divine assistance in her prison cell that Katherine begins to preach about the joys of Christendom, and converts the pagan queen to her faith. Kempe's exchange with Arnesby is to a significant extent a quarrel about who has the right to the lexicon of saintly martyrdom.[5]

Mayor Arnesby, evidently unmoved, commands Kempe to be imprisoned (likely at the town prison in Leicester's High Street, where the mayor of Leicester had the right to guard prisoners taken within the town). However, a series of events proves fortunate for Kempe. The jailer's assistant feels compassion for her and goes on to point out that they will have to imprison Kempe among men; this allows Kempe, St Katherine-like, to plead for her chastity and to be imprisoned elsewhere. Eventually the jailer leads Kempe to his house, and he and his wife guard her in a well-appointed room, letting her go to church and eat with them. Moreover, a man visiting from the town of Boston (Lincolnshire) happens to be there (1.2638)

19 The martyrdom of St Katherine from a French book of hours (c. 1450), British Library, London.

and attests to Kempe's holy reputation in his hometown and this appears to sway the mayor and his authorities to allow Kempe to be placed in the jailer's care. Like St Katherine, Kempe's detention becomes a kind of spiritual release, and this is mirrored in her sudden salvation at a moment of peril.

The entire episode at Leicester is structured through Kempe's interactions with male authority, and the paradoxical presence of St Katherine here further genders the episode in invoking a female virgin-martyr defined by the flagrant abuses to which she was subjected by the men around her. Subsequently, the mayor attacks Kempe again, in front of the abbot; the *Book* discreetly omits what the mayor alleges this time, but from Kempe's answers (1.2713–16), he seems to have conjoined gender and heresy, alleging that she is a 'strumpet', a lecherous woman, and a 'Lollard'.

Kempe's confident handling of Mayor Arnesby may have made him determined to punish her. The city's steward – one of the most influential secular officials, presiding over local courts – sends for Kempe; this man has not been securely identified, but may have been the Lancastrian careerist Sir Robert Babthorpe (d. *c.* 1436).[6] Kempe describes the steward as a 'semly' (1.2645), or handsome, man, an observation that undercuts her subsequent emphasis on her purity and virtue. However, the jailer's wife, in a moment of sorority, protects her. For Kempe, the threat to her sexual integrity, rather than the charge of heresy, seems paramount. Once the jailer has overruled his wife and taken Kempe to the steward, she is put before him, where he discusses her with many priests. Talked at in Latin, Kempe does not understand what is being said and says to the steward, 'Spekyth Englysch, yf yow lyketh [if you please], for I undyrstonde not what ye sey.' Bluntly, crudely, the steward replies, 'Thu lyest falsly in pleyn Englysch' (1.2650–51). Again, hierarchy is visible in their forms of address, as Kempe uses the honorific 'yow', the steward the familiar 'thu'.

After an initial round of questions, the steward takes Kempe by the arm and leads her into 'his chamber' (suggesting that this interview took place at his base at Leicester Castle). His gesture is both overfamiliar and threatening. Kempe comments on his 'fowyl rebawdy wordys' (foul rude words), 'desyryng, as it semyd hir, to opressyn hir and forlyn hir' (desiring, as it seemed to her, to violate her and rape her; 1.2656). The language is careful to emphasize Kempe's *perception* of the situation; if the steward was indeed Robert Babthorpe, he was still alive at the time of writing in the 1430s. However, the way the incident is reported makes us acutely aware of Kempe's panic and her powerlessness.

This brief interaction summarizes the challenges that Kempe faced; by speaking about God in 'pleyn Englysch' she laid herself open to the charge of 'Lollardy' through vernacular preaching. The steward's interest is both theological and gendered; after his interrogation of Kempe he says to her, 'Thu schalt telle me whethyr thu hast this speche of [from] God er [or] of the devyl, er ellys thu schalt gon to preson' (1.2659–60), and concludes by saying to her 'Eythyr thu art a ryth good woman er ellys a ryth wikked woman' (1.2667–8): she can be either saint or strumpet, at the poles of misogyny.

The mayor and steward at Leicester are reacting to the national context in which inquisitors began to probe heresy as part of their routine duties and launch general enquiries. Just a year before Kempe's ordeal at Leicester, in July 1416, Archbishop Chichele decreed that every bishop was to make inquiries at least twice a year into

> any heretics, any persons holding secret conventicles, any persons differing in life or morals from the behaviour of the faithful, anyone holding errors or heresies, anyone owning suspicious books written in English, anyone receiving persons suspected of errors or heresies or their favourers, or

anyone in the area who has had communication with them
or visited them.[7]

Such a 'definition' was vague; it foregrounded suspicion
over proof, asserted guilt by association, and was particularly
weighted against anyone 'differing in life or morals' in ways that
were not specifically heretical. It was in such an atmosphere of
surveillance that Margery Kempe found herself being interrogated at Leicester in the summer of 1417.

As in her previous examination by the mayor, Kempe
protects herself from the steward by appealing to God and
her husband, rather than asserting her own authority ('for the
reverens of almythy God, sparyth me, for I am a mannys wife';
1.2658–9). What she can do, however, is find power in her
own powerlessness, as she restates, echoing St Katherine, her
fearlessness of imprisonment and her devotion to abjection:
'to gon to preson I am not aferd for my Lordys lofe [my Lord's
love], the whech meche mor suffyrd for my lofe than I may for
hys' (1.2662).[8] The steward's response is to make dirty gestures
and wicked faces at Kempe (1.2664), terrifying her, to force her
to disclose how she receives speech and communication from
the Holy Ghost and not from her own knowledge or study. The
steward places Kempe back into detention, along with Thomas
Marshall and another pilgrim, a man from the town of Wisbech
near Lynn, who had been travelling with her. The next day
the two male pilgrims are interrogated again, at Leicester's
Guildhall, where they swear that Kempe is 'a good woman
of the ryth feyth' (right faith) and 'clene and chaste' in her
conduct (1.2683–4).

Kempe and her companions at Leicester were orthodox and
conventional pilgrims, but the idea of 'Lollard' heresy was so
nebulous, and the sense of illicit criminality so pervasive, that
such people were subject to a significant degree of surveillance

and inquisition. The detection of heresy or dissent is necessarily an imprecise process, but Kempe's account of her ordeals at Leicester in 1417 provides us with a detailed portrait of England as a highly regulated, even paranoid, political environment. Later in the same year Kempe went to Archbishop Chichele at Lambeth Palace to receive his letter and seal, effectively an endorsement of her devotional orthodoxy which allowed her safe passage (and was produced to that effect when she was challenged at Ely; 1.3226).

At the same time, the entire incident at Leicester is a Kempeian retelling of St Katherine's legend, of a 'holi virgine' subjected to interrogation, imprisonment and physical ordeal, and who garnered a community of people 'enflawmed with soverayne devocion' to her.[9] Elsewhere, Kempe aspires to be beheaded, like saints Katherine and Margaret, in a 'most soft deth' (1.680). The ordeal at Leicester ends when Kempe, in church, receives a religious imprimatur in the face of her secular naysayers. She goes to the abbey at Leicester, is welcomed there by Abbot Richard Rothley (d. 1420), she collapses in an abundance of devotion and gets a letter from Rothley for the Bishop of Lincoln. At the end of her difficult time in Leicester, Kempe has successfully gained the approval of senior churchmen, the abbot and dean, who 'had gret confidens that owre Lord lovyd hir' (1.2765).

20 A 'Jewish' elder peers through his eyeglasses at a book, as he ignores the young Jesus preaching. Master of the Housebook, *Life of the Virgin* series (*c.* 1490–1505), oil on wood, Landesmuseum, Mainz.

FIVE

Things

One of the first moments of divine intervention in *The Book of Margery Kempe* takes place around an unlikely object: a pair of spectacles. A priest 'whech this creatur had gret affeccyon to' (1.73), after prevaricating for over four years, eventually agrees to read a draft of Kempe's book and to continue writing for her. However, he finds that, even though he can see 'alle other thyng', his eyesight fails him when he comes to write, 'so that he myght not se to make hys lettyr' or 'mend hys penne'. So, in an elegantly informal phrasing that sounds like Kempe's reported speech, he 'sett a peyr [of] spectacles on hys nose' (1.105–6). Yet with spectacles his vision is worse than before! Kempe tells him that his spiritual enemy, the Devil, is trying to hinder him and that God will give him grace if only he continue. And then, the next time he comes to write the book, he can see perfectly well, by daylight and by candlelight!

The Book of Margery Kempe opens with a discussion of spiritual vision and correct ways of seeing: worldly vision – the bodily eye, aided by 'spectacles' – is less reliable, less effective, than devout vision. This is in keeping with mystical notions of 'negative' and 'apophatic' understandings of God (knowing God through what He is not, and knowing God by not representing Him). Accordingly, mysticism held that God's goodness and wholeness could not be understood through language or positively described. Only God's grace (the grace that intervenes to help the priest's vision *despite* his spectacles) and contemplation (a diligent, humble attentiveness) can lead to true vision.[1]

Spectacles, introduced to England in the fourteenth century, would have been an expensive item and were frequently associated with scribal crafts.[2] In medieval art early Christian 'author-scribes', especially St Jerome, sometimes wear spectacles.[3] Spectacles were already associated with scholarly diligence but were also distrusted as emphasizing the literal word rather than the spirit, and in medieval images sometimes rabbis, pagans and the 'wicked' tormentors of the saints wear spectacles. Like Kempe's scribe-priest, in trying to see properly through the body such bespectacled fools only cloud their vision. For instance, in the Mainz *Life of the Virgin* series, a 'Jewish' doctor of the Temple peers through his eyeglasses at a book in 'Hebrew' (illus. 20), rather than attending to, and learning from, the young Jesus.

Kempe's *Book* opens with an advertisement of 'correct' ways of reading, but also warns of the limits of material objects: the priest's spectacles are no help if he cannot overcome his spiritual enemy. Kempe's experience corroborates other mystical accounts of supernatural writing processes and xenoglossia (the preternatural ability to speak languages), foreshadowing the miraculous way in which Kempe's German priest in Rome will later suddenly find himself able to understand her.[4] The writing of the *Book* itself becomes a kind of set of eyeglasses, as it is through this process that the priest-scribe is better able to see to write, to glimpse the divine as manifested in Kempe's life.

Kempe's religious practice has aptly been described as 'a very material mysticism'.[5] Late medieval Christianity was characterized by its awareness of the transformative power of material objects.[6] Even though Kempe sought a contemplative path, her *Book* demonstrates a great attachment to books, souvenirs, fabrics, food, jewellery, relics. One gains a rich sense of the material world that she moved in, and the precious value of material objects in her life. Sometimes, these are artefacts with which she comes into contact, like the pair of knives given by her confessor Alan (1.4040) or, in Rome, the hampers of food she was given with which to make soup (1.2186). Other times, this material sensibility takes the form of vividly object-based imagery and similes. Kempe's God behaves to her 'as a smyth wyth a fyle' (like a blacksmith with a file; 1.1019), filing down her impurities. Kempe hears a sound 'as it had ben a peyr of belwys blowyng in hir ere' (like a pair of bellows blowing in her ear; 1.2114).[7] She has a unique vision of Christ stabbed in the chest by a stranger wielding a 'baselard knyfe' (1.4943), a fashionable, curved dagger. Kempe's tears are like angels' 'pyment' (1.3805), an expensive medicinal spiced wine.

For Kempe, religious media are not cheap substitutes for religious experience but, rather, a mode of having a religious experience. Medieval culture abounds with enlivened things, objects that transform themselves and do things to the people around them:[8] the crucifix that emits light, the eucharistic host that leaps from the mouth of the faithless, the images of the Virgin that smile at a woman who says the *Ave Maria*.[9] These lively things represent intersections of life and death, miracle and mimesis, the extraordinary and the mundane. Kempe's experiences with crucifixes show how public icons and objects could be engaged in intensely subjective encounters.

The reformist John Wycliffe had been cautiously critical about the power of images and icons, which he believed could be used for good or ill; in his sermons he expressed the wish that Christians could do without such images but acknowledged that images and icons could, if used with care, deepen devotion to God.[10] The anonymous author of *Dives and Pauper* (c. 1400) criticized laypeople who mistook religious iconography for divinity itself, leading them into a kind of idolatry: he counselled,

21 Walnut-wood figure of the Christ child in swaddling, made in Perugia (c. 1320), Bode-Museum, Berlin.

'knele, yf thu wilt, aforn the ymage, nought to the ymage' (kneel, if thou wish, before the image, but not to the image).[11] However, by the first two decades of the fifteenth century (at precisely the time at which Kempe was developing her religious persona), the 'Lollard' heresy had taken up a strident position against images and icons. The Twelfth Lollard Conclusion asserted that people spend too much time and attention making beautiful objects of art and craft and should instead simplify their devotions and refrain from such unnecessary endeavours. This complemented the broader 'Lollard' antipathy to worldly objects and temporal power, and their assertion that the doctrine of transubstantiation and the practice of pilgrimage to relics was a kind of idolatry. It is in this fraught context that Kempe's determinedly material mysticism avows and renews the role of material objects in influencing her as a devout person. At several points Kempe displays great devotion not only to relics but to purchased souvenirs – 'the mett of Cristys grave', a parchment strip showing the measurement of Christ's grave (1.1817), and a staff like Moses's rod (1.2775), bought in Jerusalem. The souvenir of Moses's rod is both Kempe's lowly walking stick but also a progenitor of the magic wand, for Kempe is certain that it will protect her. She adds that 'sche wold not a lost it for forty shillings' (1.2776), characteristically putting a financial value on a spiritual item.

In 1414, after visiting the Holy Land, Kempe travels from Venice to Rome with Richard the Irishman, two Franciscan friars, and a woman who had come with the friars from Jerusalem. This female pilgrim carries with her a 'chist' (chest, case; 1.1797) which contains an 'ymage' of Jesus in it, an artefact that catches Kempe's eye. At each point where the group rests, local women gather round the chest and clothe the little figure and kiss it, 'as thei it had ben God hymselfe' (as if it were God Himself; 1.1799). What Kempe seems to describe here is an ivory or wooden statue or doll, which were especially popular in women's religious communities. Few examples survive but those that do tend be 20–45 cm (8–18 in.) tall, often jointed, and were dressed or swaddled (see illus. 21).[12]

After seeing the holy doll, Kempe describes how the same women furnish her with a bed, lay her down on it, 'and comfortyd hir as mech as thei myth for owyr Lordys lofe' (1.1808). The devotional object models Kempe's own devout behaviour and establishes her own relationship with the other women. Thus their small image in the chest intimately corresponds with Kempe's devotional body and she becomes at once doll-like, childlike and Christlike: the icon transfers to Kempe herself.

'a fayr ymage ... clepyd a pyté': A pretty image ... called a pietà

In Norwich, Kempe records how she encountered a 'a fayr ymage of owr Lady clepyd a pyté' (1.3492), a pietà: an image of the mourning Virgin Mary holding the dead Christ. She recalls how a 'lady' wished to have dinner with her, and so Kempe goes to a Norwich church where this lady attends services. There, she sees the pietà, and

thorw the beholdyng of that peté hir mende was al holy
ocupyed in the Passyon of owr Lord Jhesu Crist and in the
compassyon of owr Lady, Seynt Mary, be whech sche was
compellyd to cryyn ful lowde and wepyn ful sor, as thei
sche schulde a deyd (1.3493–5).

through beholding that 'pity' her mind was fully occupied in
our Lord Jesus Christ's Passion and in the compassion of our
Lady, St Mary, by which she was compelled to cry very loudly
and weep very bitterly, as though she were going to die.

This is a very concise portrait of the image or object as emotional stimulus, as the act of seeing and 'beholdyng' occupies
Kempe's mind, followed by a physical, affective compulsion
('sche was compellyd') to cry and to weep. The verb 'occupien'
describes how the 'pity' enters Kempe's mind and at once con-
notes Kempe's engagement with, and possession by, the image.[13]
Grammatically, the 'sche' who was 'compellyd' to cry as though
she might die can be Kempe and/or the Virgin. Indeed Kempe
imitates both the Virgin, weeping for her dead son, and the
dead Christ, as she laments so painfully 'as thei sche schulde a
deyd'. Viewing the pietà facilitates Kempe becoming close to
the Virgin and becoming *like* her.

Kempe may have seen a mural, an alabaster sculpture, a
painted cloth, or a stone carving: the pietà appeared in a range
of forms in Norwich churches.[14] Kempe does not specify exactly
where she saw the 'pity', but the subject was one of the most popular in late medieval religious imagery. Kempe's contemporary
John Lydgate, the East Anglian poet of popular religion, wrote
the poem 'On the Image of Pity', designed to accompany a pietà
image. Lydgate's poem helps us to provide a context for Kempe's
interaction with the pietà, showing how this was not a personal,
individual or spontaneous reaction, but rather an enactment of

a popular emotional script. Lydgate's poem powerfully exhorts the viewer:

> O wretched synner! what so ever thow be,
> With hert endurat [enduring] hardar than the stone,
> Turne hidder [hither] in hast [haste], knelle [kneel] doun,
>   behold and se
> The moder [mother] of Cryst, whose hert was woo begon
>   [woebegone]
> To se her childe, whiche synne dide nevar non [who never
>   sinned],
> For thyn offence thus wounded & arayd [adorned];
> Rewe on [be ashamed of] that peyne, remembringe here upon,
> Pray to that quene, that moder is, and mayd [virgin] . . .¹⁵

Lydgate asserts that the purpose of such images is 'dewe remembraunce', proper retention in the memory, which will help cure the viewer's soul. In medieval theories of vision, to look at something was to encounter it physically as the retina was believed to give out a beam that struck the image (the theory of extramission), or the image became imprinted on the receptive faculty through entering and striking the retina (the theory of intromission).¹⁶ In other words, gazing on an image like the 'pity' was a way of penetrating one's 'hert . . . hardar than the stone' in order to receive a wound of love and grace through physical contact with the grieving intercessor, the Virgin. This exemplifies how religious media enabled dynamic movement through time and identity, since the viewer, like Kempe, is 'compelled' into an act of 'remembringe' through being touched by the image.

As with other mediated moments in *The Book of Margery Kempe*, the people around Kempe do not share her holy vision. At Norwich, seeing Kempe's reaction to the pietà, the lady's priest approaches Kempe and says 'Damsel, Jhesu is ded long sithyn'

(Lady, Jesus is long since dead). Kempe responds, incisively, 'Sir, hys deth is as fresch to me as he had deyd this same day, and so me thynkyth it awt to be to yow and to alle Cristen pepil' (1.3497–8). The image makes Jesus's death 'fresch' to her, and this is a conversation as much about the meaning and efficacy of images as it is about Kempe's sincerity. Hearing this answer, the Norwich lady is impressed and becomes Kempe's 'avoket' (1.3502), her supporter, her advocate, as the 'pity' continues to work its effects for Kempe.

'crucyfyx': Crucifix

Kempe also has several vivid encounters with crucifixes, images or sculptures of Christ on the Cross. The town of Lynn was well known for one of its crosses, which stood at St Margaret's and at which offerings were made and pilgrimage badges purchased.[17] Another cross, the 'Blackfriars Cross', a stone cross with the crucified Christ on one side, once stood by Lynn's Dominican priory where Kempe visits the supportive recluse (1.853) and where, later, she has a vision of the Virgin wrapping the infant Christ in a white handkerchief (1.4974–7).[18]

Early in her spiritual conversion, Kempe many times desires 'that the crucifix schuld losyn hys handys fro the crosse' and lovingly embrace her (1.307), a longing that Kempe understands to be vainglorious. Later, such sensual, physical visions are replaced by something more internal. At Leicester, Kempe views a painted crucifix in a church and starts to 'meltyn' (to melt) and dissolve (1.2608). Viewing the crucifix causes Christ's Passion to enter her mind and kindle the 'fyer of lofe' (1.2610) in her heart, and she cries out so 'hedowslyche' (hideously, passionately; 1.2613) that people gawp at her. Kempe describes how whenever she sees a crucifix 'sche saw owyr Lord be betyn er wowndyd' (1.1588) in her thought, a pithy description of how the material object of the crucifix becomes active in the responsive mind's eye. In the Palm Sunday procession at Lynn (1.4368–440), which culminated in a dramatic unveiling of the crucifix, the crucifix assists Kempe in putting worldly thoughts aside and focusing 'entirely' on spiritual things.

Kempe's description of the Palm Sunday rituals at Lynn develops the relationship between bodily sight and spiritual vision. By the later Middle Ages, Palm Sunday processions in England were elaborate multimedia performances, usually involving willow or yew 'palms', a painted cross, a churchyard procession, special reliquaries and shrines for the sacrament, gospel readings, children's role-playing and choristers, the singing of anthems by the congregation, and the scattering of flowers and unconsecrated hosts. Throughout England, the procession's climax was akin to that described by Kempe: a cloth, which had been hung over the crucifix at the rood screen, was drawn off to reveal Christ's crucified body to the kneeling congregation, which then sang the anthem, 'Ave Rex Noster' – 'Hail, Our King'.[19] Mass then followed.

Likewise, Kempe describes joining the churchyard procession, but 'it semyd to hir gostly sygth' (it seemed to her in her spiritual sight; 1.4370) that she is transported from Lynn to Jerusalem. Thus Kempe is not a witness or bystander or even a congregant, but an active participant in the biblical events that Palm Sunday commemorates. When the Palm Sunday crucifix is finally revealed, Kempe says

> hir thowt that sche saw owr Lord Crist Jhesu as verily in hir sowle wyth hir gostly eye as sche had seyn beforn the crucifixe wyth hir bodily eye (1.4438–40).

> she thought that she saw our Lord Christ Jesus as truly in her soul with her spiritual eye as she had seen the crucifix with her physical eye.

The material object of the crucifix therefore facilitates Kempe seeing with her 'gostly' eye of faith.

Far from emphasizing arousal or erotic affect, Kempe focuses on the act of ocular translation. Viewing leads to inward seeing, and the object of the crucifix becomes present in her receptive soul. This accords with the moral understanding of vision set out in the widely read treatise *De oculo morali* (On the Moral Eye) by Peter of Limoges (d. 1306), which argued that physical vision was morally formative.[20] For Kempe, artefacts like the pietà and the crucifix were not proxies or substitutes for religious feeling, and she is careful to show how she is not idolatrous. To view the crucifix was, for her, a way into the deepest kind of contemplation, creatively bringing together physical engagement with moral edification. It was through such vision that Christ came to be 'verily' alive for Kempe.

'my bone maryd ryng': My precious wedding-ring

While lodging on the road in Italy, somewhere between Venice and Assisi, Kempe describes how she has a ring, 'the which owyr Lord had comawndyd hir to do makyn whil she was at hom in Inglond' (1.1809–11). It had been inscribed with the legend 'Jhesus est amor meus' (Jesus is my love). Kempe wears the ring hanging from her purse, as a protective amulet against thieves. However, on the morning of her departure from her lodgings, the ring goes missing. She addresses the 'good wyfe of the hows', the landlady: 'Madam, my bone maryd ryng to Jhesu Crist, as ho seyth, it is awey!' ('Madam, what one might call "my precious wedding-ring to Jesus Christ" is gone!'; 1.1822–3). Kempe describes this as a ring that stands for her wedding to Jesus (this is before her marriage to the Godhead in Rome), although Kempe – or her amanuensis – adds the qualifier, 'as ho seyth': 'what one might call'. A trivial 'non-miracle' occurs: the landlady suddenly has a 'gylty' countenance, and the two women look under the bed. Kempe finds the ring, the landlady begs her forgiveness, and the narrative moves on. We are to understand that Kempe has touched the landlady's conscience.

Kempe's ring is replete with religious symbolism and, for her, vibrant with pious stories.[21] Rings were used as pledges of marriage and love in medieval England, and rings bearing religious mottoes and quotations were very widespread. More specifically, Kempe's 'wedding ring of Jesus' purchases on two particular traditions: the ring given to novices on taking the veil to signify their espousal to Christ, and the ring worn by vowesses to betoken their chastity and spiritual marriage to Christ. In fifteenth-century images of the Madonna and Child, the Virgin sometimes wears a wedding band, to invoke the mystical betrothal of Christ and Mary.[22] Kempe's ring is, then, a public sign of her chastity, her closeness to Christ, and of her special status akin to a nun. No rings survive from medieval England with the same motto as Kempe's, but similar examples include a vowess's ring (illus. 22) with the motto 'O cest anel de chastete: seu espose a Ihesus Crist' (O this ring of chastity weds one to Jesus Christ), or the fifteenth-century wreath-ring featuring St Margaret and St Christopher, with the motto 'tout mon cuer auez' ('you have all my heart').[23] Kempe's ring's protective, talismanic function

22 Ring of chastity to Jesus Christ. Finger-ring with inscribed hoop, c. 1300, British Museum, London.

is not unusual, with evidence of people wearing St Christopher rings especially to protect them from sudden death and while travelling.[24] Rings were at once intimate devotional symbols and public displays of wealth, but they were also matters of personal preference and adaptation, a way of marking the body and of subtly adapting one's prayers to one's own style. Versions of the words on Kempe's ring, 'Jhesus est amor meus', appear elsewhere in *The Book of Margery Kempe* and this seems to have been Kempe's motto: early on, Jesus commands Kempe 'boldly clepe me Jhesus, thi love, for I am thi love' (1.375) and later when Jesus thanks Kempe 'for the gret lofe thu hast to me', he says, 'dowtyr, thu mayst boldly seyn to me, "Jhesus est amor meus"' (1.3787; 1.3808). The phrase may be inspired by Richard Rolle's writings, and it is one of many instances of Kempe adapting versions of verbal phrases drawn from elsewhere, most frequently books and sermons.[25]

Kempe has had the ring made, she says, at God's command. It would be easy to see this as the commodification of her religious feeling, as the devoted *bourgeoise* going shopping to express her personal holiness and her own interpretation of her relationship to Jesus. When fearing that the ring has been lost in the Italian lodging house, Kempe says she 'wold not a lost the ryng for a thowsand pownde and meche mor' (1.1813). The ring gains its power in its physicality, its material worth and the threat of its physical loss: in *The Book of Margery Kempe*, 'one is kept constantly aware of the "cash nexus"'.[26] But the ring effectively punctuates Kempe's journey between Venice and Assisi and it establishes her devout identity in a territory where she can otherwise scarcely make herself understood.

'boke': Book

Unsurprisingly for a work of writing that is so concerned with
its own genesis as a book, books play an important recurring
role in *The Book of Margery Kempe*. Yet Kempe states that she
could neither read nor write and books appear as icons as much
as practical objects of literacy. Certainly, at around the same
date to Kempe somewhat similar English women – both religious and of the merchant class – could read.[27] We might note
Kempe's 'predilection for words – for repartee, for edifying conversation, for sermons, for the written word, and above all for
verbal revelations of the divine', and conclude therefore that it
is surprising that she was not literate.[28] Some have argued that
Kempe could read and write in English but was 'illiterate' in a
clerical sense, as she did not write Latin.[29] Kempe states at her
trial in Leicester that she does not know Latin (1.2651) but
expounds the Bible quoted in Latin to a cleric in York (1.2842).
She reports that her priest 'red hir so many bokys' (read so many
books to her; 1.3397–8) for seven or eight years, inspiring him
to seek out material with which he had previously been unfa-
miliar. Her Christ seems not to mind how she encounters sacred
texts, telling her that he is pleased with her for her praying
aloud, 'whether thu redist er herist redyng' (whether you read
or hear them read; 1.5187).[30] Many modern readers of Kempe
have understood these comments as a strategic 'trope of illiter-
acy', in which Kempe pretends that her *Book* was produced not
by a laywoman but a male cleric.[31]

In the later Middle Ages, reading aloud and 'active listen-
ing' – that is, learning a text from public reading – were not
thought of as signs of 'illiterate' 'deficiency', but rather benefited
both the reader and their audience. Indeed very much vernacular writing was explicitly designed to be 'heard' rather than
restricted to private reading in a book.[32] *The Book of Margery*

Kempe mentions a wide range of written material with which Kempe was familiar, the vast majority of which was read with her by priests, probably in the period 1416–20. These books are a glossed Latin bible ('the Bybyl with doctowrys'); Richard Rolle's *Fire of Love* ('Richard Hampol, hermyte, in *Incendio amoris*'); a work by Walter Hilton ('Hyltons boke'), probably his *Scale of Perfection*; Bridget of Sweden ('Seynt Brydys boke'); the *Stimulus amoris* attributed to Bonaventure ('*The Prykke of Lofe* . . . that Bonaventur wrot of hymselfe'); lives of Elizabeth of Hungary ('as is wrteyn in hir tretys') and Marie d'Oignies ('he red of a woman clepyd Maria de Oegines').[33] This list does not constitute Kempe's personal library but rather the English and Latin texts she encountered, here adduced to support her manner of living.

As well as being practical vehicles for religious writing, books were totemic items and signs of cultural authority, for women and men. This is demonstrated by the imagery of books in *The Book of Margery Kempe*. Kempe's first 'miracle', of the falling beam at Lynn, occurs as she is holding a book like a protective charm. Later, on pilgrimage, a priest is accused of stealing Kempe's sheet, but he swore 'be [by] the boke in hys hand' (1.1546) that the sheet is his; this book – probably a bible, psalter or book of hours – functions as a symbol of truthfulness. Elsewhere, an example of Kempe's wisdom occurs around a '*portose, a good lytyl boke*' (1.1312) – a breviary, a liturgical manuscript – that a hapless monk is nearly conned into buying. Kempe correctly intuits that the vendor, who claims to be from Pentney Abbey (Norfolk) near Lynn, is a dishonest man.

One of Kempe's most arresting visions, which comes to her as she falls asleep in front of an altar while at prayer, is of 'an awngel al clothyd in white as mech as it had ben a lityl childe beryng an howge boke beforn hym' (an angel, all dressed in white as if it were a little child, bearing a huge book in front of him;

1.4912–13). Kempe identifies this 'howge' heavenly book as 'the boke of lyfe' (1.4914), *the* totemic biblical book, God's muster roll of those chosen for eternal life, in which all the names and deeds of dead souls are inscribed for divine judgement.[34] Kempe's visionary book contains an image in gold of the Trinity, and Kempe asks the little angel where her name is in the book. The child-angel shows Kempe that her name is written at the foot of the Trinity. The book is a dazzling, iconic vision and yet, at the same time, Kempe cannot find, or read, her own name. As Liz Herbert McAvoy has suggested, the white-clad angel and the Trinity underscored with Kempe's name equate the *Book of Life* with *The Book of Margery Kempe*, and vice versa.[35] The angel presents the *Book* to Kempe, as patroness, and the vision combines contemplative vision and heavenly salvation with a highly materialistic sense of textual patronage. Kempe's vision is also indebted to Bridget of Sweden's stirring vision of a magnificent golden book on a pulpit, each word 'alive and uttering itself'. Bridget says that no one is reading the text of this book, but rather the words, upon being uttered, make things happen.[36] This vividly describes the cacophonous orality of the medieval book, its role as a place for multiple voices, and its exemplary status as an efficacious vehicle for engaging with the world.

'clothys': Clothes

Clothing is crucial to Margery Kempe's biography; not just the white clothes she adopted sporadically and controversially. Clothing frames Kempe's early relapse into pride, through her 'pompows' outfits, which included gold horned hats, slashed tippets on her hoods, and cloaks lined with 'dyvers colowrs', designed to be 'the mor staryng to mennys sygth' (to be more striking to people's eyes; 1.194–5). This causes her to be proud, and to be jealous of her neighbours' clothing, 'that thei schuld

ben arayd so wel as sche' (1.201). In this way, *The Book of Margery
Kempe* directly engages in one of the dominant medieval ways of
describing women: as vain, shallow, proud and worldly, interested
only in their 'array'. A fifteenth-century conduct poem for young
women, 'How the Good Wife Taught Her Daughter', advised:

> Loke thou were [wear] no ryche robys [robes],
> Ne counterfyte thou no ladys [Nor should you imitate
>   noble ladies];
> For myche schame do them betyde,
> That lese ther worschipe thorow [reputation through] ther
>   pride.[37]

As if reading Kempe's mind, the poet counsels that 'if thi
neighboris wiif hath on riche attire . . . brenne [burn] not as fier'
with jealously, but thank God for what He has given. Kempe's
Book seems to be aware of such antifeminist commonplaces to
show Kempe's early acquisitiveness. Even as she such moves
away from such finery, Kempe remains deeply aware of the meaning of clothing.

White clothes appear as a sign of stainlessness and virginity in one of Kempe's early visions. In the Bethlehem of her
mind's eye, she arranges 'whyte clothys' for the Virgin (1.409;
1.429), such clothing established early on as fitting for a virgin.
Shortly afterwards Kempe is commanded by God to wear 'clothys of whyte and non other colowr' (1.732) for her Holy Land
pilgrimage, but Kempe boldly disagrees and worries about being
labelled a dissembler:

> yf I go arayd on other maner than other chast women don,
> I drede that the pepyl wyl slawndyr me. Thei wyl sey I am
> an ypocryt and wondryn upon me (1.734–5).

if I go about attired differently from how other chaste
women do, I'm afraid that people will slander me. They
will say I'm a hypocrite and mock me.

Kempe's God replies that the more such mockery Kempe receives,
the more it pleases Him.

In 1413, when Kempe sought approval from Bishop
Repingdon at Lincoln to make her vow of chastity, she also
requested permission to wear white. Repingdon demurred, not
wishing to endorse 'so synguler a clothyng' (1.798). Shortly after,
in Constance, she is forced to wear the 'whyte canwas' (1.1431),
a rough white cloth cut short, mocking her aspirations to wear
a holy outfit. Kempe started to wear her white clothes again in
Italy in 1414, apparently as a sign of sexual purity that she envis-
ages will deter sexual harassers. In Rome, one confessor tells her
to wear black not white clothing (1.1976), an outfit which seems
to recall her earlier customary black clothing that she had worn
when she was still bearing children (1.873).[38] On 26 May 1415,
back in Norwich, Kempe once again adopted white clothing,
her new outfit bought for her by a well-to-do supporter (1.2456).

It seems significant that Kempe's white clothes recur in Italy
and her confidence grows in wearing white. Kempe had initially,
in England, resisted wearing white and met resistance to it, but
in Italy she seems to have been happier to experiment with it.
This might signal Kempe's self-definition as having been res-
urrected, an exalted messenger of God, a member of the elect
after visiting the Holy Land. She may have been informed by
religious movements like the white-robed Bianchi, enthusiasts
and flagellants who had appeared in northern Italy in 1399. The
Bianchi movement sprung up after a peasant's vision of a young
pilgrim and his weeping, white-clad mother who transpire to
be Jesus and Mary.[39] The Bianchi were considered disruptive
and, eventually, heretical, but they also had much in common

with Kempe's devotional poses: they eschewed eating meat, they listened to sermons, they went on long pilgrimages, they prayed for peace, mercy and grace and they wore white robes. Kempe may even have heard about them in 1399, as Richard II is said to have forbidden such a sect from entering London. Some fifteen years later, by the time Kempe was in Venice, the Bianchi movement had passed but was frequently recalled in chronicles, with commentators marvelling at its adherents' white outfits.

Kempe clearly knew that her adoption of white clothing would be provocative, scandalous even. In the Bible, the elect are described as wearing white, a 'raiment of snow' (Matthew 28:3), 'they shall walk with me in white, because they are worthy' (Apocalypse 3:4). The adoption of white clothing may have signified a nun's avowal, a dramatic ceremony in which clothing was used to show transformations of identity and of the soul;[40] however, women making a vow of chastity more usually wore a mantle or veil, together with a darkly coloured robe.[41] The *Book of Vices and Virtues* develops an extended analogy between white robes and virginity, the purpose of white being more clearly to show any spot of earth (representing covetousness), blood (worldly desire) or fire (sin).[42] Another likely inspiration for Kempe's clothing is St Bridget of Sweden's vision of the Virgin at the Nativity clad in a 'white mantill' (see illus. 23), a vision that had a tremendous influence on representations of the Virgin in late medieval iconography.[43] In 1414 Kempe is likely to have seen Niccolò di Tomasso's altarpiece showing the Virgin in white, at St Bridget's house in Rome.[44]

The meanings of both her white and her earlier black clothing remain ambiguous, but these outfits seem to have been a complex rejoinder to the fashionable, particoloured extravagance of her

23 The Nativity with the Virgin Mary in white, Book of Hours (c. 1500), Walters Art Museum, Baltimore, Maryland.

God wilt
dencken
in mijn
hulpe.
Here tot
mi te hel
pen haeste. Glorie si
den vader. Jnitius.
Om scepper gheest
vande dine dien
res inwendicheit vervul
le mit hemelscher graci
en die herten die du ghe
scepen heues. Du biste

earlier life in Lynn. They demonstrate her awareness of clothing as a legible medium, a thing to be viewed and appraised but also, through controversy, a way of gaining agency and autonomy.

'stokfysch': Stockfish

Stockfish is hard dried fish (usually cod in medieval England) and was a staple of the late medieval English diet. It was imported from Norway and Iceland, traded across the Baltic and, with a shelf life of up to seven years and a surprising culinary versatility and nutritional value, it would have been omnipresent.[45] It was by no means a luxury product and Lynn was a major centre for its import. Indeed, Stockfishrow was the former name of one of medieval Lynn's main streets, parallel to the quay (now King Street), where stockfish was traded and Kempe's father is recorded in 1379–80 as supplying this staple.[46]

Kempe's Christ-God mentions stockfish to her twice. In both cases stockfish is referred to on account of its materiality. Early in Kempe's spiritual conversion, Jesus speaks to her one day in St Margaret's Church in Lynn, telling her to give up the things she loves most, 'that is etyng of flesch' and instead to be nourished by His 'flesch' and 'blod', 'the very body of Crist in the sacrament of the awter'. Christ tells her that the world will be amazed by her, but that 'Thow schalt ben etyn and knawyn of the pepul of the world as any raton knawyth the stokfysch' (You shall be consumed and knawed at by the worldly people like any rat gnaws at the stockfish; 1.382–4). Later on, God tells Kempe, his 'Dowtyr', that she is so 'buxom' (obedient) to his will, she

> clevyst as sore onto me as the skyn of stokfysche clevyth to a mannys handys whan it is sothyn, and wilt not forsake me for no schame (1.2124–6).

cleaves as tightly to me as the skin of stockfish cleaves to a man's hands when it is boiled, and you will not forsake me for any shame.

The image of stockfish is particularly arresting: in the first instance, the 'raton' (rat) gnaws at the stockfish, a vile, pestiferous, thieving kind of eating, contrasted by Christ with the holy eating of His body in the Eucharist. In the second example, the skin of the stockfish – which becomes rubbery and sticky when boiled – becomes a potent and evocative image of Kempe's attachment to God. The stockfish sacralizes Kempe's everyday existence, as familiar dried fish is transformed into a sacred idiom: that is to say, Kempe's Christ-God speaks through the imagery of fifteenth-century Norfolk.

Stockfish has the consistency of wood (stockfish literally means 'log fish') and a special 'stockfish hamer', a small mallet, was used to beat the dried fish to make it useable in cookery. Kempe's references to stockfish would have gained part of their potency through their gendered echoes because, in fifteenth-century English proverbs, beating stockfish was compared to the beating of a woman and a husband's right to beat his wife. One saying went:

Ther be 4 thyngs take gret betyng [beating]:
A stockfisch, A milston [millstone], A fedirbed [feather bed], A wooman.[47]

Another piece of 'wisdom' literature said:

Ther wer 3 wold be betyn [beaten], 3 wold be betyn ther wer:
A myl [millstone], a stoke-fysche, and a woman.[48]

A stockfish was therefore something proverbially to be beaten like a woman. This echoes another of Kempe's godly metaphors, that of her God who will behave with her like a blacksmith with a file: she is to be struck, beaten, rubbed and boiled, an exemplary recipient of injury. In God's simile, of Kempe's cleaving to him like stockfish cleaves to a man's hand, this idiom is rehabilitated, from domestic violence to divine proximity and intimacy. The image of stockfish complements and extends Kempe's mode of gaining power through abjection and of merging the domestic, the everyday, the material, with the divine.

'as motys in the sunne': Like dust-motes in the sun

For a long period following her mystical marriage to the Godhead in Rome in 1414, Kempe experiences flickering visions, of 'many white thyngys flying al abowte hir' (many white things flying all around her), 'as thykke in a maner as motys in the sunne' (as thick as [dust]-motes in the sun; 1.2047–8).

One might dismiss these bright specks in Kempe's vision as an ocular malady, eye floaters or retinal disintegration. Yet Kempe does not experience these specks as an illness, but as a sign of divine favour. This flying matter comforts Kempe and, even though she worries about its meaning, it is revealed to be a sign from God that He and His angels are with her wherever she is, protecting her from the Devil and evil men. The motes appear everywhere: in church and in her room, while eating and while praying, when walking and when sitting, in light and in darkness. Kempe suggests that everyday life is full of dusty matter but also that Christian, human history begins and ends with dust: 'Dust thou art, and into dust thou shalt return' (Genesis 3:19). If the world is full of God, and all things are created by God, then it follows that dust too is not the remainder but the essence of a world enlivened by material things. Similarly, the godly presence of dust is teasingly evoked by Chaucer's Wife of Bath, who laments, in a phrasing that Kempe seems to echo, that fairies have been chased away by the charity and prayers of a great number of friars in every land and region, 'As thikke as motes in the sonne-beem'.[49]

As Carolyn Steedman has written, '[dust] is about circularity, the impossibility of things disappearing, or going away, or being gone. Nothing *can be* destroyed.'[50] Kempe's dust-like motes are tiny and quotidian but also holy and universal. This directly parallels Julian of Norwich's famous vision of 'a littil thing the quantitye of a hesil nutt' (a little thing the size of a hazelnut), a thing that is revealed by Julian to represent 'all that is made' in God's creation. Like a dust mote or a hazelnut, the minuscule encapsulates the cosmological and the universal. As Julian says of the little hazelnut-like object:

> I mervellid how it might lesten, for methowte it might suddenly have fallen to nowte for littil. And I was answered in my understondyng. *It lesteth and ever shall, for God loveth it; and so all thing hath the being be the love of God.*[51]

> I wondered how it could last, for it seemed to me so small that it might have disintegrated suddenly into nothing-ness. And I was answered in my understanding, 'It lasts, and always will, because God loves it; and in the same way everything has its being through the love of God.'[52]

Julian does not see a hazelnut, but rather something tiny *like* a hazelnut, the same quantity as a hazelnut. Likewise, Kempe does not see dust but something 'dust-like', and her description of the strange tranquillity of this matter is beguiling and beautiful. This is Kempe's eloquent motif for the circularity and endurance of the physical world, and the spiritual comfort Kempe derives from her material yet mystical encounters with this world.

INTERLOGE:

'a gret fyer', Lynn, 1421

FIRE IS THE key element described in *The Book of Margery Kempe*, both the threatening flames of execution by burning and the delectable 'fire of love' kindled in the soul. A specific fire brings Kempe and the local milieu of mercantile Lynn back into focus: the fire at the Trinity Guildhall in Lynn on 23 January 1421. This is a historically attested event, and the Guildhall complex was rebuilt in its aftermath.[1] As a dateable moment in Kempe's unruly chronology, it helps us to understand her engagement with her home town and her continuing struggles to establish herself, many years after she had started on her journey of public devotion and self-transformation. By this point, Kempe was about fifty years old and had proved herself as an orthodox pilgrim in many places; but proving herself to the guildsmen and churchmen of Lynn remained a struggle for her.

The Trinity Guildhall (properly the Guildhall of the Holy and Undivided Trinity) faces St Margaret's Church and would have been a very familiar locale to Kempe, just a few moments by foot from the Burnham family's front door. Kempe's *Book* describes how, one night, a huge fire engulfs the 'gylde halle of the Trinité' (1.3847). The *Book* describes Kempe being present there and, seeing fire threatening church and town, she bursts into loud crying, weeping 'ful habundawntly'. Even though the local people have frequently asked her to stop her crying, this time they let her cry, in their desperation that, through her, God might show them some mercy and staunch the fire. Kempe's account of the fire makes her central to what happens next, as she assumes the role of a divine.

Kempe's confessor comes to her and asks if he should take the
sacrament towards the fire. Earlier in her *Book* Kempe is content
to display her supervision by her confessors. Here, the confessor
seeks her advice, as if she is an intercessor to the divine. Faith
in the sacrament's ability both to kindle and to staunch flames
reflects pan-European beliefs. In Amsterdam in 1345 a eucharist
wafer had been vomited by a dying man and was disposed of in a
fire but, miraculously, it did not burn.[2] The 'Miraculous Host' of
Amsterdam soon became the object of veneration and pilgrimage. Likewise in 1383, at Wilsnack in Brandenburg, a place to
which Kempe would later make a pilgrimage, three unharmed
hosts, each bearing a spot of blood, were found after an otherwise all-consuming fire.[3] Similar preachers' tales show eucharistic
hosts giving out pillars of flame, turning to burning coals in the
mouths of sinful priests, and not burning when set into an oven
or furnace.[4]

Thus Kempe's confessor takes the sacrament towards the
fire, exhorted by Kempe, who has been told by Jesus that 'it
schal be ryth wel'. Kempe is in church at this point but follows
the sacrament out towards the fire and, seeing the conflagration,
'cryed wyth lowde voys and gret wepyng'. 'Good Lord, make
it wel', she says, 'and sende down sum reyn er sum wedyr that
may thorw thi mercy qwenchyn this fyer and esyn myn hert'
(1.3867–8). Sparks from the fire threaten to leap from the burning Guildhall to St Margaret's Church ('a solempne place and
rychely honowryd', the *Book* piously adds). Suddenly 'three worschepful men' walk into the church and Kempe sees snow on
their clothing. '"Lo, Margery," they say, "God hath wrowt gret
grace for us and sent us a fayr snowe to qwenchyn wyth the fyr."'
And so even though the Guildhall burns, St Margaret's is saved,
'thorw myrakyl and special grace' (1.3872–7).

Snow is rarely described in medieval literature. A widely read
medieval encyclopaedia, Bartholomew the Englishman's *On the*

Properties of Things, emphasized the positive qualities of snow: when snow lies on the land, says Bartholomew, it enriches the soil by closing the earth's pores and causing the plants' roots to draw together.[5] Snow 'helith and hidith stinkynge place', and helps hunters to catch wild animals. Over and above this, snow is known for 'lightnesse of his substaunce', it 'maketh no sowne noithir noise in his fallynge doun to th'erthe, but fallith priveiliche and softeliche out of privey place of the eyre, and settith himseil upon th'erthe and spredith al aboute'. Moreover, in Bartholomew's account, snow 'with his whitnesse and fairenesse comfortith iyen to biholde' (comforts the eyes to behold). Bartholomew's account of snow's gentle falling, its genesis in a 'privey place' of the atmosphere, and its universal spread and beauty, is strikingly similar to Christ's gentle appearance from the air to Kempe in her bedchamber, to the dust-like omnipresence of God, and to the miraculous appearance of the snow to staunch the Lynn fire. I mention this passage from Bartholomew because it helps us to understand how snow could, in later medieval England, be easily amenable to being understood as

24 The Miracle of the Snow at Santa Maria Maggiore, Rome, detail from Taddeo di Bartolo, *Madonna and Child with Saints* (1411), polyptych with predella made for the Societa di San Francesco, Volterra.

a quasi-divine sign. Indeed, the 'three worschepful men' who appear in snowy attire ('Lo, Margery') call to mind the three wise men who likewise appear as a miraculous sign at Christ's nativity, sometimes depicted as taking place in a snow-covered Bethlehem.[6] Kempe may have been familiar, from her time in Rome, with the widespread story of the miracle of the church of Santa Maria Maggiore, where a miraculous snowfall in August was said to have marked out the site and form of the church the Virgin wished to be built in her honour (see illus. 24).[7]

Kempe's account is, as far as we know, historically accurate insofar as the Trinity Guildhall did burn in January 1421; this was an unusually cold year in East Anglia, and so even Kempe's snowfall is factually plausible.[8] But the story does not just record a gripping incident; as one scholar has argued about this passage, 'God is in Margery as he is in the church.'[9] By the early 1420s Kempe had assumed a public persona as a seer of Lynn and a protectress of St Margaret's, saintly in her ability to deliver her town from peril. Kempe is both exemplar for and protectress of the community, a community centred on her beloved church.

SIX

Feelings

*T*he *Book of Margery Kempe* is a rich and unique document in the cultural and social history of emotions.
As a record of one person's 'feelings' and 'stirrings',
the *Book* provides both a lexical record of emotional reactions,
and a social record of emotional effects. Kempe's key expressions of feeling – joy, crying, desire, shame – can show how
fifteenth-century subjectivity was emotionally constituted. This
approach owes much to the recent development of the 'history
of emotions', in which emotions are not considered unchanging
over time, but rather as expressions of specific social and religious contexts. The historian of emotions Barbara Rosenwein
has explored the emotional force of Kempe's writing by looking
at the terms she uses for feelings that were 'in' her heart or 'filled'
her heart (Rosenwein calls the heart 'a touchstone of emotion'
in Kempe's times).[1] Kempe's emotional 'sequences' were often
highly 'dramatic' and scripted to a typical pattern: she starts
with despair, moves through a sense of sinfulness, followed by
a dread of damnation or fear of God's abandonment, followed
in turn by tears of compunction, culminating in the joy or bliss
associated with God's love or with knowing God.[2]

'joye': Joy

As they approach Jerusalem in 1414, Kempe and her fellow pilgrims reach a dusty, rocky summit. There's an old church, around
which clusters a town. But neither Kempe nor any of the pilgrims
are looking at the church or the town; instead, their guide directs
their gaze into the distance, to see the object of their journey, the
holy city of Jerusalem:

> Than, for joy that sche had and the swetnes that sche
> felt in the dalyawnce of owyr Lord, sche was in poynt to
> a fallyn of hir asse, for sche myth not beryn the swetnesse
> and grace that God wrowt in hir sowle (1.1556–9).

> Then, for the joy that she had and the sweetness she felt
> in conversing with our Lord, she was on the verge of fall-
> ing off her ass, for she could not bear the sweetness and
> grace that God performed in her soul.

Kempe's near-fall as she reaches the zenith of her pilgrimage
is a microcosm of that disjunction, characteristic of her mixed
life, between the divine communication she thought she was
having ('dalyawnace of owyr Lord') and what the people around
her believed to be happening: two German pilgrims believe
she is ill ('seke') and 'put spycys in hir mowth to comfort hir'
(1.1560–61). For Kempe, the view of Jerusalem, shimmering in
the distance stimulates 'joy' and 'swetnes', an emotional response
to a specific sight, a glimpse of the 'cyté of hevyn', from a specific place within the sacred landscape; the people beside her
believe she is suffering from a physical ailment.

Kempe almost certainly experienced this 'joy' at the summit
known as Mount Joy (now Nabi Samwil, Palestine), a short distance from Jerusalem. It's the highest of the hills surrounding

Jerusalem on its western side. Mount Joy, long reputed to be the burial place of the prophet Samuel, was a well-established stopping point for pilgrims to take their first view of the Holy City. The site affords spectacular views in all directions; one can clearly see the Mount of Olives and distantly, less distinctly, the Church of the Holy Sepulchre and the Dome of the Rock. This would have represented for Kempe and her fellow pilgrims the reaching of the destination after an arduous journey. Medieval pilgrim guidebooks routinely enjoined pilgrims to weep and to kiss the ground here, to manifest the joy of reaching Jerusalem. Kempe feels joy, almost overwhelmingly, through the medium of sight but she does not mention either Samuel's tomb or the multi-confessional building (illus. 25) in which it was housed.[3]

Nabi Samwil (literally, 'the prophet Samuel') was a holy site for all Christians, as well as Jews and Muslims. The building at the top of the hill had been a Premonstratensian monastery during the Crusader period, but following the fall of Jerusalem in 1187 it had been abandoned as a church. At the time Kempe visited, it was a mosque and a synagogue (today it is church, mosque and synagogue in one). Local and visiting Jews and Muslims, as well as Eastern Christians, would have populated the site, and in Kempe's interaction with Mount Joy we might discern one of her common strategies: through emotional reaction and devotional vision, she is able to elide or obliterate competing narratives and inconvenient circumstances. Thus one of the functions of Kempe's overwhelming feeling of joy is to refocus her and her story on her own interaction with the landscape, rather than the more ambiguous shared space behind her.

Medieval joy (Latin *gaudium*) was a specific and complex emotion, a devotional passion rather than a universal feeling. Joy was often used to describe the achievement of pious or righteous people who had successfully transcended worldly concerns or were counted among the saved. The Joys of Our Lady were

25 Mount Joy (Nabi Samwil), Palestine.

a popular late medieval litany of the Virgin's special joys, from the Annunciation to her heavenly Coronation, marking the moments (originally five, but later fifteen) when her earthly life was touched by divinity. For Thomas Aquinas (1225–74), the passion of *gaudium* (joy) represents the 'achievement' or fulfilment of good; this joy is hard-won and felt especially in God's presence.[4] In Walter Hilton's mystical tract on spiritual ascent, *The Scale of Perfection* (*c.* 1387, written for a female recluse), 'joy' is a spiritual feeling in God's realm, generally collocated with 'hevenly' or 'ghostly'. For Hilton, 'the sovereyne Joye' is 'love in heven'. The sweetness of joy is often only briefly tasted, joy is glimpsed ('not clerly, but half in derkenes, the whyche shal be fulfylled & openly clered in the blysse of heven').[5] To attain joy is a huge labour, a painful test. In particular, such devout joy, the 'joy of heaven' written about in mystical texts, was especially associated with the heavenly Jerusalem, an eschatological joy.

Kempe's overwhelming 'joy' on seeing Jerusalem is a specific feeling that reflected her sense of hard-won ascension to the *heavenly* Jerusalem and the presence of the divine, a cherished mental state rather than a physical passion, and a feeling that could only be engendered in the presence of God. This is a moment of attaining union with God and Christ, who are here conversing with her in her mind. As God says elsewhere to Kempe, He will welcome her to Heaven 'wyth al maner of joye and gladnes . . . evyr to dwellyn wyth me in joy and blysse' (1.1202–3). Later, when a visiting priest reads to his mother and to Kempe about 'how owr Lord, seyng the cite of Jerusalem, wept therupon' (1.3378), Kempe, on hearing 'how owr Lord wept', herself weeps painfully and loudly. Christ's view of Jerusalem causes him to weep; Kempe's compunction causes her to weep; this, in turn, leads to communal joy and solace. Kempe, the priest and his mother 'joyyd and wer ryth mery in owr Lord' (rejoiced and were very merry in our Lord; 1.3382). To glimpse the beatific vision of God was the ultimate goal of mystical experience, and Kempe's joy at Mount Joy is a moment of contemplative unity with God that she hopes will presage the glorious end of the pilgrimage of life. Her companions' misunderstanding that she is unwell shows that they have not yet felt or understood such unity.

'cryeng': Crying

One of Kempe's most memorable emotional states concerns tearfulness or, in her terms, a 'cryeng . . . so lowde and so wondyrful that it made the pepyl astoynd' (astonished; 1.1582–3). Kempe's crying has already been discussed, when at Norwich she 'roars', prostrated. Crying was not a sign of 'irrational' emotion or a sign of madness or instability, but was often, for Kempe, devotionally rewarding and strategic.

In Jerusalem, at Calvary, Kempe has her first divinely inspired bout of tears, an example of a crying that is transformative. Kempe experiences the sight of Jesus's tortured body 'in the sygth of hir sowle' as if He himself is hanging 'befor hir bodily eye in his manhode' (1.1614–15). Her internal vision sees 'hys precyows tendyr body', torn and scourged. This body is, she says, 'mor ful of wowndys than evyr was duffehows of holys' (more full of holes than any dove-cote ever was), hanging on the Cross with the Crown of Thorns on His head. Kempe continues,

> hys blysful handys, hys tendyr fete nayled to the hard tre, the reverys of blood flowing owt plenteuowsly of every membr, the gresly and grevous wownde in hys precyows syde schedyng owt blood and watyr for hir lofe and hir salvacyon (1.1619–21).

> His blissful hands, His tender feet nailed to the hard tree, the rivers of blood flowing out plentifully from every limb, the grisly and grievous wound in His precious side shedding forth blood and water for her love and for her salvation.

The prose builds through its repetitive structure, its cumulative clauses, its concise listing of Passion symbolism, and the memorable comparison of Christ's wound-ridden body to a dove-cote. The culmination is not Christ's collapse but Kempe's:

> sche fel down and cryed wyth lowde voys, wondyrfully turnyng and wrestyng hir body on every syde, spredyng hir armys abrode as yyf sche schulde a deyd, and not cowde kepyn hir fro crying, and these bodily mevyngys for the

fyer of lofe that brent so fervently in hir sowle wyth pur
pyté and compassyon (1.1622–5).

she fell down and cried out with a loud voice, marvellously
twisting and writhing in her body on every side, spreading
out her arms wide as if she should have died, and could not
keep herself from crying from these physical movements,
due to the fire of love that burned so fervently in her soul
with pure pity and compassion.

The modern term 'crying' does not properly encompass all
that Kempe experiences, as her entire body engages in a memorable display. By spreading her arms 'abrode' she seems to mimic
Christ's body on the Cross, as the devotional past overwhelms
her physical self, the sacred memory encompassing her present
moment.

In Jerusalem Kempe visited the Latin Calvary, as worshipped
by western pilgrims, an altar at an outcrop of rock on a raised
platform above the Greek Calvary, situated near the Church of
the Holy Sepulchre's main doorway. Here, Kempe emulated St
Bridget of Sweden, who was also moved to tears, 'wepinge and
hevi', at Calvary.[6] Kempe also 'literally enacts the medieval
reading of Mary's *compassio* at Christ's crucifixion as the labor
pains she did not suffer at Christ's birth'.[7] At Calvary, Kempe
is at once the suffering Christ, the empathetic Virgin and the
devoted pilgrim in the style of Bridget of Sweden.

It is easy to be seduced by Kempe's emphasis on her personal
reactions, but crying was an essential part of the medieval
Jerusalem pilgrimage: pilgrims not only cried their way around
Jerusalem but were directed where to cry. The Mount of Olives,
and the Church of *Dominus flevit* where Jesus is said to
have wept over Jerusalem, became especially well known for
ritualistic displays of mournful weeping. Kempe would likely

have been shown the stone columns inside the Church of the Holy Sepulchre always dripping water, known as 'the stones which wept for Our Lord's Death'.[8] As Burchard of Mount Zion (d. 1285) wrote of Jerusalem in his widely read *Description of the Holy Land*, 'O God, how many devout tears have been shed in that place by those seeing there the joy of the whole earth, the city of the great King!'[9] Jerusalem was a city of ritualized, public tears, replete with places that celebrated and encouraged crying. Here crying was neither individualized nor secret, but publicly valorized and spatially provoked. Kempe's tears and roaring at Jerusalem were part of an established geography of emotional performance.

In medieval England, tears were thought to appear in the eyes because of strong emotion but were not necessarily connected with sadness or distress. Crying could be physiological or emotional but was, above all, a sign of compunction (from Latin 'compungere', to sting or prick), the authentic moment at which a feeling or an idea was etched on the soul. So when Kempe cries, she shows or performs the authenticity of God working actively and sorely in her soul, in her heart. In Middle English we often find the striking phrase 'blodi tears'. For instance, a fourteenth-century verse sermon judges the 'sinful man': 'Wel aght [ought] thi hert throghute cleve [spilt], / Thin eiine [eyes] blodi teris [bloody tears] wepe.[10] This connection between tears and blood reflects Hippocratic medical theory, which held that tears were humours from the brain and so, like any bodily humour, an excess needed to be purged by the body, just as blood had to be let. Tears were considered warm and moist (hence for Kempe they are kindled by the fire of love) and as such they were closest to blood, the warm, wet humour.[11]

At Calvary, Kempe's fire of love is kindled with 'pyté and compassyon'. Compassion is literally a 'suffering with', *cum passionem*, a translation of suffering from one body to another. An

extended section of Kempe's *Book* explains and interprets her
tears, describing how her great compassion, 'so gret peyn to
se owyr Lordys peyn' (1.1578), that she could not keep herself from crying and roaring. Kempe's crying is compassionate
and intersubjective (between her and Christ) and empathic (a
shared feeling of pain), and it is caused by combining 'mental'
and 'physical' stimuli to tears, both seeing and thinking about
Christ's pain. Kempe goes on to explain how her crying was
influenced by viewing both religious media and actual violence:

> whan sche saw the crucyfyx, er yf sche sey a man had a
> wownde er a best . . . er yyf a man bett a childe befor hir er
> smet an hors er another best wyth a whippe, yyf sche myth
> sen it er heryn it, hir thowt sche saw owyr Lord be betyn
> er wowndyd lyk as sche saw in the man er in the best, as
> wel in the feld as in the town, and be hirselfe alone as wel
> as among the pepyl (1.1586–90).

> when she saw the crucifix, or if she saw a person or a beast
> . . . who was wounded, or if a man beat a child in front of
> her, or struck a horse or another beast with a whip, if she
> could see it or hear it, in her thought she saw our Lord
> being beaten or wounded, just as she saw it in the man
> or the beast, either in the fields or in town, and alone by
> herself as well as among people.

Seeing or hearing stimulates Kempe's tears, but through
a mental movement towards a memory of Christ's Passion.
Kempe does not cry out of emotional grief for victims, but
because violence stimulates thoughts of Christ. This crying,
the *Book* explains, 'come nevyr wythowtyn passyng gret swet-
nesse of devocyon and hey contemplacyon' (never came without
unsurpassed sweetness of devotion and high contemplation;

1.1597), demonstrating its pleasure, its valued significance, and its intellectual effectiveness. Crying, for Kempe, was a form of knowledge.

'peyne': Pain

One's own experience of being ill is famously hard to define in words, and being ill is always a chaotic and multifaceted experience. It is therefore no surprise that the 'diagnosis' of Kempe has been such a significant but disparate element in readers' reactions to her. Many readers of *The Book of Margery Kempe* find themselves drawn to medical, psychiatric and psychoanalytical diagnoses of its protagonist. Such medically inflected analysis attended early readings of Kempe's *Book* in the 1930s.[12] Kempe herself describes various kinds of 'bodyly sekenesse' (physical illness) and disorders of 'mende' (mind, head).

Illness and wellness are not, for Kempe, two separate realms. Rather, illness and wellness are parts of the same realm through which, like the ever-turning wheel of fortune, they pass unpredictably, in and out of her life as immediate personal conditions linked to her spiritual health. This is made clear in the memorable use of the rhetorical figure of oxymoron (the joining of two opposing ideas) in the *Book*'s first pages:

> ower mercyfulle Lord Cryst Jhesu havyng pety and compassyon of hys handwerke and hys creatur turnyd helth into sekenesse, prosperyté into adversyté, worshep into repref, and love into hatered (1.15–17).

> our merciful Lord Jesus Christ, having pity and compassion for His handiwork and His creature, turned health into sickness, prosperity into adversity, esteem into disgrace, and love into hatred.

The *Book* opens as a kind of anti-cure, a 'compassionate' movement from health into sickness, and does so in a way that puts this movement into a pattern, both rhetorical and cosmological, of other kinds of transformation. Compassion, a suffering that is intersubjective and shared, and the cure of prayers are the *Book*'s key values.

Being unwell provides Kempe with valuable moments of self-care and renewal. The *Book* opens with its vivid description of Kempe's crisis during her first pregnancy and labour, during which 'sche was labowrd wyth grett accessys' (she was afflicted with great attacks of fever; 1.132), 'seke or dysesyd', and out of her 'mende' (her mind, the seat of emotion, imagination, thought and reason). Later in the *Book*, Kempe is punished by God (as the *Book* describes it) with 'many gret and divers sekenes' – sometimes identified by modern readers as Kempe's menopause – during which she had 'flyx' (something like dysentery or diarrhoea), weakness, 'a gret sekenes in hir hevyd and sithyn in hir bakke' (a severe illness in her head and then in her back; 1.3242), followed by an eight-year period of having 'an other sekenes' in her right side, which caused her to vomit and to groan:

> Sumtyme sche had it onys in a weke contunyng sumtyme thirty owrys, sumtyme twenty, sumtyme ten, sumtyme eight, sumtyme four, and sumtyme two, so hard and so scharp that sche must voydyn that was in hir stomak as bittyr as it had ben galle, neythyr etyng ne drynkyng whil the sekenes enduryd but evyr gronyng tyl it was gon. Than wolde sche sey to owr Lorde, blysful Lord, why woldist thu becomyn man and suffyr so meche peyne for my synnes and for alle mennys synnes that schal be savyd, and we arn so unkende, Lord, to the, and I, most unworthy, can not suffyr this lityl peyne? (1.3245–52)

Sometimes she had it once a week, sometimes for thirty hours, sometimes twenty, sometimes ten, sometimes eight, sometimes four, and sometimes two, so hard and so sharp that she had to void everything that was in her stomach, as bitter as if it was gall, neither eating nor drinking while the illness endured, but always groaning until it had gone. Then she would say to our Lord, 'Oh blissful Lord, why did you wish to become a man and suffer so much pain for my sins and for all men's sins that shall be saved, and we are so unkind, Lord, to you, and I, the most unworthy cannot suffer this little pain?'

One of Kempe's (or her amanuensis's) favourite rhetorical devices, the repetitive clauses 'sumtyme . . . sumtyme . . . sumtyme', gives a sense of the onerousness of Kempe's illness. The extreme bitterness of gall was a common adage, stemming from the biblical account of the gall offered in mockery to the suffering Christ ('they gave him wine to drink mingled with gall', Matthew 27:34). Kempe's account draws attention to the way in which she describes what it is to 'suffyr' in body and soul. Illness is easily assimilated for Kempe into religious experience, as to 'suffyr' encompasses both physical and spiritual affliction and for Kempe the two are always linked. Her diseased or distressed body is both similar to Christ's 'peyne' yet nothing in comparison to it, and in common with much late medieval spirituality Christ's suffering body offers Kempe her most potent exemplar of the transformative potential of suffering and affliction and the valued status of the unwell person.

The word 'peyn(e)' and related terms like 'peynful' appear in *The Book of Margery Kempe* over eighty times, mostly in the second parts of Book 1, dealing with Kempe's mature life as a contemplative in the period 1417–30. 'Peyn' and suffering take on an insistent, forceful, sharp form in the *Book* through alliteration, for example, 'peynes and passyons', 'peyn and pony-schyng', 'peyn that thei mythyn preysyn', 'peynys of Purgatory', and 'suffred sche many scornys', 'suffred hir to sey', 'strong for to suffyr'. Kempe's 'peyne' is often felt by one person but caused by another and, in the majority of cases, refers to pain suffered either by Kempe or by Christ. Pain is, in Kempe's account, sent by God and is a way of displaying her wickedness, 'the gret abhominacyon that sche had of hir synnys' (2.630), via the medium of her body.

Pain is not the same as illness. Pain is, for Kempe, a treasured sign of her wretchedness and sinfulness. Illness, meanwhile, is repeatedly used in the *Book* in incidents of transformation. For example Kempe describes how she became so occupied in her mind by viewing 'Jhesus Crist with hys wowndys bledyng' (1.4182) that she could not bear to see a 'lazar' (leper) or other sick people with wounds or scars. This then in turn causes her great distress, 'for sche myth not kyssyn the lazerys whan sche sey hem er met wyth hem in the stretys for the lofe of Jhesu' (1.4184–5).

To show one's love of a leper was part of a spiritual economy of compassionate public charity. It is therefore unsurprising that the souls of 'lazerys' (lepers) appear in Kempe's prayers, along with 'seke' (sick) and 'bedred' (bedridden) men and women. Kissing lepers was a well-established sign of devotion, and fea-tures in the lives of many of Kempe's favourites such as Francis of Assisi, Marie d'Oignies, Catherine of Siena and Bridget of Sweden.[13] Kempe tells her confessor that she has 'gret desyre' to kiss lepers, and he warns her that she may not kiss male lepers but she can kiss women. So she 'went to a place wher seke women dwellyd whech wer ryth ful of the sekenes and fel down on hir kneys beforn hem, preyng hem that sche myth kyssyn her mowth for the lofe of Jhesu' (1.4192–4). She kisses two of the leprous women, with crying and 'good wordys', and she urges them to thank God for their illness. One of these

female lepers is herself much like Kempe – a self-styled virgin
vexed by her 'gostly enemy'. The reference to her virginity is on
account of the fact that leprosy was often regarded as a venereal
or sexually transmitted disease and so, like Kempe, this leper is
a tempted woman striving to be godly (and this reinforces and
echoes Kempe's reluctance to kiss male lepers, on account of her
sensitivity to being accused of lechery).[14] This leper becomes
the recipient of Kempe's prayers, and this episode culminates in
Kempe spiritually assisting the troubled leper, acting as confessor
to her, touching her soul, transforming her from vexed wretch
to recipient of grace:

> the sayd creatur went to hir many tymys to comfortyn
> hir and preyd for hir, also ful specialy that God schulde
> strength hir ageyn hir enmye, and it is to belevyn that he
> dede so (1.4203–5).

> the said creature went to her many times to comfort
> her and to pray for her, most especially that God should
> strengthen her against her enemy, and it is to be believed
> that He did so, blessed may He be!

Kempe shows that, far from being sick herself, she is effica-
ciously carrying out one of the corporal Works of Mercy, the
visitation of the sick. The word 'lazar' is etymologically cognate
with the biblical Lazarus, sick and 'full of sores' (Luke 16:20) –
and the care of lepers was a common act of public pious charity.
As Guy de Chauliac's medieval medical handbook says, even
if the world hates lepers, God does not hate them; rather 'God
. . . luffed Lazer [Lazarus], the leprouse man, more than other
men.'[15] Lepers were not removed from medieval society but, as
Kempe shows, were symbolically and physically very much a
part of the world. In Kempe's day there was a main hospital at

26 St Elizabeth of Hungary tends the needy and ill; a disfigured leper is in the lower right-hand corner, Church of St Peter Mancroft, Norwich (*c.* 1440).

Lynn, dedicated to St Mary Magdalen, where some lepers were treated, and there were at least four smaller 'lazar houses', or leper hospitals, just outside the town.[16]

In particular, Kempe seems to be mimicking St Elizabeth of Hungary (1207–31), a Thuringian princess whose mystical visions Kempe certainly knew (1.3644).[17] Elizabeth was well known for her care of lepers, and is shown tending to the sick in artworks, including in the stained glass at the church of St Peter Mancroft, Norwich, which dates from the 1430s–40s.[18] Elizabeth is shown dispensing bread to beggars (illus. 26), a blind man and, in the right-hand corner, a leper whose illness has eaten away his face. The ascetic St Radegund may also have offered Kempe an authorizing model for the enthusiastic kissing of female lepers.[19] In her legend, Radegund is described as 'seizing . . . leprous women in her embrace, her heart full of love, she kissed their faces'.[20]

Arthur W. Frank has written eloquently about the figure of the 'wounded storyteller', seeing the potential in illness for creating narrative. Frank argues that 'ill people' need to tell their stories, 'in order to construct new maps and new perceptions of their relationships to the world'; these stories are themselves narratives of embodiment, both told about the body but speaking via a body that has experienced its own unwellness.[21] This is true for Kempe, and it is one of the reasons her readers feel so intimate with her: her body and her *Book* are both media for suffering. However, when we try to diagnose Kempe according to post-medieval medicine we engage a culture of medicine that is quite alien to Kempe's. Illness for Kempe is about miracles, valued suffering and spiritual *salus* (both health and salvation).

The incident with the lepers comes towards the end of the *Book*, as if to chart the progress Kempe has made in converting her own periods of extreme illness into her ability to heal the pain of others. Shortly after the story of kissing the lepers, there is a somewhat separate, but important, narrative of illness, describing John Kempe's old age. In describing her own health, Kempe is 'successfully ill' insofar as she is a witness to her own transformation, and her *Book* bears out Richard Rolle's conception of the 'medicyne of words', in which praying, reading and writing purge both body and soul of illness.[22]

'desyr': Desire

'Desyr', in Middle English, can be a state of longing, or it can be a craving, physical desire, the deadly sin of sexual lust. One scholar argues that 'sexuality predominates among [Kempe's] sins, and that she never succeeded in integrating it into her overall personality in a way that could satisfy her natural instinct'.[23] Sexuality is just one part of Kempe's 'desyr', one of her favourite words (it appears over a hundred times in her *Book*), describing her yearnings, from emotional craving to physical lust and lechery. The diabolical aspect of lust is reflected in Kempe's 'horybyl' and 'abhominabyl' hallucination of priests' genitals. At one point Kempe says, piously, 'I take lytil heed of a mannys bewté er [or] of hys face' (1.2795–6) but this is at odds with what the *Book* tells us elsewhere, as she notes how good-looking several men are (1.1718; 1.2015; 1.2645). In fact, Kempe's *Book* narrates her movement from carnal desire to spiritual yearning, from her sexual lust to her love of Jesus. When she sees handsome ('semly', 1.2017) men in Rome, they cause her to think of Christ, the 'most semly, most bewtyuows, and most amyable' (1.170) man she ever saw.

According to Richard Rolle, only the name of Jesus can do away with 'fleschly desire and grevous temptaciones'.[24] *The Book of Vices and Virtues* says lechery has two branches: of the heart and of the body; Kempe experiences both. Lechery of the heart includes thinking about a person's likeness ('nyse lokers to loken on'), delighting in this likeness, and the development of 'the grete brennynge wille' (the great, burning intention) to sin with the person.[25] Lechery of the body includes all manner of 'lecherous biholdyng', 'heryng', 'spekynge', 'handlynge', and is like other fleshly lusts: 'outrageous etynges and drynkynges and esy beddynges and delicious and softe schertes and smokes and swote robes of scarlet' (extravagant food and drink and comfy bedding and delicious and soft shirts and smocks and pleasant scarlet robes).[26]

We see Kempe's sexual lexicon at several points in the *Book*, including in her account of Jesus as a lover. After Kempe's marriage to the Godhead in Rome, Jesus tells her that a wife should be 'homly' (intimate) with her husband, that they must 'ly togedir and rest togedir in joy and pes [peace]'. And this, He says, is how it should be between Kempe and Himself.

> Therfore most I nedys be homly wyth the and lyn in thi bed wyth the. Dowtyr, thow desyrest gretly to se me, and thu mayst boldly, whan thu art in thi bed, take me to the as for thi weddyd husbond, as thy derworthy derlyng, and as for thy swete sone, for I wyl be lovyd as a sone schuld be lovyd wyth the modyr and wil that thu love me, dowtyr, as a good wife owyth to love hir husbonde. And therfor thu mayst boldly take me in the armys of thi sowle and kyssen my mowth, myn hed, and my fete as swetly as thow wylt (1.2098–108).

> Therefore I must be intimate with you and lie in your bed with you. Daughter, you really desire to see me, and boldly you can: when you are in bed take me to yourself as your wedded husband, as your dear darling, as your sweet son, for I wish to be loved as a son should be loved by the mother, and wish that you love me, daughter, as a good wife ought to love her husband. And therefore you may boldly take me in your soul's arms and kiss my mouth, my head, and my feet as sweetly as you wish.

Jesus strikingly takes the role of Kempe's mother (the Lynn hermit earlier describes Kempe as suckling at Christ's breast; 1.1397) but here different kinds of kinship merge within Kempe's relationship with Jesus: mother, son, husband, wife, father, daughter. Alliterations like 'derwerthy derlyng' and 'swete sone' make this a strikingly lyrical moment and these alliterations appear elsewhere, establishing a rhetorical patterning of Kempe's relationships.[27] It is also an intensely erotic piece of writing, as Kempe is enjoined to kiss and embrace Jesus like a wife to her husband, in ways that boldly suggest her active role, including the memorable detail of her kissing His feet.

The sexual desire of Kempe's Jesus translates the bride and bridegroom of the biblical Canticles, but also transcends Kempe's marriage to John Kempe by placing herself with Jesus as part of a married couple, going to bed, consummating their relationship, 'wythoutyn any schame er dred'. This sexualized Jesus is far from Kempe's creation.[28] Catherine of Siena had married Jesus, making a wedding ring from His foreskin, and drinking blood from His side-wound.[29] Kempe seems to be influenced by the sexualized register of texts like the thirteenth-century *Ancrene Wisse* (Knowledge for Anchoresses) and *Hali Meithhad* (Holy Virginity) and *A Talkyng of the Love of God*, a fourteenth-century set of meditations written for nuns. *A Talkyng of the Love of God* envisions an erotic ecstasy of kissing and licking Christ's body, including licking His feet, vigorously leaping on Him like a greyhound:

> I lepe on him raply as grehound on herte . . . the blood I
> souke of his feet, that sok is ful swete. I cusse and I cluppe
> . . . I walewe and I souke, I not whuche while, and whon
> I have al don yit me luste more. Thenne fele I that blood
> in thought of my Mynde as it weore bodilich, warm on my
> lippe, and the flesch on his feet bifore and beohynde so
> soft and so swete to cusse and to cluppe.[30]

> I leap at Him swiftly as a greyhound at a hart . . . I suck
> the blood from His feet, that sucking is very sweet. I kiss

and I embrace . . . I writhe and I suck, I do not know for
how long, and when I'm sated I want yet more. Then I feel
that blood in my imagination as if it were physical, warm
on my lips and the flesh on His feet in front and behind so
soft and so sweet to kiss and to embrace.

Alliteration, active verbs, repetition, internal rhymes and the
agency of the sensual first person all show the feverish eroticism
of the vision of the incarnate Christ.[31] Such mystical eroticism is
not over-literal, and in fact Kempe is theologically cautious, her
erotic encounter with the handsome bridegroom/Christ proceed-
ing out of her marriage with the Godhead.[32] Far from lechery,
erotic mystical language describes the intense longing and the
personal urgency of achieving joyous union with Jesus.

'schame': Shame

Shame was, in medieval Christian terms, a beneficial feeling,
an opportunity to reflect on one's sinfulness and one's mis-
placed attachment to worldly reputation; as Jesus tells Kempe,
those 'that dredith the schamys of the world may not parfytely
lovyn God' (1.3749–50). Kempe's *Book* is replete with incidents
involving shame, 'reputacyon', 'slawndyr' (slander), 'bakbytyng'
(backbiting) and the 'angwisch' of being part of – or excluded
from – a 'felaschep' or community. We might see Kempe's main
strategies for dealing with shame either as reinterpreting scorn as
divine favour or defending herself against shame by denying it.[33]
One notorious incident, which took place in the early 1430s, can
help us to understand Kempe's feelings of shame.

On returning from the Continent after her last pilgrimage, to
Wilsnack and Aachen, Kempe enters London. She is a woman
in her sixties, bedraggled and clothed like a pauper, with an
old scar on her hand. Her entry to the city recalls Christ's *via*

dolorosa, as she enters the city 'clad in a cloth of canvas' (2.548), 'in maner of a sekkyn gelle' (a kind of coarse sackcloth), exactly the same description of the humiliating garment she was forced to wear some twenty years earlier on her way to Venice. Kempe is well known in London but she wishes to remain unknown, embarrassed by her lack of money, until she can borrow some funds, so she 'bar a kerche befor hir face' (wore a handkerchief across her face; 2.552). Kempe's attire in the rough canvas smock is a pose of humility, an important tool to promote her unique relationship with Christ; nonetheless, she remains ashamed of her sartorial inelegance. The 'kerche befor hir face' is not only an ineffective disguise but recalls St Veronica, who placed her handkerchief or veil on Christ's face on his way to Calvary, the imprint of his sweat making the *vernicle* (*vera icona*, true icon). Kempe's entry to London, replete with symbolism of ignominy and victimhood, inaugurates her last trip to the city, which turns out to be a study in embarrassment. Someone guesses Kempe's identity, 'Mar. Kempe of Lynne' (2.553), the only time her full name is given in the *Book*. This person comments loudly on Kempe's hypocrisy: 'A, thu fals flesch, thu schalt no good mete etyn' (Oh, you false flesh, you'll eat no good meat; 2.554). It's a slur on Kempe, inferring that she won't eat good meat but she will reach for other delicacies. Even as the elderly Kempe makes her way through the busy streets of London with her face covered, she has become infamous as a holy fraud.

Kempe explains that the story had long before – about 20 to 25 years previously – been contrived, at the Devil's instigation, by some person or persons unnamed. Kempe was said to have sat down for supper on a fish-day (that is, a day on which she observed the conventional Christian fast from meat on Fridays, sometimes on a Wednesday, and at Lent, Advent and Pentecost). Offered cheap herring and finer pike, she reached for the pike, like a greedy hypocrite. Thus, *The Book of Margery*

Kempe explains, a kind of proverb developed against her, that people said of her, 'Fals flesch, thu schalt ete non heryng' (2.570–71), that is, the hypocrite won't eat cheap food like herring. In fifteenth-century England herring was proverbially cheap ('not worth a red herring') whereas pike was proverbially desirable ('as healthy as a pike').[34]

An honourable widow, living in London, gives Kempe a warm welcome, and one evening Kempe is invited to a great dinner including guests from Cardinal Henry Beaufort's household (with which Kempe was connected through her confessor Sleightholme, through Beaufort's sister Countess Westmorland, and probably via Lynn with Beaufort's brother Thomas Beaufort).[35] The dinner is going very well, the diners are 'in her myrthys' (enjoying themselves; 2.581), when a guest at the table repeats a gossipy proverb about someone about whom it is said 'Thu fals flesch, thu schalt non etyn of this good mete' ('You false flesh, you shall eat none of this good meat'; 2.582). This causes much hilarity. The groups chatters away, laughing about the phrase. Kempe enquires gently if they know about whom this proverb was said. Someone replies that they have heard about 'a fals feynyd ypocrite in Lynne whech seyth sweche wordys, and, leevyng of [putting aside] gret metys, sche etith the most delicyows and delectabyl metys that comyn on the tabyl' (2.586–8). Kempe discloses that this is she. She states that she is 'not gylty in this mater' (2.592), and the ashamed diners find themselves 'rebukyd' and corrected by her.

This episode brings together Kempe's alleged gluttony and hypocrisy, as well as offering a study of externally imposed shame rather than internally generated guilt. In *The Form of Living*, Richard Rolle set out clearly the dangers of delight in food and drink, but equally he warned of the dangers of excessive abstinence. Moderation in appetite was, according to Rolle, a virtue of the soul.[36] Kempe struggled to achieve such moderation. Early on, Kempe's Christ tells her to forego eating meat, the thing she loves most in the world (1.379). She enjoys a 'gret dyner' with a group of monks (1.614), 'a dyner of gret joy and gladnes' with Alan of Lynn (1.4039) and dines with a Norwich lady (1.3490). As several scholars have noted, mealtimes, like clothing, are a public stage for Kempe, an opportunity to promote herself and to practise her piety socially.[37] She repeatedly receives food from wealthy or influential benefactors, and often disrupts mealtimes by speaking her truth.

The London meal is a final example of the difficult but ultimately edifying nature of Kempe's mixed life: people are spiteful, the Devil is everywhere in the world and, wherever she goes, shame follows success. It is after this dinner that Kempe seems to reconcile the mixed life by rejecting quiet, measured equilibrium: she goes out into the London streets and speaks 'boldly and mytily' wherever she is, against 'swerars' and 'lyars' and people who dress in 'pompows aray'. She refuses to flatter, and she makes herself radically independent: 'sche sparyd hem not, sche flateryd hem not, neithyr for her giftys, ne for her mete, no for her drynke' (2.596–8). Kempe claims no longer to care what the world thinks of her, but instead she is 'comfortyd in the swet dalyawns of owr Lord': she refuses to 'mesuryn hirself' according either to her own will or the 'discrecyon' of other people, but only as God leads her, 'in sobbyng ful boistowsly and wepyng ful plenteuowsly' (2.605–6).

This spell in London is Kempe's last description of her engagement with the wider, secular world: subsequently, she goes to Sheen and Syon, west of London, to receive a great Birgittine indulgence, and then makes her final journey home to Lynn. That is to say, after the excruciating London meal she focuses on her future, heavenly perfection, rather than on the benefits of revelling in her worldly shamefulness. In the years that follow, she will stay home in Lynn, dictating *The Book of*

Margery Kempe and remembering this and other moments of shame. The *Book* stands at a junction in Kempe's mixed life: she claims to have freed herself from caring about worldly opinion, and yet, in having the *Book* written, she paradoxically presents herself and her life back to a public that repeatedly and painfully shamed her.

SEVEN

Old Age

K empe recalls how she suffers from a long 'sekenes' from around 1418 until about 1426. Almost no part of Kempe's story covers the later 1420s, and the narrative restarts, probably in 1432, with the return from Prussia of Kempe's eldest son, John Jr, his death, and then the death of John Kempe. The *Book* opens with an account of Kempe's illness and closes with a return to illness and physical care as its central themes.

The *Book* discreetly omits fraught events in Norfolk and beyond during this period. In September 1428 three 'Lollards', William White, Hugh Pye and John-William Waddon, were burned at the stake in Norwich. In the following years, Margery Baxter (1429) and Hawise Moon (1430), women whose anticlericalism, irreverence and social backgrounds mirror Kempe's, were tried for heresy in Norwich.[1] Nicholas Drye of Lynn, who was tried for heresy at Lynn in August 1430, was probably known to Kempe.[2] Drye abjured and was fined. Like Baxter and Moon, this was enough for him not to be put to death. In January 1429 the mayor of Lynn reported that three of the town's prominent citizens (John Wythe, John Springwell and Thomas Chevele) had recently been arrested by the bishop's steward and accused of heresy.[3] This was likely motivated by rumour rather than evidence, and nothing came of it. However, these men would have been well known to Kempe, since they were all prominent burgesses and members of the town's merchant elite, and had held high civic office.[4] On 30 May 1431 Joan of Arc was burned in Rouen, under the aegis of Kempe's former tormentor, the Duke of Bedford.

The *Book* tells us nothing about such significant incidents. Kempe would almost certainly have known about them, especially as she elsewhere mentions some of the people – Thomas Netter; the Duke of Bedford; Bishop William Alnwick – involved in these events.[5] Bishop Alnwick (d. 1449) appears in *The Book of Margery Kempe* as a wise judge in a dispute over two chapels in Lynn (*c*.1360) but was still Bishop of Norwich until 1436: that is, during the period when Kempe was first composing her *Book*, from around 1432/3.

The silence of *The Book of Margery Kempe* about this historical moment is perhaps all the more noteworthy as Kempe details her earlier citations for heresy, as at York, Cawood, Hessle, Leicester and near Ely in 1417. The accounts of accusations of 'Lollard' heresy given in Kempe's *Book* carefully presents Kempe as a falsely accused innocent, which in turn presents her as a Christlike martyr before illegitimate or corrupt authorities. Margery Baxter used a similar strategy during her heresy trial in Norwich, denouncing Bishop Alnwick as a 'Caiaphas', the Jewish high priest who plotted to kill Jesus (Matthew 26:57–67).[6]

'a man in gret age': An old man

Kempe's *Book* is divided into two separate 'books'. Book I seems to have been designed to stand alone, detailing Kempe's life up to about 1430, and closes with the death of her first scribe. Book II, a pacier and more organized narrative than Book I, was written by another scribe in 1438, according to Kempe's 'owyn tunge' (2.8). Book II contains no mystical material and briskly describes, among other things, John Kempe's death and Kempe's dealings

with her eldest son, also called John.[7] Book II effectively restarts
Kempe's life with stories of physical decline, especially of her
husband John Kempe, in the late 1420s and then, in 1432, his
death and that of John Kempe Jr. The *Book* is a unique document
in this regard, as we have no other such medieval accounts of
the burden of a wife caring for a person with something like what
we might now call senility or dementia.

Old age in medieval England was represented both as a state
of wisdom and of bodily frailty, in which one should prepare for
a 'good death' by readying one's soul.[8] In 'The Parlement of the
Thre Ages', a late fourteenth-century poem, Youthe, Medill
Elde (Middle Age) and Elde (Old Age) debate with each other
about the vices of each generation.[9] Elde is 'a laythe lede' (an
ugly person), 'Croked and courbede, encrampeschett for elde;/
Alle disfygured was his face and fadit his hewe' (crooked and
bent, contorted by old age; his face all disfigured and pale of
complexion). Elde mumbles and moans for mercy, 'envyous and
angrye'. Yet Elde wins the debate, because he can advise the
younger characters to amend their ways while they can. Elde
has the last, grim words: 'Dethe dynges one my dore, I dare no
lengare byde' (Death knocks at my door, I dare stay no longer).

Kempe's marriage is a significant narrative arc in *The Book of
Margery Kempe*, charting her transformation from materialistic
young wife, the agony of her first childbirth, her spiritual marriage
to the Godhead, to her husband's death and her widowhood. John
Kempe disappears from large sections of the *Book* and it is hard
to reconstruct his life. Lynn Staley has described the complexity
of the Kempes' marriage, while highlighting John's tolerance of
his wife's embarrassing and at times humiliating postures.[10] In
the Kempes' discussion at York about Margery's chastity, John is
a shrewd negotiator and largely gets what he wants: the payment
of his debts.[11] But Margery Kempe, or her amanuensis, thought
her husband was socially beneath her: 'hym semyd nevyr forto

a weddyd hir' (he never seemed a likely man to have married her; 1.198). Likewise, the Kempes' fourteen children barely warrant a mention in *The Book of Margery Kempe*, as the narrative focuses on its protagonist's contemplation, her care for Christ and the Virgin, rather than her domestic duties.

The decline of John Kempe is a particularly affecting part of *The Book of Margery Kempe*. Over the age of sixty ('a man in gret age'), John Kempe has an accident, losing his footing on the stairs and fracturing his head ('hys hevyd undyr hym grevowsly brokyn'; 1.4242). The wound has to be stitched and filled with five 'teyntys' (linen plugs; 1.4243), a humble version of Christ's five wounds. Margery Kempe must therefore come home (the couple had been living apart to fulfil their vow of chastity, and to allow Kempe space for unhindered contemplation). Everyone expects John to die from his injuries but God's intervention keeps him alive. God then requests that Kempe look after him, promising her the same reward for looking after her husband as she would receive for going to church and praying. Thus Margery and John Kempe are reunited through illness, and she 'kept hym yerys aftyr as long as he levyd' (looked after him for years afterwards, as long as he lived; 1.4281).

The medieval medical manual, the *Cyrurgie* of Guy de Chauliac (d. 1368), contains much information about the dangers of, and treatments for, head injuries. According to Chauliac, the perilous symptoms of a head injury include 'agewe, quakyng, crampe, ravynge and swowning, lesynge of the voice, goyng out, derkenesse and redenesses and goggeliyednesse' (acute fever, trembling, cramp, delirium and fainting, loss of voice, protrusion of the eyes, blindness and inflammation and squinting).[12] Chauliac counsels that those who have suffered a head injury must be kept from 'colde', and the patient should be 'sette by brennynge coles and to schette the wyndowes and to have candel-light', and to bind the head with a ram's skin.[13]

Kempe follows such advice and her portrait of her husband's debility is poignant, closing the long chapter on the Kempes' worldly marriage.[14] After his accident, John Kempe 'turnyd childisch agen and lakkyd reson' (1.4282), a closing counterpart to the portrait of Kempe losing her own mind that opens the *Book*. Kempe tends him; he shits, 'as a childe', in his clothes wherever he is, and needs a constant fire burning beside him. Kempe complains about 'waschyng and wryngyng' his linens and 'hir costage in fyryng' (the expense of keeping a fire burning; 1.4286), but she converts this to spiritual profit. She was 'glad' to be punished by her husband's body, with which she had once indulged her 'fleschly lustys' (1.4288). She 'servyd hym and helpyd hym, as hir thowt, as sche wolde a don Crist hymself' (1.4290), imagining Christ, rather than John Kempe, as her master. Kempe can turn her personal trials into her own rewarding domestic Calvary. In doing so she provides a unique portrait, one that seems many years ahead of its time in its ambivalent sympathies for John Kempe's physical and mental decline.

Similarly, Kempe's travails with her eldest son, a merchant, are converted to glory. Kempe frequently counselled her son to 'leevyn the worlde and folwyn Crist' (2.15) and he started to avoid her. In time, the son went abroad and fell into 'the synne of letchery' (2.27). Soon after, his complexion changed, covered in 'whelys and bloberys as it had ben a lepyr' (spots and pustules as if he were a leper; 2.28). He loses his job and understands, as his mother had warned him, that God has cursed him. As many readers have noticed, this closely parallels Bridget of Sweden's difficulties with her degenerate son Karl.[15] But John Kempe Jr's story also directly parallels his mother's. His attachment to worldly goods is followed by chastising and punishment. His lechery leads to his physical malady. He is shunned by the townspeople of Lynn. His mother prays for him and in doing so casts herself as the Virgin Mary, offering prayers for 'the frute of

hir wombe' (2.48), echoing the angel Gabriel's address to the
Virgin ('Blessed art thou among women, and blessed is the fruit
of thy womb', Luke 1:42). Kempe's prayers are answered: her
son is released from his illness, he marries a Prussian woman and
together they have 'a fayr mayde child' (2.55), a granddaughter
for Kempe. Like his mother, the son abandons his fashionable
clothes (2.66), his conversation brims with 'vertu' (2.67), he
undertakes many pilgrimages 'to Rome and to many other holy
placys' (2.80), always returning to his wife and child as he was
obliged. Margery Kempe becomes her son's model for spiritual
conversion and the mixed life, and thereby proves his mother's
way of life.

In the early 1430s, John Kempe Jr, living in Gdańsk, wants
to visit his mother in Lynn. They exchange letters, and Margery
Kempe writes to her son predicting that whether he comes home
by land or sea he shall 'come in safté' (2.90). So, in the second
half of 1431, John Kempe Jr visits Lynn. One Sunday lunchtime
he suddenly feels unwell. He takes to his sickbed for a month,
then dies (2.105). For Kempe, this confirms and corroborates
the prediction she had made in her letter to him: her son really
has come home safely, not to his home in Lynn but to Heaven,
'wher deth schal nevyr aperyn' (2.107).

Likewise, a short time afterwards, John Kempe, Margery
Kempe's husband, dies. The *Book* states, laconically, that he
'folwyd the sone the wey whech every man must gon' (followed
the son the way every person should go; 2.108). Kempe becomes
an independent widow, although she had long since separated
herself from her husband.[16] After the men's deaths, Kempe
becomes more like her younger self, embarking on a challenging
adventure defined by her spirited disobedience.

Last days

John Kempe Jr's Prussian widow lives with Kempe for about eighteen months. During this period, a daughter, Kempe's grand-daughter, is left with friends in Gdańsk (2.96). In 1433 the daughter-in-law makes plans to return to the Baltic. Kempe suggests to her confessor that she chaperone her daughter-in-law to Ipswich to take the boat to Prussia, but her confessor points out her infirmity: 'Ye hirtyd but late yowr foote, and ye ar not yet al hool, and also ye arn an elde woman. Ye may not gon' ('You recently hurt your foot, and you're not yet fully healed, and also you're an old woman. You can't go'; 2.135). Kempe contrives, through taking a local hermit named Reginald ('Reynald') with them, to go to Ipswich anyway. At Ipswich, she decides to board the ship and go to Prussia, disobeying her confessor and the hermit. Kempe's daughter-in-law turns against her, and does not want her on the voyage (2.186). This part of her *Book* foregrounds Kempe's wilful submission to 'the mevyng' of her 'spiryt', the guiding or the steer she receives from God, and her corresponding disobedience to her spiritual counsellors. Just as she refused to confess at the beginning of the *Book*, so she continues to refuse to submit to her confessors' advice towards its end, presenting herself as beyond any advice other than that she receives from God. When word reaches Lynn that Margery Kempe has gone to Prussia, people are utterly astonished; some say it's 'a womanys witte and a gret foly' (womanly spirit and a great folly) for Kempe, 'a woman in gret age', to go overseas without any notion of how she will return. Book II – and Kempe's life in the 1430s – seems to be repeating her earlier life, when she set off for Jerusalem and Rome and left behind Lynn's spiteful naysayers.

The journey is an ordeal. The boat is blown off-course, to Norway, where Kempe spends Easter. She relies on the kindness of the ship's captain to look after her, finding another surrogate spiritual son: he 'was as tendyr to hir as sche had ben hys modyr' (2.254). Kempe eventually spends six weeks in Gdańsk, where there was a large English community, and she fortuitously meets a merchant from Lynn who assists her (2.287). She then sails along the north German coast to the Hanse port of Stralsund, and thence to see the famous blood relic at Wilsnack, a pilgrimage site some 190 km (118 mi.) to the south of Stralsund. The region is aflame with wars between the Teutonic Knights and the Hussites (thought to be in league with the English 'Lollards'), and there were frequent trading disputes between the Hanse ports and English traders.[17] Both these conflicts are referred to (2.268–9; 2.285; 2.305–6), and hinder Kempe's making her way back home.

Kempe crossed Germany in June 1433. The weather is terrible – there is thunder, lightning and rain – and she is very unwell. She sleeps in a bed made of 'but a lityl strawe' (2.332). She travels with a guide but not happily: like her pilgrim companions twenty years previously, he keeps trying to get away from her (2.303) and is irked by her constant crying (2.316). On the way to Aachen a monk takes a dislike to her, chastising and reproaching her, calling her 'ypocrite' (2.366). She thinks she hears the local people calling her 'English tail' (2.389), a common jibe that the English have tails.[18] Her guide abandons her. She fears she will be raped. She joins a group of poor people who stop by the wayside, take off their clothes and pick at the fleas and parasites that torment them. Nonetheless, she progresses and this, says her *Book*, 'was gret merveyl and myracle that a woman dysewsyd of goyng and also abowtyn three scor yer of age schuld enduryn cotidianly to kepyn hir jurney' (was a great marvel and miracle that a woman unaccustomed to walking, and also about sixty years of age, should daily endure to keep her pace on her journey; 2.329–30).

Kempe reaches the important pilgrimage city of Aachen by St Margaret's Day, 13 July 1433. On that day she views the cathedral's celebrated relic of the Virgin Mary's smock, a garment said to have been worn at the Nativity. After her visit to Aachen, Kempe limps home to England. She heads for Calais, then an English territory. She's about sixty years old, she has fleas and bugs biting at her skin, she's dressed in filthy clothes. The journey remains one of 'angwisch and disese and meche lettyng' (anguish and distress, and much difficulty; 2.412). However, she is going home to Lynn and so the overall narrative of her *Book* is one of 'exile and return' – Kempe has been to the edges of western Christendom, upended her life, made herself unpopular, imperilled and poor, but now goes back to the place from which she came.

Kempe goes to Calais, then to London, where the humiliating dinner takes place. She seems to have spent many months – almost a year – in London, and on 1 August 1434 received the famous Lammas Indulgence at the grand Birgittine monastery at Syon. In another moment of providence and traveller's good luck, at Syon she bumps into Reginald the hermit (2.638), who had previously escorted her from Lynn to Ipswich, and returns to Lynn with him in the summer of 1434, only to be chastised by her confessor for disobediently travelling overseas.

The final, somewhat separate, part of the *Book* does not deal with Kempe's death, but rather her prayers. Suddenly, Kempe's first-person voice appears in an extended sequence of prayers that show her devotional priorities and preoccupations. Kempe's prayers start by addressing God then the Virgin and the whole court of Heaven and repudiating the Devil. They then take the form of intercessory prayers, repeating the opening formula, 'I crye yow mercy' to Jesus: mercy for her tears, for the people who are converted by her, for her confessors, for the King of England, for Jews, 'Saracens', heathens, heretics, lepers and many others.

The prayers seem to be offered as a model, perhaps the closest the *Book* gets to teaching its readers.[19] The prayers end by appealing to Kempe's audience:

> for alle tho that feithyn and trustyn er schul feithyn and
> trustyn in my prayerys into the worldys ende, sweche grace
> as thei desiryn, gostly er bodily, to the profite of her sowlys,
> I pray the, Lord, grawnt hem for the multitude of thi mercy.
> Amen (2.798–800).

> for all those that have faith and trust, or shall have faith
> and trust, in my prayers until the world's end, such grace
> as they desire, spiritually and physically, to the profit of
> their souls, I pray you, Lord, grant them for the abundance
> of your mercy. Amen.

So, the *Book*'s conclusion is a model of universal prayerfulness and a strong assertion of Kempe's role as an intercessor on behalf of the Christian community. We are asked to emulate and trust Kempe, for future salvation.

Margery Kempe's own death is unrecorded. The last pieces of evidence about her are her membership payments of 20 shillings in April 1438 and May 1439 to Lynn's Guild of the Holy Trinity.[20] These suggest that in later life, far from retreating from the worldly, social sphere of burgess-class Lynn, Kempe returned to it and embraced it.

At one point, when she is isolated and despised, Kempe seems to be assured by God that she will become a saint, venerated at St Margaret's. He says,

> In this chirche thu hast suffyrd meche schame and reprefe
> for the gyftys that I have govyn the and for the grace and
> goodnes that I have wrowt in the, and therfore in this

cherche and in this place I schal ben worschepyd in the
(1.3698–700).

In this church you have suffered much shame and reproof
for the gifts I have given you, and for the grace and the
goodness I have performed in you, and therefore in this
church and in this place I shall be worshipped in you.

As far as we know, such a prediction never came to pass. Even
as Kempe's life was put into the form of something like a saint's
life in *The Book of Margery Kempe*, there is evidence neither of
offerings at Kempe's grave nor of a shrine to her.[21] Kempe tried
her hardest to craft a testimony of her life, to curate a lasting,
posthumous image, but in death she finally had to submit to the
vicissitudes of 'reputacyon'.

EIGHT

Writing and Rediscovery

*T*he *Book of Margery Kempe* was written late in Kempe's life. It discloses the actual dates of writing as being between 23 July 1436 and summer 1438, in the years after Kempe had returned from her last pilgrimage to Wilsnack, Aachen and Syon.

The *Book of Margery Kempe* opens with an account of the difficulties of its composition. In the 1410s, clerics had begged Kempe to have made 'a booke of hyr felyngys and hir revelacyons' (1.60) but at God's command she had waited to do so. Kempe narrated Book 1 of her *Book* in the early 1430s to an Englishman who had lived in German-speaking Europe for many years (this may well have been her son); he then died (1.69–72). Around 1432, Kempe's priest looked at what had been written but could make little sense of the handwriting. He delayed a further four years, put off by malicious gossip about Kempe, and eventually told Kempe to approach another person to help her write her *Book* (1.84–5). This man could also make no sense of it. The priest felt a pang of conscience, and returned to Kempe to help her with her *Book* (1.92–7). He could suddenly, miraculously and without spectacles, read it, and thus the *Book* was completed.

Almost all medieval authorship was collaborative but, in resolving to compose her own book, Kempe was unusual but not unique as a female 'author'.[1] Alongside Julian of Norwich, whom Kempe describes as a wise anchorite rather than as a writer, we may consider two further instructive examples from a similar period to Kempe and Julian: the unnamed author of *A Revelation of Purgatory* (1422) and the writings of Eleanor Hull (d. 1460).

The anonymous *Revelation of Purgatory* was written by a woman who, like Julian of Norwich, had withdrawn from the world. It is a remarkably vivid account of purgatory, describing how the anchoress was visited over three nights, beginning specifically on 10 August 1422, by a terrifying revenant named Margaret, a Winchester nun. The author of the *Revelation* was experienced in visionary religious culture, and her visions provide a good idea of the spectacular spirituality of mortifying moral punishment in which Kempe lived. The revenant Margaret appears 'full of stronge wondes als scho hade bene drawene with kames' (covered in vicious wounds as if she had been cut open with combs), followed by 'a littill hounde and a littill catte, alle one fyre brynnynge' (a little dog and a little cat, all on fire and burning).[2] Over the following nights she describes horrific visions of Purgatory, including one of devils cutting nuns' lips apart with razors as a punishment for kissing, and removing their tongues and placing adders and toads on them, in retribution for slander and lechery. The dog and the cat are revealed to be the nun's pets she kept as 'mawemetts' (idols) during her lifetime, on whom she had placed too much worldly affection, and she is condemned to have them follow her around, tormenting her, until she is fully cleansed of sin. *A Revelation of Purgatory* is intensely invested in the body and its renunciation, a terrifying account of the torments that were thought to follow sinfulness. Like Kempe's *Book*, *A Revelation of Purgatory* urges its readers to recognize the importance of contrition, the severe process of being pounded to pieces (*contritus*) in one's soul for one's sins.

Meanwhile, Eleanor Hull (née Malet), daughter and wife of Lancastrian retainers, was from a more elevated social class than Kempe.[3] Hull herself served Joan of Navarre, Henry iv's widow, and she had received gifts from Henry v, including the gown he had worn to ride through London on the day following his coronation.[4] Hull retired, as a widow, to the Benedictine priory of Sopwell (Hertfordshire) in the 1420s where she wrote a remarkable commentary on the psalms. Hull's commentary is aligned with *The Book of Margery Kempe* insofar as both are deeply concerned with the act of their own writing and their engagement with multiple authorities and potential audiences. Hull's learned, dense and finely crafted commentary merges her individual voice with those of the Bible and post-biblical texts, a more literary version of Kempe's 'public interiority'. Moreover, Hull successfully negotiated patriarchal structures in a way not dissimilar to Kempe, through the patronage of her learned friend, Roger Huswyf (*fl.* 1458), and her book was probably adopted and preserved by monks at St Albans Abbey. Huswyf was a kind of spiritual companion of Hull's throughout her life, and in her will she left him two breviaries, a psalter and a 'blue byble of Latyn' (a Latin bible bound in blue fabric).[5]

Kempe may have had rudimentary grounding in how to read in English, and the burgess class would have been suffused with written documents concerning trade, law and regulation.[6] From her mercantile background, Kempe would have been very familiar with the role of the professional scribe – known as a 'scrivener' or, in Kempe's terms, 'writer' or 'secretari'. Kempe's descriptions of the reading and writing of *The Book of Margery Kempe* attest to a book being passed between various people around Lynn, with the production of the *Book* a shared and communal iterative process. Rebecca Krug has compellingly argued that the writing of the *Book* is a work of consolation in pursuit of spiritual joy, a collaborative and social act involving confessors and scribes, ultimately fulfilling Kempe's long-held wish to have a book.[7]

The consensus is that the narrative of *The Book of Margery Kempe* as we have it is, more or less, as dictated by Kempe, but turned into continuous prose and variably edited by her amanuenses.[8] If we trust its own account of itself, *The Book of Margery Kempe* is best thought of as a collaborative document, in which individual experience merges with the imprimatur of confessors and scribes, rendering it a collectively produced version of Kempe's life.

'devoute ancres': Devout anchoress

The *Book* survives in one fifteenth-century manuscript (London, British Library Add. MS 61823, illus. 27) and in two highly abbreviated early printed editions (of *c.* 1501 and 1521). The original manuscript of *The Book of Margery Kempe* is presumed lost or destroyed. The unique surviving copy of the *Book* was copied in the later 1440s from this lost archetype by one Richard Salthouse, a young monk at Norwich cathedral priory.[9] Here, the manuscript would have been part of the massive monastic library comprising at least 1,350 volumes.[10] However, by the early sixteenth century the manuscript had reached Mount Grace (Yorkshire), a Carthusian monastery some 320 km (200 mi.) north of Norwich. At Mount Grace, *The Book of Margery Kempe* would have joined a collection of English and Latin devotional and mystical texts.[11] Between four and six annotators, including Carthusians of Mount Grace, enthusiastically annotated their manuscript of *The Book of Margery Kempe*, finding within it abundant evidence of mystical visionary experience. For example, alongside Kempe's account of her boisterous weeping at St Stephen's Church, Norwich, an annotator has written 'fyre of love' in the margin, to highlight Kempe's allusive experience of spiritual heat. Below this, the same annotator has written the word 'vyker', as if to highlight Richard Caister's presence and

status. In some places, Kempe's words were corrected (for example, her unusual, graphic description of Christ being stabbed by
a stranger with a 'baselard knyfe' (1.4943) has been struck
through, although remains legible (f. 100v)).[12]

Around the same time that the book was being read as evidence
of spiritual practice by the monks at Mount Grace, in Westminster
it was mined by the printer Wynkyn de Worde for a short set of
religious extracts. The resulting book, *A shorte treatyse of contemplacyon* (c. 1501), foregrounded its protagonist's contemplative
prayerfulness and private revelation, and removed most of the
biographical material. Kempe, as a character or as a historical
subject, was largely written out. A similar version was published
in 1521 by Henry Pepwell, another London printer.[13] Pepwell
refers to Kempe as an 'devoute ancres called Margery kempe of
Lynne', the only evidence that Kempe might have formally taken
up an eremitical vocation (directly contradicting the record of
her membership of the Guild of the Holy Trinity in 1438–9).[14]
Everything points to the early sixteenth-century, pre-Reformation
reception of *The Book of Margery Kempe* as an orthodox, religious
text, and the posthumous construction of Kempe as a respected
visionary, even as de Worde and Pepwell's versions effectively delete
Kempe from her own story as an unruly and distinctive protagonist.
Their versions excerpt key moments of prayerfulness from *The Book
of Margery Kempe*, transforming it into a much less experimental
account of mystical conversation and prayer, with the repeated
characterization of Kempe as Christ's 'doughter'. The resulting text
was undoubtedly more marketable, but largely silences Kempe's
distinctive voice and biography. These early sixteenth-century
pamphlet versions of Kempe would have been cheap and widely
disseminated, printed in runs of about three hundred to five hundred
copies, although only one copy of each survives.

Their texts were precisely the kind of popular piety decried
by the Protestant reformers and destroyed during the English

fyre of love

vyker

27 The unique manuscript of *The Book of Margery Kempe*, with marginalia ('fyre of love', 'vyker'), British Library, London.

Reformation. The analogous example of the visionary nun Elizabeth Barton (c. 1506–1534), 'The Holy Maid of Kent', is informative, as a huge quantity of written material circulated about Barton, almost none of which survives today. Barton, like Kempe, experienced severe bouts of illness as a young woman which were followed by visionary experiences and revelations. Her mystical spirituality was explicitly modelled on Bridget of Sweden and Catherine of Siena and, like them, Barton started to make political prophecies. She was eventually hanged by Henry VIII for prophecies against his reforms of the English Church. A pamphlet describing her visions and her mystical communication with the Virgin Mary, published in the late 1520s and called A *Marveilous Woorke*, circulated widely but not a single copy survives. Likewise, the manuscript life of Barton, the *Nun's Book*, written by her confessor, has perished.[15] The royal Act of Attainder by which Barton was put to death in 1534 demanded that the public surrender any books, scrolls, or writings about Barton's revelations, on pain of a fine or of imprisonment. This was evidently very successful, given the paucity of surviving written material about Barton, who was well on the way to becoming a saint. The erasure of Barton's reputation is a clear case of sixteenth-century publishing censorship, as publications about the 'old religion' were explicitly targeted by the reformers, and the lives of people like Margery Kempe or Elizabeth Barton deliberately destroyed. It is no surprise that such scant remains of Kempe's textual reputation survive, and the lack of surviving material cannot be read as evidence that her story was not well known in pre-Reformation England.

'undisciplined clutter'

The whereabouts of the unique surviving manuscript of *The Book of Margery Kempe* were unknown for several hundred years. The manuscript was certainly at Mount Grace around the 1510s, and possibly at the London Charterhouse in the 1530s.[16] The circumstances in which the manuscript reappeared in the twentieth century are characteristically Kempeian: a story of chance, disorder and layered histories.[17]

In July 1934, in a small Georgian mansion called Southgate House in the village of Clowne (Derbyshire), some young people were playing ping-pong. Somebody accidentally stood on the ball. In the search for a replacement, the house's owner, William Butler-Bowdon, rifled through some cupboards and found 'an entirely undisciplined clutter of smallish leather bound books'. One of these was a medieval missal (a mass-book); the other a long work in Middle English.[18] It so happened that one of the guests then staying at Southgate House was Charles Gibbs-Smith of London's Victoria & Albert Museum. He saw that the long Middle English book might be of importance, and invited his colleague Albert Van de Put to inspect it. Van de Put then asked the eminent scholar of mysticism, Evelyn Underhill, for advice. She in turn suggested the museum consult three people: Roger Huddleston, a Benedictine monk at Downside Abbey in Somerset; the renowned Cambridge medievalist (and author of ghost stories) Montague Rhodes James; and the American scholar of medieval mysticism, Hope Emily Allen, then living in London at a Thameside house in Chelsea. Neither Huddleston nor James recognized the manuscript, but Allen, who saw it in mid-August 1934, recognized it as relating to Margery Kempe, whom she knew from the sixteenth-century printed editions.

On 27 December 1934, a letter from Hope Emily Allen in the London *Times* announced the rediscovery of *The Book of Margery Kempe*.[19] The letter opened with a spirited invocation of Kempe's gender and her extraordinary importance: 'Sir, – It was said regretfully (not long ago) by a distinguished historian that in the Middle Ages old ladies did not write their reminiscences.

The reminiscences of a medieval old lady have lately come to light . . .' Allen describes Kempe's *Book* as being 'crammed with highly interesting narratives of real life', that 'a neurotic strain ran through [Kempe's] religious life', and closed with the asseveration that 'now, after an interval of 400 years, [Kempe] is likely to become famous'.[20] A modern English translation of the *Book* was published in 1936 and Kempe suddenly became prominent.[21] *The Children's Newspaper*, a widely read British weekly for younger readers, ran a long story on Kempe entitled 'Margery Goes A-Weeping: An Indomitable Old Tramp'. It evoked Kempe as a 'queer figure in the streets', 'a sturdy mother' of 'fanatic fervour'.[22]

Hope Emily Allen worked (with friction and animosity) with the American philologist Sanford Brown Meech on the Middle English edition of *The Book of Margery Kempe*, which was published in 1940, as the Second World War raged. The first

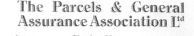

28 The first consignment of printed copies of *The Book of Margery Kempe*, lost to enemy action, 1941.

shipment of *The Book of Margery Kempe* to Allen, then back in upstate New York, was lost in enemy action (see illus. 28), as if symbolic of her difficulties in apprehending Kempe and fulfilling her work on her *Book*.

Allen was occupied for many years on a 'volume II', which was never published. It remains a chaotic jumble of notes, jottings and redrafts, stored in seven boxes at Allen's *alma mater*, Bryn Mawr College, Pennsylvania. One gains the impression that Allen had reworked her materials so much that completion became impossible; since she wrote in a letter to the Oxford medievalist Helen Gardner in 1944, 'my materials are volumninous [*sic*] and I was very much overstrained the last few years before the war, hence everything has gone slowly. I do not want a long book but it takes me time to be succinct. I wish you could see the masses of rewritings strewn about me.'[23] It is hard not to see a parallel between the disorderly and convoluted genesis of *The Book of Margery Kempe* and the discordant, halting and ultimately unfulfilled work that Allen did with Kempe's *Book*.

The reactions that had attended Kempe since around 1410 continued in the twentieth century, as her *Book* both attracted devotees and inflamed readers' ire. A certain 'K. M.' of Baltimore wrote a brief note to Allen in June 1943, saying: 'Dear Miss Allen – Margery Kempe would have been unbearable in the flesh, but I rather enjoy reading her, though she gets tiresome in spots.'[24] The reaction in print was similar.[25] Kempe has since been recast and reinterpreted in various popular media, including a high-camp wartime thriller, Colin Curzon's *Love in a Barrage Balloon* (1942), the plot of which literally hinges on *The Book of Margery Kempe*. Trying to recall who Kempe is, the novel's hero, Mark Antony, muses:

'Trying to find Margery Kempe,' replied Mark Antony, looking out of the window. 'The damn name is familiar,

but I can't place it. Margery Kempe. Is she a film-star
or a tennis-player, or a woman who's been cured after
suffering excruciating agony in the left leg for fifteen
years?'

Curzon wittily juxtaposes Kempe's 'medieval' suffering with
twentieth-century glamour, a 'film-star or a tennis-player', taking
to the extreme the idea that Kempe can be whatever her readers want her to be. When he remembers who Kempe is, Mark
Antony characterizes her thus: 'Margery Kempe was the eccen-
tric mystic of the early Middle Ages who travelled around making
herself public inconvenience number one. She had written a
book of pseudo-mysticism remarkably in advance of her time
in confused thinking.' Curzon's light-hearted but rather spiteful
description brings together a number of trends in how *The Book
of Margery Kempe* was received in the twentieth century. Kempe's
eccentricity and her interventions of 'public inconvenience' were
easily identified and condemned, and yet she was 'remarkably in
advance of her time' in speaking to her twentieth-century audience, not the 'proper' medieval person this audience had been
trained to expect.

At the other end of the spectrum, a short, religiously orien-
tated biography of Kempe, *Margery Kempe: Genius and Mystic*,
appeared in 1947, written by Katharine Cholmeley. Cholmeley
sought to show the Catholic orthodoxy and sincerity of Kempe's
spirituality, and Cholmeley's book opens with an obedient submission to the Apostolic See, 'which alone has power and
authority to pronounce as to whom rightly belong the Character
and Title of Saint or blessed.' Cholmeley argued that 'Margery's
revelations, which . . . can be held as authentic as those of Juliana
of Norwich, are of value for all time.'[26]

The Book of Margery Kempe is now more widely read than
ever, from university syllabi to theatrical productions. Since

the 1980s Kempe has been widely studied, building on interest in mysticism and women's experience among feminist theorists and historians. This is in part a consequence of the fact that in the era of mysticism 'for the first time in Christian history . . . a particular kind of religious experience is more common among women than men'.[27] It is also because Kempe's *Book* solicits a variety of responses, protean in its applicability to new ways of being read. Another version of Kempe appears in Robert Glück's dazzlingly original novel *Margery Kempe* (1995, repr. 2020), retelling Kempe's story through graphically sexual interactions with Christ ('Jesus kisses her too quickly, jamming his tongue down her throat . . .') and descriptions of her characters' inner lives and desires.[28] These are interspliced with the narrator Bob's love and lust for L., an erotic knight-hero with whom Bob is deliriously, hopelessly smitten. 'If I say I love you too often, it's partly amazement at the strength of my desire,' muses Bob, and it's not clear whether this voice should be identified with Kempe, Jesus, Bob himself or all three.[29] Glück, like Kempe, 'depends on the tension between maintaining an impersonation and breaking it'; his Kempe is a bold 'failed saint', who 'tried to change her future by recasting herself in the medium where she was strong'.[30] Both Kempe and Glück's Bob are consumed with desire and with anguish, narrating the 'quandary of wanting and not wanting'.[31]

Recently, in her novel *The Testaments*, the Canadian writer Margaret Atwood included a rich vein of allusions to medieval culture, used in the dystopian realm of Gilead as models for godly female conduct; these include the 'Margery Kempe Retreat House', to which one tearful woman is sent, being told ominously, 'You'll be a different woman soon.'[32] In Matthew Kneale's comic historical fiction *Pilgrims*, the self-righteous, self-interested character of Matilda Froome is explicitly modelled on Kempe.[33] More broadly, Kempe's embrace of shame and her unsuccessful

attempts to become a saint eloquently foreshadow the contemporary genre of autobiography-as-failure, in which the anti-hero
revels in their unfulfillment. As the narrator of one such book,
Chris Kraus's *I Love Dick*, says, 'Isn't the greatest freedom in
the world the freedom to be wrong?'[34] Or, in a similar vein, the
anguished storyteller of Karl Ove Knausgaard's *My Struggle*, who
says, 'I wanted to open the world by writing, for myself, at the
same time this is also what made me fail.'[35] Such sentiments
carry over Kempe's delight in recording her failures and slights
against her while wallowing in the pain of being an outsider and
a disappointment to oneself, with the now-familiar framing of
an unreliable narrator.

Kempe's ability to engage a wide variety of audiences is borne
out by her lively, if contested, presence on social media in the
digital age;[36] Kempe has numerous digital detractors online,
as well as a vibrant fan community. There are, at the time of
writing, around eighteen different *Twitter* accounts by or for
'Margery Kempe' and, since 2018, a Margery Kempe Society (@
MargerySociety), 'supporting and promoting the scholarship,
study, and teaching of *The Book of Margery Kempe*'. Kempe and
her *Book* have come a long way, but her ability to polarize opinion, just as she did at Lambeth Palace more than six hundred
years ago, remains intact. *The Book of Margery Kempe* speaks to
contemporary culture as an exploration of the subject as author,
untidily wavering between envy, ambition, inadequacy and
stringent self-criticism. Kempe asserts the validity of her own
experience and authority while attempting to repudiate social
acclaim, as she struggles with the demands of the mixed life.
In this way, *The Book of Margery Kempe* remains a captivating
account of what it is to try repeatedly to change oneself, to seek
words adequate to a difficult situation, and to maintain one's faith
in the future in a profoundly imperfect world.

29 Ruins of the chapel of St Michael, Mintlyn, Norfolk.

Envoie

Kempe's strident gift of 'plentyuows terys and boystows sobbyngys' (1.2515) was repeatedly mistrusted, both by Kempe and those around her. One day, perhaps around 1418–20, two priests, well disposed to her, take her to the countryside outside Lynn. They want to test the sincerity of her tears in an isolated place. The priests lead her to the little church, now an isolated ruin (illus. 29), of St Michael in the village of Mintlyn, beside the main road from Lynn to Norwich. Mintlyn speaks eloquently about medieval and modern ideas of place, and to our loss of the landscapes of Kempe's Middle Ages.

The priests want to see if Kempe's tears are for the benefit of an audience, or if they are divinely inspired, even in the countryside, 'a good . . . distawnce fro any other hows' (1.4750). Kempe and the two priests are accompanied by a child or two, perhaps some of Kempe's own. After praying for a time, Kempe 'brast owt in boistows wepyng and sobbyng and cryid as lowde, er ellys lowder, as sche dede whan sche was amongys the pepil at hom' (1.4754–6). On the way home, the party encounters other women carrying children, and Kempe asks if they have any young boys, because her mind is 'so raveschyd into the childhood of Crist' (1.4761), causing her again to fall down and weep so bitterly that 'it was merveyl to her it' (it was a marvel to hear; 1.4762). The verdict of the priests is that, by crying in both private and public, in the countryside and in town, Kempe has proved the authenticity of her tears.

I went to Mintlyn one early May afternoon. It had been a rainy morning, but the afternoon was warm and sunny. By the time I reached the ruins, the sky was brilliantly blue, the wet grass glistened in the sunlight. The ruins lie off a small, unpaved lane, with asparagus fields on either side. Three hares leapt from the hedgerows and ran together into the next field, where they jumped and sparred, before disappearing into the woodland beyond.

Mintlyn is mentioned in the Doomsday Book, when it was a significant settlement, with 21 houses. After the great plague of 1347–51, the village shrank, and seems to have died out entirely by the sixteenth century. The church became ruined and was abandoned around 1680 and has been allowed to crumble.[1] The modern Kings Lynn bypass road is close by; thousands of motorists drive past, unaware of the ruins marooned in the fields.

Medieval Christianity transformed everyday spaces into holy places through familiarity, use and ritual, endowing them with spiritual value. Kempe's excursion to Mintlyn evokes a landscape busy with religiosity, alive with chapels and shrines, a setting in which Christ and the Virgin Mary could be readily summoned and emotional reactions felt. In the process of the English Reformation, holy places like chapels, wells, hermitages and wayside shrines were ruined in what has been called 'the progressive desacralization of the landscape', accompanied by 'a desire to preserve mutilated remnants of [Catholic] idolatry as enduring evidence of Protestantism's glorious triumph'.[2] Ruined churches were hoped to be salutary lessons against the religion practised by Margery Kempe and her like. Yet, through Kempe's *Book*, a memory of this place endures. It is a place of visionary connection, where one can imagine Kempe, the two priests and the children in a site that was becoming deserted even in the fifteenth century but remained resonant with access to the divine. It was part of Kempe's familiar landscape, a landscape that was a surrogate text for her experiences.

Mintlyn is today overgrown and largely forgotten, a scarred monument of medieval England, eloquent in its incompleteness but impossible to reconstruct in its totality. Its ruins allow us to glimpse something unique in the past but also to fill the gaps with our projections and desires. Similarly, *The Book of Margery Kempe* is a partial memorial, one that helps us vividly to conjure some parts of a life while leaving so much that is unknown. Yet far from being broken, *The Book of Margery Kempe* offers something radical: an eager testament constituted by shame, embarrassment and torment; a description of extremes of failure and joy; the relentless pursuit of fantastical possibilities that other people wished to prevent; and a bold self-definition of one's own life as holy.

CHRONOLOGY

c. 1373	Birth of Margery, daughter of John Burnham of Lynn
1391	Bridget of Sweden canonized
c. 1393	Margery Burnham marries John Kempe
1401	William Sawtry, formerly of Lynn, burned as a heretic in London
1409	Promulgation of Thomas Arundel's Constitutions, regulating orthodoxy and heresy
c. 1409	Kempe stops eating meat
c. 1412	Kempe receives a divine directive to visit Rome, Jerusalem and Santiago
1413	Kempe visits Norwich, York and Bridlington. Later in the year, leaves Yarmouth for Jerusalem. Kempe's father, John Burnham, probably died this year
1414	Kempe travels to Venice. Visits Jerusalem and the Holy Land. Kempe travels via Assisi to Rome, where she spends many months
1415	Council of Constance confirms Bridget of Sweden as a saint. Kempe returns to England. Visits Norwich
c. 1416	Death of Julian of Norwich
1417	Kempe travels to Santiago de Compostela via Bristol. Afterwards is held and interrogated at Leicester and undergoes tribulations at York, Cawood, Hull, Hessle and Beverley; also visits London
c. 1418	Kempe returns to Lynn and starts to suffer from an illness, which will endure for eight years
1420	Kempe visits the grave of Richard of Caister at Norwich
1421	(23 January) Lynn Guildhall engulfed by fire
1428	Completion of the rebuilding of Lynn's Guildhall of the Holy Trinity
1431	(30 May) Joan of Arc, aged nineteen, burned at the stake in Rouen. (12 June) A John Kempe, probably Kempe's son, recorded trading between Gdańsk and Boston
c. 1432	Approximate date of the first attempts at writing down Kempe's revelations; death of Kempe's husband and of her oldest son

1433   Kempe sails from Ipswich to Gdańsk via Norway; visits
            Wilsnack and Aachen, returning to Dover via Calais
1434   Kempe visits Sheen and Syon
1436   (23 July) Kempe's priest begins to rewrite Book I
1438   (February–April) admission of 'Margeria Kempe' to the
            Lynn Guild of the Holy Trinity, Lynn. (28 April) Kempe's
            priest begins to rewrite Book II
1439   (22 May) Further mention of 'Margerie Kempe' in the
            Lynn Guild records the last evidence suggesting Kempe
            was still alive
c. 1501   Wynkyn de Worde publishes *A shorte treatyse of
            contemplacyon taught by our lorde Jhesu cryste, taken out of
            the boke of Margerie kempe of lyn*
1521   Henry Pepwell publishes extracts from Kempe's *Book* as
            part of *A veray devoute treatyse*, a collection of mystical
            works

ABBREVIATIONS

BMK: *The Book of Margery Kempe*, ed. Sanford Brown Meech and Hope Emily Allen, EETS o.s. 212 (London, 1940)

CBMK: *A Companion to the Book of Margery Kempe*, ed. John H. Arnold and Katherine J. Lewis, revd edn (Cambridge, 2010)

EAN: Ann Eljenholm Nichols, *The Early Art of Norfolk* (Kalamazoo, MI, 2002)

EETS: Early English Text Society (o.s. = original series, e.s. = extra series, s.s. = supplementary series)

GL: *Gilte Legende*, ed. Richard Hamer with Vida Russell, 3 vols, EETS o.s. 327, 328, 339 (2006–12)

IE: *Index Exemplorum: A Handbook of Medieval Religious Tales*, ed. Frederic C. Tubach (Helsinki, 1969)

KLBA: King's Lynn Borough Archives

ODNB: *Oxford Dictionary of National Biography*, at www.oxforddnb.com

TNA: The National Archives, Kew, London

REFERENCES

Foreword: A Note on this Book

1 Hermione Lee, *Biography: A Very Short Introduction* (Oxford, 2009), pp. 2–3.

1 Creature

1 John Mirk, *Instructions for Parish Priests*, ed. William Edward Peacock, EETS O.S. 31 [1868] (London, 1902), pp. 3–4.
2 From the *Trotula* (an eleventh-century gynaecological handbook translated into Middle English in the fifteenth century); Beryl Rowland, ed., *Medieval Woman's Guide to Health: The First English Gynecological Handbook* (London, 1981).
3 Rowland, *Medieval Woman's Guide to Health*, p. 134.
4 Ibid., p. 138.
5 Ibid., p. 155.
6 See Helen M. Hickey, 'The Lexical Prison: Impairment and Confinement in Medieval and Early Modern England', *Parergon*, LXXVII/2 (2017), pp. 133–57; Claire Trenery and Peregrine Horden, 'Madness in the Middle Ages', in *The Routledge History of Madness and Mental Health*, ed. Greg Eghigian (London, 2017), pp. 62–80.
7 'They put on him a purple garment' (John 19:2).
8 'O God my God, look upon me: why hast thou forsaken me?' (Psalm 21:2); Matthew 27:46; Mark 15:34.
9 John Gower, *Confessio Amantis*, ed. Russell A. Peck and Andrew Galloway (Kalamazoo, MI, 2004), vol. VII, pp. 106–7, at https://d.lib.rochester.edu.
10 John Van Engen, 'Multiple Options: The World of the Fifteenth-century Church', *Church History*, 77 (2008), pp. 257–84.
11 Walter Hilton, 'Epistle on the Mixed Life', in *English Mystics of the Middle Ages*, ed. Barry Windeatt (Cambridge, 1994), pp. 110–30. See also Hilary Carey, 'Devout Literate Laypeople and the Pursuit of the Mixed Life in Late Medieval England', *Journal of Religious History*, XIV/4 (1987), pp. 361–81.
12 Hilton, 'Epistle on the Mixed Life', p. 113.

13 Ibid., pp. 118–19. See also Naoë Kukita Yoshikawa, *Margery Kempe's Meditations: The Contexts of Medieval Devotional Literature, Liturgy and Iconography* (Cardiff, 2007), pp. 120–33.

2 The Town of Bishop's Lynn

1 Alan Dyer, 'Ranking Lists of English Medieval Towns', in *The Cambridge Urban History of Britain*, vol. 1: 600–1540, ed. D. M. Palliser (Cambridge, 2000), pp. 758–60. The 1377 Poll Tax returns, which indicate populations over age fourteen, show London as England's largest city (23,314), York second (7,248), Norwich fifth (3,952) and Lynn eighth (3,127).

2 BMK, pp. 358–68; Anthony Goodman, *Margery Kempe and Her World* (London, 2002), pp. 49–50.

3 See Dorothy Owen, *The Making of King's Lynn: A Documentary Survey* (Oxford, 1984), pp. 39–40.

4 See Charity Scott-Stokes, 'Margery Kempe: Her Life and the Early History of Her Book', *Mystics Quarterly*, XXV/1–2 (1999), pp. 10–68, on the social make-up of Kempe's Lynn.

5 *Red Register of King's Lynn*, ed. Holcombe Ingleby (King's Lynn, 1919–22), vol. II, p. 124, confirmed in KLBA KL/C 39/35.

6 Reproduced in BMK, p. 360; see also George Holmes, *The Good Parliament* (Oxford, 1975).

7 See Susan Maddock, 'Margery Kempe's Home Town and Worthy Kin', in *Encountering the Book of Margery Kempe*, ed. Laura Kalas and Laura Varnam (Manchester, 2021). I am exceptionally grateful to Susan Maddock for sharing her work on Kempe's family with me.

8 Scott-Stokes, 'Margery Kempe', p. 58; Maddock, 'Margery Kempe's Home Town'.

9 Goodman, *Margery Kempe*, pp. 15–35. He is described as being unwell in December 1412 and he was certainly dead by October 1413 (Goodman, *Margery Kempe*, p. 50), but probably died before his daughter embarked for Jerusalem in May/June. There is no evidence, however, that Kempe received a large legacy from her father, and it was unusual for married women to receive their father's fortune.

10 Owen, *Making of King's Lynn*, p. 331.

11 Virginia Jansen, 'Trading Places: Counting Houses and the Hanseatic "Steelyard" in King's Lynn', in *King's Lynn and the Fens: Medieval Art, Architecture and Archaeology*, ed. John McNeill (London, 2017), pp. 66–82.

12 Sebastian Sobecki, '"The writyng of this tretys": Margery Kempe's Son and the Authorship of Her *Book*', *Studies in the Age of Chaucer*, XXXVII (2015), pp. 257–83.

13 Goodman, *Margery Kempe*, pp. 64–5.

14 Ibid., p. 223.

15 From the England's Immigrants database, at www.englandsimmigrants. com.

16 Canterbury Cathedral Archives, DCC-ChAnt/M/462/2.

17 TNA C 1/71/9.

18 TNA SC 8/104/5183.

19 Maddock, 'Margery Kempe's Home Town'.

20 See Sarah Pearson, 'Medieval Houses in English Towns: Form and Location', *Vernacular Architecture*, XL (2009), pp. 12–13.

21 Goodman, *Margery Kempe*, p. 50; Scott-Stokes, 'Margery Kempe', p. 20.

22 Goodman, *Margery Kempe*, p. 51.

23 Ibid., pp. 42–8.

24 Wolfgang Riehle describes it as 'a paradoxical juxtaposition of down-to-earth worldly materialism and desire for spiritual experience'; *The Secret Within: Hermits, Recluses, and Spiritual Outsiders in Medieval England*, trans. Charity Scott-Stokes (Ithaca, NY, 2014), p. 247.

25 Susan Maddock, 'Society, Status, and the Leet Court in Margery Kempe's Lynn', in *Town Courts and Urban Society in Late Medieval England, 1250–1500*, ed. Richard Goddard and Teresa Phipps (Woodbridge, 2019), pp. 200–219.

26 Goodman, *Margery Kempe*, p. 65.

27 Ibid., p. 66; Susan Maddock, 'Mapping Margery Kempe's Lynn', *The Annual: The Bulletin of the Norfolk Archaeological and Historical Research Group*, 26 (2017), pp. 3–14.

28 W. Nelson Francis, ed., *The Book of Vices and Virtues*, EETS o.s. 217 (Oxford, 1942), p. 136.

29 See Maddock, 'Society, Status', pp. 213–15.

30 On urban women and milling, see P.J.P. Goldberg, *Women, Work, and Life Cycle in a Medieval Economy* (Oxford, 1992), pp. 135–8.

31 See Judith M. Bennett, *Ale, Beer, and Brewsters in England: Women's Work in a Changing World, 1300–1600* (New York, 1996). An Agnes Kempe appears in the Lynn records in 1434 involved in ale production, and could be Margery Kempe's daughter or daughter-in-law (Maddock, 'Mapping Margery Kempe's Lynn', p. 9).

32 John Lydgate, 'A ballade on an Ale-seller', in *The Minor Poems of John Lydgate*, ed. Henry Noble McCracken, EETS o.s. 192 (London, 1934), vol. II, p. 431.

33 *EAN*, p. 247.

34 The borough of Lynn was a single parish with St Margaret's its parish church (St Nicholas and St James were 'daughter' or parochial chapels of St Margaret's, and All Saints was the parish church of South Lynn).

35 For a full discussion, see Laura Varnam, 'The Importance of St Margaret's Church in *The Book of Margery Kempe*: A Sacred Place and an Exemplary Parishioner', *Nottingham Medieval Studies*, 61 (2017), pp. 197–243.

36 Nelson Francis, ed., *Book of Vices*, pp. 37, 249.

37 *GL* 1:461.

38 *GL* 1:462.

39 Kempe sets the scene in Advent 'on a Friday before Crystmes Day' (1.365). This might indicate the December 'Ember Day', a Friday in Advent of fasting and penance, or Christmas Eve (Christmas Day fell on a Saturday in 1395, 1400 and 1406).

40 *GL* 1:40.

41 It appears that he dies while she is away in 1414–15, as she laments that her 'ankyr', her 'syngular solas & comforte' (1.3367; 1.3996) has been taken away.

42 *GL* 1:334.

43 *GL* 1:336.

44 *BMK* 372; Wereham is 21 km (13 mi.) southeast of Lynn.

45 See Naoë Kukita Yoshikawa, *Margery Kempe's Meditations: The Context of Medieval Devotional Literature, Liturgy and Iconography* (Cardiff, 2007).

3 Places

1 Norwich had around forty parish churches whereas the borough of Lynn was a single parish with St Margaret's being its parish church. Norwich's population was probably about 10,000 at this time (E. Rutledge, 'Immigration and Population Growth in Early Fourteenth-century Norwich', *Urban History Yearbook*, 15 (1988), p. 27).

2 See Kate Parker, 'Lynn and the Making of a Mystic', in *CBMK*, pp. 61–3.

3 Norman Tanner, *The Church in the Later Middle Ages* (London, 2008), pp. 56–69; see also Tanner, *The Church in Late Medieval Norwich, 1370–1532* (Toronto, ON, 1984).

4 See *EAN*, p. 81; Sarah Stanbury, *The Visual Object of Desire in Late Medieval England* (Philadelphia, PA, 2015), pp. 76–93.

5 Vicar (1397–1402) of Sedgeford, about 22 km (14 mi.) from Lynn. On Caister, see Norman P. Tanner, 'Richard Caistor', ODNB.

6 Discussed in Tanner, *Church in Late Medieval Norwich*, pp. 232–3.

7 Ibid.

8 Kempe falls or lies down to pray at, for example, 1.415; 1.888; 1.906; 1.572; 1.1621; 1.1929; 1.2400; 1.2941; 1.4133; 1.4193; the Virgin swoons at 1.1665; 1.4475–7; 1.4538.

9 See Mary Carruthers, 'On Affliction and Reading, Weeping and Argument: Chaucer's Lachrymose Troilus in Context', *Representations*, XCIII/1 (2006), p. 9; see also Anthony Bale, 'Where Did Margery Kempe Cry?', in *Fluid Bodies and Bodily Fluids in Premodern Europe*, ed. Anne Scott and Michael Barbezat (Leeds, 2019), pp. 15–30.

10 See Kimberley-Joy Knight, 'Lachrymose Holiness and the Problem of Doubt in Thirteenth- and Fourteenth-century Hagiographics', in *Doubting Christianity: The Church and Doubt*, ed. Frances Andrews, Charlotte Methuen and Andrew Spicer, Studies in Church History, LII (Cambridge, 2016), pp. 118–34.

11 Anthony Goodman, *Margery Kempe and Her World* (London, 2002), p. 139.

12 Anthony Bale, 'Richard Salthouse of Norwich and the Scribe of *The Book of Margery Kempe*', *Chaucer Review*, LII/2 (2017), pp. 173–87.

13 Derek Keene, 'A New Study of London Before the Great Fire', *Urban History Yearbook, 1984* (Leicester, 1984), pp. 11–21.

14 See Ian Forrest, *The Detection of Heresy in Late Medieval England* (Oxford, 2005), pp. 86–9; Simon Forde, 'Repyndon [Repington, Repingdon], Philip', ODNB.

15 She mentions it again at 1.844; 1.2834; 1.2917; 1.2963; 1.3005.

16 Other parts of the palace surviving that would have been there when Kempe visited include the chapel, its tiled floor and its undercroft, and parts of the Gothic frontage, which would, in Kempe's day, long before the embankment of the Thames, have been on the river's waterfront. The so-called Lollards' Tower (or Water Tower) was built by Archbishop Chichele in the early 1430s, long after Kempe visited.

17 See Nicholas Watson, 'Censorship and Cultural Change in Late Medieval England: Vernacular Theology, the Oxford Translation Debate, and Arundel's *Constitutions* of 1409', *Speculum*, LXX/4 (1995), pp. 822–64; Ian Forrest, 'English Provincial Constitutions and Inquisition into Lollardy', in *The Culture of Inquisition*, ed. Mary Flannery and Katie Walter (Woodbridge, 2013), pp. 45–59.

18 On Sawtry's trial, see A. K. McHardy, 'De heretico comburendo, 1401', in *Lollardy and the Gentry in the Later Middle Ages*, ed. Margaret

Aston and Colin Richmond (Stroud, 1997), pp. 112–26.

19 David Wilkins, *Concilia Magnae Britanniae et Hiberniae* (London, 1737), vol. III, p. 255.

20 See Kantik Ghosh, *The Wycliffite Heresy: Authority and the Interpretation of Texts* (Cambridge, 2009), p. 148.

21 Vincent Gillespie, 'Chichele's Church: Vernacular Theology in England after Thomas Arundel', in *After Arundel: Religious Writing in Fifteenth-century England*, ed. Vincent Gillespie (Turnhout, 2011), pp. 32–3.

22 John Mirk, *Instructions for Parish Priests*, ed. William Edward Peacock, EETS o.s. 31 (London, 1868, rev. 1902), p. 13.

23 Ibid.

24 Similarly, Bridget of Sweden was derided for her 'febill clethinge' (worn-out clothing); *The Liber Celestis of St Bridget of Sweden*, ed. Roger Ellis, EETS o.s. 291 (Oxford, 1987), p. 3.

25 Louise Ropes Loomis, ed. and trans., *The Council of Constance: The Unification of the Church* (New York, 1961), p. 108.

26 See C.M.D. Crowther, 'Correspondence between England and the Council of Constance', *Studies in Church History*, 1 (1964), pp. 184–206.

27 Loomis, *Council of Constance*, pp. 91–100.

28 Ibid., pp. 133–4.

29 See Anna Fredriksson, 'Challenging and Championing St Birgitta's *Revelations* at the Councils of Constance and Basel', in *A Companion to Birgitta of Sweden*, ed. Maria Oen (Leiden, 2019), pp. 103–31; Rosalynn Voaden, *God's Words, Women's Voices* (Woodbridge, 1999).

30 Genelle Gertz, *Heresy Trials and English Women Writers, 1400–1670* (Cambridge, 2012), p. 50.

31 Loomis, *Council of Constance*, pp. 109–10.

32 Netter only returned from Constance in 1420 and in 1424 he presided over a gathering of the Carmelite provincial chapter at Lynn; see Anne Hudson, 'Netter [Walden], Thomas (c. 1370–1430)', ODNB.

33 Kevin Alban, *The Teaching and Impact of the 'Doctrinale' of Thomas Netter of Walden, c. 1374–1430* (Turnhout, 2010).

34 See Naoë Yoshikawa, 'The Making of *The Book of Margery Kempe*: the Issue of *Discretio spirituum* Reconsidered', *English Studies*, XCII/2 (2011), pp. 119–37.

35 Gary M. Radke, 'Nuns and Their Art: The Case of San Zaccaria in Renaissance Venice', *Renaissance Quarterly*, LIV/2 (2001), pp. 430–59.

36 See Ruth Nisse Shklar, 'Cobham's *Daughter: The Book of Margery Kempe* and the Power of Heterodox Thinking', *Modern Language Quarterly*, 56 (1995), pp. 277–304.

37 British Library Cotton MS Appendix VIII, ff. 108r–112v.

38 *BMK*, pp. 287–8; Clarissa Atkinson, *Mystic and Pilgrim: The Book and the World of Margery Kempe* (Ithaca, NY, 1983), p. 48.

39 For context see Nicole Chareyron, *Pilgrims to Jerusalem in the Middle Ages*, trans. W. Donald Wilson (New York, 2005); Sylvia Schein, 'Bridget of Sweden, Margery Kempe, and Women's Jerusalem Pilgrimage in the Middle Ages', *Mediterranean Historical Review*, XIV/1 (1999), pp. 44–58.

40 Quotation adapted from Francis of Assisi, *Early Documents: The Prophets*, ed. Regis Armstrong et al. (New York, 1999), p. 501.

41 For relevant material from Bridget, see Anthony Bale and Sebastian Sobecki, eds, *Medieval English Travel: A Sourcebook* (Oxford, 2019), pp. 151–8.

42 See Colin Morris, *The Sepulchre of Christ and the Medieval West* (Oxford, 2005).

43 Felix Fabri, *The Book of Wanderings*, ed. and trans. Aubrey Stewart, 2 vols, Palestine Pilgrims' Text Society, nos 7–10 (London, 1896), vol. II, p. 342.

44 Matthew 4:2; Mark 1:13; Luke 4:2.

45 See Bale and Sobecki, *Medieval English Travel*, pp. 232–61.

46 Tertius Chandler and Gerald Fox, *3000 Years of Urban Growth* (New York, 1974), p. 92.

47 John Capgrave, *Ye Solace of Pilgrimes: A Description of Rome circa AD 1450*, ed. C. A. Mills (London, 1911), p. 25.

48 Rebecca Krug, *Margery Kempe and the Lonely Reader* (Ithaca, NY, 2017), pp. 185, 45.

49 For the history of the Hospice see John Allen, ed., *The English Hospice in Rome: The Venerable Sexcentenary Issue*, revd edn (Leominster, 2005); Debra J. Birch, 'Pilgrimage to Rome in the Middle Ages: Continuity and Change', *Studies in the History of Medieval Religion*, 13 (Woodbridge, 1998).

50 Allen, ed., *English Hospice in Rome*, pp. 265, 66. See also Margaret Harvey, *The English in Rome, 1362–1420: Portrait of an Expatriate Community* (Oxford, 2008), pp. 58–9.

51 See Sarah Salih, 'At Home: Out of the House', in *The Cambridge Companion to Medieval Women's Writing*, ed. Carolyn Dinshaw and David Wallace (Cambridge, 2003), pp. 124–40.

52 For these moments from Catherine's medieval biography see

Raymond of Capua, *The Life of Catherine of Siena*, trans. George
Lamb (London, 1960), pp. 121–5, 131, 147.

53 See P. H. Cullum, '"Yf lak of charyte be not ower hynder-awnce":
Margery Kempe, Lynn, and the Practice of the Spiritual and Bodily
Works of Mercy', in CBMK, pp. 177–93.

54 Patrizia Marchetti, *La casa delle Oblate di Santa Francesca Romana a
Tor de' Specchi* (Rome, 1996).

55 Guy Boanas and Lyndal Roper, 'Feminine Piety in Fifteenth-century
Rome: Santa Francesca of Rome', in *Disciplines of Faith: Studies in
Religion, Politics, Patriarchy*, ed. Jim Obelkevich, Lyndal Roper and
Raphael Samuel (New York, 1987), p. 180.

56 Giovanni Mattiotti, *Il dialetto Romanesco del Quattrocento*, ed. Giorgio
Carpaneto (Rome, 1995), p. 3.

57 Cullum, '"Yf lak of charyte"'.

INTERLOGE: 'my weddyd wyfe', Rome, 1414

1 *The Liber Celestis of St Bridget of Sweden*, ed. Roger Ellis, EETS o.s.
291 (Oxford, 1987), pp. 238–9; see also pp. 284–6.

2 See Naoë Kukita Yoshikawa, *Margery Kempe's Meditations: The
Context of Medieval Devotional Literature, Liturgy and Iconography*
(Cardiff, 2007), pp. 55–6.

3 John Capgrave, *Ye Solace of Pilgrimes: A Description of Rome circa* AD
1450, ed. C. A. Mills (London, 1911), pp. 102–3.

4 Anthony Bale and Sebastian Sobecki, eds, *Medieval English Travel:
A Sourcebook* (Oxford, 2019), p. 256.

5 *Manuale et processionale ad usum insignis ecclesiae Eboracensis*, ed. W. G.
Henderson, Surtees Society, 63 (Durham, 1875), p. 19 (appendix 1).

6 Dyan Elliott, *The Bride of Christ Goes to Hell: Metaphor and
Embodiment in the Lives of Pious Women, 200–1500* (Philadelphia,
PA, 2011), p. 185.

7 Ibid., p. 178.

8 Ibid., pp. 215–16.

9 Naoë Kukita Yoshikawa, 'Margery Kempe's Mystical Marriage and
Roman Sojourn: Influence of St Bridget of Sweden ', *Reading Medieval
Studies*, XXVIII (2002), pp. 39–57: p. 40.

4 Friends and Enemies

1 Richard Rolle, *The Fire of Love and the Mending of Life*, ed. Ralph
Harvey, EETS o.s. 106 (London, 1896), pp. 90–91. Further

references to Rolle's *Fire of Love* are given parenthetically in
the text.

2 On these terms see Rebecca Krug, *Margery Kempe and the Lonely
Reader* (Ithaca, NY, 2017), pp. 24–57.

3 See Genelle Gertz, *Heresy Trials and English Women Writers, 1400–
1670* (Cambridge, 2012), pp. 49–52.

4 Anthony Goodman, *Margery Kempe and Her World* (London, 2002),
p. 89.

5 These manuscripts are now London, British Library, Royal MS 3
D.iii, ff. 1r–44v; Oxford, Lincoln College, MS Lat. 69, ff. 197r–234v.
See Naoë Kukita Yoshikawa, *Margery Kempe's Meditations: The
Context of Medieval Devotional Literature, Liturgy and Iconography*
(Cardiff, 2007), p. 64.

6 Susan Maddock, 'Margery Kempe's Home Town and Worthy Kin',
in *Encountering the Book of Margery Kempe*, ed. Laura Kalas and
Laura Varnam (Manchester, 2021).

7 Janette Dillon, 'Margery Kempe's Sharp Confessors', *Leeds Studies in
English*, XXVII (1996), pp. 131–8.

8 A. C. Spearing, 'Margery Kempe', in *A Companion to Middle
English Prose*, ed. A.S.G. Edwards (Cambridge, 2004), pp. 83–97;
see also Charity Scott-Stokes, 'Margery Kempe: Her Life and the
Early History of Her Book', *Mystics Quarterly*, XXV/1–2 (1999),
p. 16; Sebastian Sobecki, '"The writyng of this tretys": Margery
Kempe's Son and the Authorship of Her *Book*', *Studies in the Age
of Chaucer*, XXXVII (2015), pp. 280–81; Springold's identity as
amanuensis is rejected by Goodman, *Margery Kempe*, p. 91.

9 KLBA, KL/C 53/1. I am grateful to Susan Maddock for this reference.

10 Rotha Mary Clay, *The Hermits and Anchorites of England* (London,
1914), pp. 232–3.

11 E. A. Jones, ed., *Hermits and Anchorites in England, 1200–1550*
(Manchester, 2019), p. 66.

12 'Synodal Statutes of Bishop Richard de Wich for the Diocese of
Chichester', in *Councils and Synods*, vol. II: *AD 1205–1313*, ed. F. M.
Powicke and C. R. Cheney (Oxford, 1964), pt 1, p. 465.

13 For cases of recluses being associated with heresy, see Jones, *Hermits
and Anchorites*, pp. 156–8, 160–66, 193–7.

14 It is conceivable that this was Kempe's contemporary, the well-
known anchorite and political seer Emma Raughton of All Saints
North Street, York.

15 Kempe's likely kinsman, William Lok, burgess of Lynn, had provided
in his will of 16 October 1408 for a man to make a pilgrimage to

Santiago de Compostela on his behalf (Dorothy Owen, *The Making of King's Lynn: A Documentary Survey* (Oxford, 1984), pp. 251–2), so Kempe was not the first person from her social milieu to undertake this journey; Lok also left monies for pilgrimages to other sites Kempe would later visit (Canterbury, Hailes, Beverley and Bridlington).

16 Joan was Henry IV's legitimized half-sister and the full sister of Cardinal Henry Beaufort, Bishop of Winchester, about whom Kempe has an intuition that he lives when others say he is dead (1.4076) and who was also at Constance in 1414. Meanwhile, Thomas Beaufort, Joan and Henry's brother, was deeply involved in Lynn trade from 1403 until the 1420s; by 1416 Beaufort had a house and staithe in Lynn and would therefore have been known to Kempe (Goodman, *Margery Kempe*, pp. 33–4).

17 For comparative material see Robert Brian Tate and Thorlac Turville-Petre, eds, *Two Pilgrim Itineraries of the Later Middle Ages* (Santiago, 1995).

18 'Legende vom h. Blute zu Hayles', in *Altenglische legenden*, ed. Carl Horstmann (Heilbronn, 1881), pp. 275–81.

19 The laxness of the rule at Hailes, and its precarious finances, were often commented on in the period from the 1380s to the 1440s (Michael Carter, 'Abbots and Aristocrats: Patronage, Art and Architecture at Hailes Abbey in the Late Middle Ages', *Journal of the British Archaeological Association*, 171 (2018), p. 159).

20 On the imagery of holy surrogacy see Laura Kalas, *Margery Kempe's Spiritual Medicine: Suffering, Transformation and the Life-course* (Cambridge, 2020), pp. 123–5.

21 David Lawton, *Voice in Late Medieval English Literature: Public Interiorities* (Oxford, 2017).

22 See Susan Dickman, 'Margery Kempe and the Continental Tradition of the Pious Woman', in *The Medieval Mystical Tradition In England*, ed. Marion Glasscoe (Cambridge, 1986), vol. IV, pp. 150–68.

23 On Bridget see Maria H. Oen, ed., *A Companion to Birgitta of Sweden and Her Legacy in the Later Middle Ages* (Leiden, 2019).

24 See R. B. Dobson, 'Easton, Adam (c. 1330–1397)', ODNB; Miriam Wendling, ed., *Cardinal Adam Easton, c. 1330–1397* (Amsterdam, 2020).

25 Anthony Bale and Daniela Giosuè, 'A Women's Network in Fifteenth-century Rome: Margery Kempe Encounters "Margaret Florentyne"', in *Encountering The Book of Margery Kempe*, ed. Varnam and Kalas.

26 See Gunnel Cleve, 'Margery Kempe: A Scandinavian Influence on Medieval England?', in *The Medieval Mystical Tradition in England* , ed. Marion Glasscoe (Cambridge, 1992), vol. v, pp. 163–78; Naoë Kukita Yoshikawa, 'Margery Kempe's Mystical Marriage and Roman Sojourn: Influence of St Bridget of Sweden', *Reading Medieval Studies*, xxviii (2002).

27 This was a plenary indulgence originally granted to pilgrims to Bridget's foundation at Vadstena, Sweden, and 'transferred' to Syon by Henry v and confirmed by the Pope in 1425. For a fifteenth-century description see John Audelay, 'Salutation to St Bridget', in *Poems and Carols*, ed. Susanna Fein (Kalamazoo, mi, 2009), at https://d.lib.rochester.edu; Krug, *Margery Kempe*, pp. 52–3.

28 *The Liber Celestis of St Bridget of Sweden*, ed. Roger Ellis, eets o.s. 291 (Oxford, 1987), p. 459.

29 Ibid., pp. 1–3.

30 Ibid., p. 459.

31 See Nirit Ben-Aryeh Debby, 'Reshaping Birgitta of Sweden in Tuscan Art and Sermons', in *Companion to Birgitta*, ed. Oen, pp. 223–46; Maria H. Oen, 'The Iconography of *Liber Celestis revelacionum*', ibid., pp. 186–222.

32 'Fire of love' is not exclusively Rolle's formulation; it is used, for example, by Jacques de Vitry in his life of Marie d'Oignies, a text also known to Kempe or her scribes.

33 They are now widely regarded as having been written or rewritten by Johanne de Caulibus, a fourteenth-century Tuscan Franciscan. See Sarah McNamer, 'The Origins of the *Meditationes vitae Christi*', *Speculum*, lxxxiv/4 (2009), pp. 905–55; Peter Tóth and Dávid Falvay, 'Diverse Imaginations of Christ's life: New Light on the Date and Authorship of the *Meditationes vitae Christi*', in *Devotional Culture in Medieval England and Europe*, ed. Stephen Kelly and Ryan Perry (Turnhout, 2014), pp. 17–105.

34 Michael Sargent, ed., *Nicholas Love's 'The Mirror of the Blessed Life of Christ'* (Exeter, 2004), p. 10.

35 Ibid.

36 Ibid., pp. 171–2.

37 See Denise Despres, 'Franciscan Spirituality: Margery Kempe and Visual Meditation', *Mystics Quarterly*, xi (1985), pp. 12–18; Yoshikawa, *Margery Kempe's Meditations*, pp. 82–3; Barbara Newman, 'What Did It Mean to Say "I Saw"? The Clash between Theory and Practice in Medieval Visionary Culture', *Speculum*, 80 (2005), pp. 30–32.

38 In St Bridget's revelations, Christ likens himself to an apothecary making a 'holesom drinke' (*Liber Celestis*, p. 437).

39 See Jill Bennett, 'Stigmata and Sense Memory: St Francis and the Affective Image', *Art History*, XXIV/1 (2001), pp. 1–16; Suzannah Biernoff, *Sight and Embodiment in the Middle Ages* (Basingstoke, 2002).

40 Mary Carruthers, *The Book of Memory: A Study of Memory in Medieval Culture*, 2nd edn (Cambridge, 2008), p. 60.

41 Jennifer Bryan, *Looking Inward: Devotional Reading and the Private Self in Late Medieval England* (Philadelphia, PA, 2008), p. 123.

42 Edwin D. Craun, *Ethics and Power in Medieval English Reformist Writing* (Cambridge, 2010).

43 As Alastair Minnis explains, Kempe is aware of the canonical distinction between public and private speech. See Alastair Minnis, 'Religious Roles: Public and Private', in *Medieval Holy Women in the Christian Tradition, c. 1100–c. 1500*, ed. Alastair Minnis and Rosalynn Voaden (Turnhout, 2010), pp. 47–8.

44 *Liber Celestis*, p. 465.

45 IE #526; IE #517.

46 See Jennifer Brown, *Fruit of the Orchard: Reading Catherine of Siena in Late Medieval and Early Modern England* (Toronto, ON, 2019).

47 See Catherine of Siena, *The Dialogue*, ed. and trans. Suzanne Noffke (London, 1980).

48 For a sympathetic overview of Bedford's career, see Alec Myers, '*A vous entier*: John of Lancaster, Duke of Bedford', *History Today*, 10 (1960), pp. 460–68.

49 See BMK, pp. 316–17.

50 *The Bridgettine Breviary of Syon Abbey*, ed. A. J. Collins, Henry Bradshaw Society, 96 (Oxford, 1985), p. iv.

51 See Daniel Hobbins, *The Trial of Joan of Arc* (Cambridge, MA, 2009).

52 Margaret Aston, 'Lollard Women Priests?', *Journal of Ecclesiastical History*, 31 (1980), pp. 441–61.

53 The Devil and demons were often familiar, 'weak', ordinary or 'hazily' apprehended by those who encountered them. See Alain Boureau, *Satan the Heretic: The Birth of Demonology in the Medieval West*, trans. Teresa Lavender Fagan (Chicago, IL, 2006); Sari Katajala-Peltomaa, *Demonic Possession and Lived Religion in Later Medieval Europe* (Oxford, 2020).

54 Tamás Karáth, 'Good or Evil: The Ambiguity of Interpretation in Medieval English Devotional Writing', in *Does it Really Mean That? Interpreting the Literary Ambiguous*, ed. Kathleen Dubs (Cambridge, 2011), pp. 22–34.

55 *The York Plays*, ed. Richard Beadle, 2 vols, EETS s.s. 23–4 (Oxford, 2009–13), vol. I, pp. 23–8.

56 Frances Gussenhoven, 'The Serpent with a Matron's Face: Medieval Iconography of Satan in the Garden of Eden', *European Medieval Drama*, 4 (2001), pp. 207–30.

57 Michael Jones, 'Joan [Joan of Navarre]', ODNB; Michael Bailey, *Fearful Spirits, Reasoned Follies: The Boundaries of Superstition in Late Medieval Europe* (Ithaca, NY, 2013).

58 P. L. Heyworth, ed., *Jack Upland, Friar Daw's Reply, and Upland's Rejoinder* (Oxford, 1968), l.899–901 (p. 100).

59 See especially Renate Blumenfeld-Kosinski, 'The Strange Case of Ermine De Reims (*c.* 1347–1396): A Medieval Woman Between Demons and Saints', *Speculum*, LXXXV/2 (2010), pp. 321–56.

60 Dyan Elliott, 'Seeing Double: John Gerson, the Discernment of Spirits, and Joan of Arc', *American Historical Review*, CVII/1 (2002), pp. 26–54.

61 This text is translated in Brian Patrick McGuire, ed. and trans., *Jean Gerson: Early Works* (New York, 1998), pp. 288–333.

62 For an overview see Norman Cohn, *Europe's Inner Demons: The Demonization of Christians in Medieval Christendom*, revd edn (Chicago, IL, 2000).

63 See ODNB, 'Kyteler [Kettle], Alice, *fl.* 1302–24'; Cohn, *Europe's Inner Demons*, pp. 196–201.

64 Gábor Klaniczay, '*Miraculum* and *Maleficium*: Reflections Concerning Late Medieval Female Sainthood', in *Problems in the Historical Anthropology of Early Modern Europe*, ed. R. Po-Chia Hsia and R. W. Scribner (Wiesbaden, 1997), p. 66.

65 Katajala-Peltomaa, *Demonic Possession*, pp. 159–64.

66 See Jessica Freeman, 'Sorcery at Court and Manor: Margery Jourdemayne, the Witch of Eye next Westminster', *Journal of Medieval History*, XXX/4 (2004), pp. 343–57.

INTERLOGE: 'fals strumpet', Leicester, 1417

1 St Katherine's influence on Kempe is charted fully by Katherine Lewis, *The Cult of St Katherine of Alexandria in Medieval England* (Woodbridge, 2000), pp. 242–55; for an earlier analogous use of the legend, by a twelfth-century Benedictine nun, see Tara Foster, 'Clemence of Barking: Reshaping the Legend of Saint Catherine of Alexandria', *Women's Writing*, XII/1 (2005), pp. 13–27.

2 Osbern Bokenham, *Legendys of Hooly Wummen*, ed. Mary S.

Serjeantson, EETS o.s. 206 (London, 1938), pp. 181–2.

3 See Anthony Bale, 'God's Cell: Christ as Prisoner and Pilgrimage to the Prison of Christ', *Speculum*, XCI/1 (2016), pp. 1–35.

4 Bokenham, *Legendys*, pp. 172–201; see also GL 2:900.

5 On Kempe's self-fashioning as a saint, see Katherine Lewis, 'Margery Kempe and Saint Making in Later Medieval England', CBMK, pp. 195–215; Samuel Fanous, 'Measuring the Pilgrim's Progress: Internal Emphases in *The Book of Margery Kempe*', in *Writing Religious Women: Female Spiritual and Textual Practices in Late Medieval England*, ed. Denis Renevey and Christiania Whitehead (Cardiff, 2000), pp. 157–76.

6 Anthony Goodman, *Margery Kempe and Her World* (London, 2002), pp. 144–5; BMK, p. 311; Mary Bateson, ed., *Records of the Borough of Leicester* (London, 1901), p. 231.

7 Ian Forrest, *The Detection of Heresy in Late Medieval England* (Oxford, 2005), p. 48.

8 St Katherine says 'neither faire words ne drede of turnementes' (nor dread of torments) can separate her from her 'spouse' Jesus (GL 2:900).

9 GL 2:904.

5 Things

1 On definitions and terminology of mysticism see Vincent Gillespie, 'Preface', in *The Cambridge Companion to Medieval English Mysticism*, ed. Samuel Fanous and Vincent Gillespie (Cambridge, 2011), pp. ix–x; and Nicholas Watson, 'Introduction', ibid., pp. 1–28.

2 See John Dreyfus, 'The Invention of Spectacles and the Advent of Printing', *The Library*, sixth series, X/2 (1988), pp. 93–106.

3 For an excellent discussion of the idea of spectacles in Kempe's England see Shannon Gayk, *Image, Text, and Religious Reform in Fifteenth-century England* (Cambridge, 2010), pp. 45–83.

4 See Christine Cooper-Rompato, *The Gift of Tongues: Women's Xenoglossia in the Later Middle Ages* (University Park, PA, 2010).

5 Sarah Beckwith, 'A Very Material Mysticism: The Medieval Mysticism of Margery Kempe', in *Medieval Literature: Criticism, Ideology and History*, ed. David Aers (Brighton, 1986), pp. 34–57; see also Sheila Delaney, 'Sexual Economics, Chaucer's Wife of Bath, and *The Book of Margery Kempe*', *Minnesota Review*, V/1 (1978), pp. 104–15.

6 See Caroline Walker Bynum, *Christian Materiality: An Essay on Religion in Late Medieval Europe* (Cambridge, MA, 2011).

7 The image is taken from St Bridget, *The Liber Celestis of St Bridget of Sweden*, ed. Roger Ellis, EETS o.s. 291 (Oxford, 1987), p. 207.

8 My approach here is influenced by 'thing theory', describing the agency of the object. See Bill Brown, 'Thing Theory', *Critical Inquiry*, XXVIII/1 (2001), pp. 1–22; Fiona Candlin and Raiford Guins, *The Object Reader* (London, 2009).

9 On these specific miracles see IE #1383, #2667, #439. See also Amy Knight Powell, *Depositions: Scenes from the Late Medieval Church and the Modern Museum* (New York, 2012).

10 See W. R. Jones, 'Lollards and Images: The Defense of Religious Art in Later Medieval England', *Journal of the History of Ideas*, 34 (1973), pp. 27–50.

11 Priscilla Heath Barnum, ed., *Dives and Pauper*, 3 vols, EETS o.s. 275, 280, 323 (Oxford, 1976–2004), vol. I, p.85.

12 Margaretha Ebner (d. 1351), a Dominican nun whose piety was probably known to Kempe, had her own Christ-child figure; she tended, swaddled and cuddled it, and rocked it to sleep. See Rosemary Drage Hale, 'Rocking the Cradle: Margaretha Ebner (Be)holds the Divine', in *Performance and Transformation: New Approaches to Late Medieval Spirituality*, ed. Mary Suydam and Joanna Ziegler (New York, 1999), pp. 211–39.

13 Laura Varnam, 'The Crucifix, the *Pietà*, and the Female Mystic: Devotional Objects and Performative Identity in *The Book of Margery Kempe*', *Journal of Medieval Religious Cultures*, XLI/2 (2015), p. 224.

14 EAN, pp. 85–6.

15 John Lydgate, 'On the Image of Pity', in *Minor Poems*, ed. Henry Noble McCracken, EETS e.s. 107 (London, 1911), pp. 297–9.

16 See Suzannah Biernoff, *Sight and Embodiment in the Middle Ages* (Basingstoke, 2002).

17 EAN, p. 80.

18 The Blackfriars Cross is now at the Lynn Museum. On medieval devotion to the crucifix, see Sara Lipton, '"The Sweet Lean of His Head": Writing about Looking at the Crucifix in the High Middle Ages', *Speculum*, LXXX (2005), pp. 1172–208.

19 See Eamon Duffy, *The Stripping of the Altars: Traditional Religion in England, 1400–1580* (New Haven, CT, 1992), pp. 23–7.

20 Kathleen Kamerick, 'Art and Moral Vision in Angela of Foligno and Margery Kempe', *Mystics Quarterly*, XXI/4 (1995), pp. 148–58.

21 Bridget of Sweden compares the soul to a ring. *Liber Celestis*, p. 247.

22 A magnificent example is the Zbraslav Madonna (Prague, National Gallery), made for the Cistercians in the 1380s; the Madonna's

finger-ring once had a jewel fitted to the panel.

23 London, British Museum [D]712; [D]742. William Wykeham left some beads with the motto 'Jhesus est amor meus' to Archbishop Arundel (BMK, p. 297).

24 See Diana Scarisbrick, *Rings: Jewelry of Power, Love, and Loyalty* (London, 2007), pp. 136–45; Marian Campbell, *Medieval Jewellery in Europe, 1100–1500* (London, 2009), pp. 72–97.

25 The monogram 'Ihc [Jesus, the holy name] est amor meus' appears in a manuscript of Rolle's writings (British Library Add. MS 37049, f. 37r). Similarly, Kempe's motto is close to that of the Birgittine Order, 'amor meus crucifixus est', or 'my love is crucified' (Naoë Kukita Yoshikawa, 'Margery Kempe's Mystical Marriage and Roman Sojourn: Influence of St Bridget of Sweden', *Reading Medieval Studies*, XXVIII (2002), p. 44). See Rebecca Krug, *Margery Kempe and the Lonely Reader* (Ithaca, NY, 2017), pp. 110–28; Ann Killian, 'Sermon Verses and *The Book of Margery Kempe*', *Studies in the Age of Chaucer*, XLI (2019), pp. 211–37.

26 Delaney, 'Sexual Economics', pp. 104–15.

27 See the further examples given in Caroline Barron, 'Education and Training of Girls in Fifteenth-century London', in *Court, Counties, and the Capital in the Later Middle Ages*, ed. Diana Dunn (Stroud, 1996), p. 152.

28 Charity Scott-Stokes, 'Margery Kempe: Her Life and the Early History of Her Book', *Mystics Quarterly*, XXV/1–2 (1999), p. 22.

29 Jacqueline Jenkins, 'Reading and *The Book of Margery Kempe*', in CBMK, pp. 113–28.

30 This complex issue is interrogated more fully by Jenkins, ibid., p. 118, arguing that hearing rather than reading texts was preferred as a contemplative act.

31 Lynn Staley, *Margery Kempe's Dissenting Fictions* (University Park, PA, 1994), pp. 4, 36.

32 Joyce Coleman, *Public Reading and the Reading Public in Late Medieval England and France* (Cambridge, 1996), pp. 84–8, on 'the social context of medieval aurality'. On the perceived physical benefits of reading aloud, see Daniel McCann, *Soul-health: Therapeutic Reading in Later Medieval England* (Cardiff, 2018), pp. 5–8.

33 See 1.33909–92; 1.3642–4; 1.3926.

34 As described in Ezekiel 9:4; Revelation 3:5, 13:8, 17:8, 20:12, 20:15, 21:2.

35 Liz Herbert McAvoy, '"An awngel al clothyd in white": Rereading the Book of Life as *The Book of Margery Kempe*', in *Women and*

Experience in Later Medieval Writing: Reading the Book of Life,
ed. Annette Mulder-Bakker and Liz Herbert McAvoy (Basingstoke,
2009), pp. 103–22.

36 Bridget Morris, ed., *The Revelations of St Birgitta of Sweden*, vol. IV:
The Heavenly Emperor's Book to the Kings, The Rule, and Minor Works
(Oxford, 2015), p. 77.

37 'How the Good Wife Taught Her Daughter', in *Codex Ashmole 61:
A Compilation of Popular Middle English Verse*, ed. George Shuffelton
(Kalamazoo, MI, 2008), at https://d.lib.rochester.edu.

38 See Mary C. Erler, 'Margery Kempe's White Clothes', *Medium
Aevum*, LXII/1 (1993), p. 79.

39 See Daniel Bornstein, *The Bianchi of 1399: Popular Devotion in Late
Medieval Italy* (Ithaca, NY, 1993), pp. 43–4.

40 See Sarah Salih, *Versions of Virginity* (Cambridge, 2001), pp. 132–3;
Barbara Harvey, *Monastic Dress in the Middle Ages: Precept and
Practice* (Canterbury, 1988); Desiree Koslin, 'The Robe of Simplicity:
Initiation, Robing, and Veiling of Nuns in the Middle Ages', in
Robes and Honor: The Medieval World of Investiture, ed. Stewart
Gordon (New York, 2001), pp. 255–74. Wedding dresses in the
Middle Ages were not by custom white.

41 Erler, 'Margery Kempe's White Clothes', p. 79.

42 Nelson Francis, ed., *The Book of Vices and Virtues*, EETS o.s. 217
(Oxford, 1942), pp. 253–4.

43 *Liber Celestis*, pp. 485–6; see also Nirit Ben-Aryeh Debby, 'Reshaping
Birgitta of Sweden in Tuscan Art and Sermons', in *A Companion to
Birgitta of Sweden and Her Legacy in the Later Middle Ages*, ed. Maria H.
Oen (Leiden, 2019), pp. 223–46; Maria H. Oen, 'The Iconography of
Liber Celestis revelacionum', ibid., pp. 186–222.

44 Hannah Lucas, '"Clad in flesch and blood": The Sartorial Body and
Female Self-fashioning in *The Book of Margery Kempe*', *Journal of
Medieval Religious Cultures*, XLV/1 (2019), pp. 29–60. There are also
several Birgittine Nativity scenes in Norfolk sculpture, for example,
at Burnham Deepdale and at Norwich cathedral: EAN, p. 60.

45 See Justyna Wubs-Mrozewicz, 'Fish, Stock, and Barrel: Changes in
the Stockfish Trade in Northern Europe, c. 136–1560', in *Beyond the
Catch: Fisheries of the North Atlantic, the North Sea and the Baltic, 900–
1850*, ed. Louis Sicking and Darlene Abreu-Ferreira (Leiden, 2008),
pp. 187–208.

46 KLBA, KL/C 39/38. I am grateful to Susan Maddock for this reference.

47 Lucy Toulmin Smith, ed., *The Boke of Brome: A Commonplace Book
of the Fifteenth Century* (London, 1886), p. 13.

48 Thomas Wright, ed., *Songs and Carols of the Fifteenth Century*, Percy Society, XXIII (London, 1848), p. 5.

49 'The Wife of Bath's Prologue', *The Riverside Chaucer*, gen. ed. Larry D. Benson (Oxford, 1987), D.868 (p. 117).

50 Carolyn Steedman, *Dust: The Archive and Cultural History* (New Brunswick, NJ, 2001), p. 164.

51 Georgia Ronan Crampton, ed., *The Shewings of Julian of Norwich* (Kalamazoo, MI, 1994), pp. 148–9, at https://d.lib.rochester.edu.

52 Julian of Norwich, *Revelations of Divine Love*, trans. Barry Windeatt (Oxford, 2015), p. 7.

INTERLOGE: 'a gret fyer', Lynn, 1421

1 See Susan Maddock, 'The Two Halls of the Trinity Guild in Lynn', *The Annual: The Bulletin of the Norfolk Archaeological and Historical Research Group*, 9 (2000), pp. 11–19; William Richards, *The History of Lynn*, 2 vols (King's Lynn, 1812), vol. I, p. 467; Anthony Goodman, *Margery Kempe and Her World* (London, 2002), pp. 48–9. On this context, see Michael D. Myers, 'A Fictional-true Self: Margery Kempe and the Social Reality of the Merchant Elite of King's Lynn', *Albion*, XXXI/3 (1999), pp. 377–94.

2 See Charles Caspers and Peter Jan Margry, *Het Mirakel van Amsterdam: Biografie van een betwiste devotie* (Amsterdam, 2017).

3 Caroline Walker Bynum, *Wonderful Blood: Theology and Practice in Late Medieval Northern Germany and Beyond* (Philadelphia, PA, 2007), pp. 25–6.

4 IE #2654, #2685, #2690.

5 This and subsequent references to Bartholomew come from *On the Properties of Things: John Trevisa's Translations of Bartholomaeus Anglicus De Proprietatibus Rerum: A Critical Text*, ed. M. C. Seymour et al., 3 vols (Oxford, 1975–88), vol. I, pp. 588–9.

6 For example, London, British Library Add. MS 18850 (*The Bedford Hours*), f. 65r, showing snowy hills behind the stable (incidentally, this manuscript was given by Kempe's tormentor, John Duke of Bedford, to Henry VI at Christmas 1430).

7 Lucy Donkin, 'Sta. Maria Maggiore and the Depiction of Holy Ground Plans in Late Medieval Italy', *Gesta*, LVII/2 (2018), pp. 225–55.

8 Kathleen Pribyl, Richard C. Cornes and Christian Pfister, 'Reconstructing Medieval April–July Mean Temperatures in East Anglia, 1256–1431', *Climatic Change*, CXIII/2 (2012), p. 404, showing that

'cold years . . . cluster in the first decade of the fifteenth century and the early 1420s'.

9 Laura Varnam, 'The Importance of St Margaret's Church in *The Book of Margery Kempe*: A Sacred Place and an Exemplary Parishioner', *Nottingham Medieval Studies*, 61 (2017), p. 202.

6 Feelings

1 Barbara H. Rosenwein, *Generations of Feeling: A History of Emotions, 600–1700* (Cambridge, 2016), pp. 193–210.

2 Ibid., p. 205.

3 See Anthony Bale, 'From Nidaros to Jerusalem; from Feginsbrekka to Mount Joy', in *Tracing the Jerusalem Code*, ed. Kristin Aavitsland and Line Bonde (Berlin, 2020), vol. 1, pp. 187–93.

4 Thomas Aquinas, *Commentary on Saint Paul's Epistles to the Galatians by St Thomas Aquinas*, trans. Fabian Larcher and Richard Murphy (Albany, NY, 1966), pp. 179–80.

5 Walter Hilton, *The Scale of Perfection*, ed. Thomas H. Bestul (Kalamazoo, MI, 2000), at https://d.lib.rochester.edu.

6 Anthony Bale and Sebastian Sobecki, eds, *Medieval English Travel: A Sourcebook* (Oxford, 2019), p. 153.

7 Nancy Bradley Warren, *Spiritual Economies: Female Monasticism in Later Medieval England* (Philadelphia, PA, 2001), p. 101.

8 Felix Fabri, *The Book of Wanderings*, ed. and trans. Aubrey Stewart, 2 vols, Palestine Pilgrims' Text Society, nos 7–10 (London, 1896), vol. II, p. 357.

9 Burchard of Mount Sion, *Description of the Holy Places*, ed. John R. Bartlett (Oxford, 2019), p. 109.

10 'Sarmun', in *Poems from BL MS Harley 913 'The Kildare Manuscript'*, ed. Thorlac Turville-Petre, EETS o.s. (Oxford, 2015), p. 26.

11 See Laura Kalas Williams, '"Slayn for Goddys lofe": Margery Kempe's Melancholia and the Bleeding of Tears', *Medieval Feminist Forum*, LII/1 (2016), pp. 84–100.

12 Other early assessments of Kempe's illnesses are summarized in *The Book of Margery Kempe*, ed. and trans. Anthony Bale (Oxford, 2015), p. xxix; see also Laura Kalas, *Margery Kempe's Spiritual Medicine: Suffering, Transformation and the Life-course* (Cambridge, 2020).

13 For contexts see Julie Orlemanski, 'How to Kiss a Leper', *Postmedieval*, III/2 (2012), pp. 142–57.

14 See Rosalynn Voaden, 'Beholding Men's Members: The Sexualizing of Transgression in *The Book of Margery Kempe*', in *Medieval Theology*

and the Natural Body, ed. Peter Biller and A. J. Minnis (York, 1997), pp. 175–90.

15 Guy de Chauliac, *Cyrurgie*, ed. Margaret S. Ogden, EETS o.s. 265 (London, 1971), p. 381.

16 At Cowgate, West Lynn, Setchey and Gaywood. BMK, p. 332.

17 See Susan Dickman, 'Margery Kempe and the Continental Tradition of the Pious Woman', in *The Medieval Mystical Tradition in England*, ed. Marion Glasscoe (Cambridge, 1986), vol. IV. While Elizabeth was known in England, Kempe is likely also to have encountered her cult as she passed through the city of Perugia on her way from Assisi to Rome in 1414; Elizabeth of Hungary's cult was strong in Perugia, where she had been canonized by Pope Gregory IX in the Dominican convent in 1235.

18 See Christopher Woodforde, *The Medieval Glass of St Peter Mancroft, Norwich* (Norwich, 1935), pp. 47–8; Christine M. Boeckl, *Images of Leprosy: Disease, Religion, and Politics in European Art* (Kirksville, MO, 2011).

19 Radegund's kissing of lepers itself recalls the famous incident of St Martin of Tours (d. 397) who kissed a poor leper and cured him.

20 See Venantius Fortunatus, 'Life of St Radegund', ed. Martha Carlin, at https://people.uwm.edu/carlin/ venantius-fortunatus-life-of-st-radegund.

21 Arthur W. Frank, *The Wounded Storyteller: Body, Illness, and Ethics*, 2nd edn (Chicago, IL, 2013), p. 3.

22 See Daniel McCann, *Soul-health: Therapeutic Reading in Later Medieval England* (Cardiff, 2018), pp. 81–110.

23 Wolfgang Riehle, *The Secret Within: Hermits, Recluses, and Spiritual Outsiders in Medieval England*, trans. Charity Scott-Stokes (Ithaca, NY, 2014), p. 247.

24 Richard Rolle, 'Oleum effusum', in *Uncollected Prose and Verse*, ed. Ralph Hanna, EETS o.s. 329 (Oxford, 2007), p. 4.

25 Nelson Francis, ed., *The Book of Vices and Virtues*, EETS o.s. 217 (Oxford, 1942), p. 43.

26 Ibid., p. 44.

27 1.3805; 1.4537; 1.4564; 1.4654.

28 See Lara Farina, *Erotic Discourse in Early English Religious Writings* (Basingstoke, 2006).

29 Raymond of Capua, *The Life of Catherine of Siena*, trans. George Lamb (London, 1960), pp. 99–105, 147–9; the foreskin is in *The Letters of Catherine of Siena*, ed. and trans. Suzanne Noffke, 4 vols (Tempe, AZ, 2000–2008), #221.

30 Salvina Westra, ed., *Talking of the Love of God* (The Hague, 1950), p. 61.

31 For an insightful reading of this passage see McCann, *Soul-health*, pp. 130–33.

32 Riehle, *Secret Within*, p. 254.

33 Rebecca Krug, *Margery Kempe and the Lonely Reader* (Ithaca, NY, 2017), pp. 96–100.

34 See Bartlett Jere Whiting, *Proverbs, Sentences, and Proverbial Phrases, from English Writings mainly before 1500* (Cambridge, MA, 1968), #H367 (p. 281), #P195 (p. 458).

35 Given the Countess of Westmorland's earlier patronage of Kempe, this dinner might well have taken place at one of the Countess's London homes. These were The Erber, at Dowgate near the Hanse Steelyard (where Cannon Street station now stands), and Westmorland Place (near Aldersgate, where the Barbican complex now stands). See *British Historic Towns Atlas*, at www.historictownsatlas.org.uk.

36 E. A. Jones, ed., *Hermits and Anchorites in England, 1200–1550* (Manchester, 2019), p. 102.

37 See especially Melissa Raine, '"Fals flesh": Food and the Embodied Piety of Margery Kempe', *New Medieval Literatures*, 7 (2005), pp. 101–26; Hwanhee Park, 'Mealtime Sanctity: The Devotional and Social Significance of Mealtimes in *The Book of Margery Kempe*', *Parergon*, XXXVI/1 (2019), pp. 61–80.

7 Old Age

1 See Norman Tanner, 'Lollard Women: Wives of Norfolk', ODNB.

2 In Norman Tanner, ed., *Heresy Trials in the Diocese of Norwich 1428–31* (London, 1977), pp. 173–4.

3 Maureen Jurkowski, 'Lollardy and Social Status in East Anglia', *Speculum*, LXXXII/1 (2007), p. 129.

4 Moreover, Springwell, a Lynn spicer or apothecary, had been admitted as a burgess in 1412, the same year as John of Wereham, the Lynn mercer who witnessed the 'miracle' of the church masonry falling on Kempe.

5 Thomas Netter, the prior provincial of the English Carmelites and zealous anti-Lollard, appears in Kempe's *Book* (Chapter 68) as the man to whom complaints are made about her closeness to Alan of Lynn (a Carmelite) and as the man who forbade Alan from speaking with Kempe. Netter was present in Norwich in 1428 at William White's trial and, as a powerful enemy of Kempe's, her *Book* keeps

its distance from him (Tanner, *Norwich Heresy Trials*, p. 9).

6 Ibid., p. 46.

7 Sebastian Sobecki, '"The writyng of this tretys": Margery Kempe's Son and the Authorship of Her *Book*', *Studies in the Age of Chaucer*, XXXVII (2015), pp. 257–83, proves the historicity of John Kempe Jr's Gdańsk connections.

8 See Amy Appleford, *Learning to Die in London, 1380–1540* (Philadelphia, PA, 2015).

9 See Warren Ginsberg, *The Parlement of the Thre Ages* (Kalamazoo, MI, 1992), at https://d.lib.rochester.edu.

10 Lynn Staley, *Margery Kempe's Dissenting Fictions* (University Park, PA, 1994), pp. 62–3.

11 See David Aers, 'The Making of Margery Kempe: Individual and Community', in *Community, Gender, and Individual Identity: English Writing, 1360–1430*, ed. David Aers (Brighton, 1988), pp. 34–57.

12 Guy de Chauliac, *Cyrurgie*, ed. Margaret S. Ogden, EETS o.s. 265 (London, 1971), p. 237.

13 Ibid., p. 240.

14 See Sheila Delaney, 'Sexual Economics, Chaucer's Wife of Bath, and *The Book of Margery Kempe*', *Minnesota Review*, V/1 (1978).

15 Clarissa Atkinson, *Mystic and Pilgrim: The Book and the World of Margery Kempe* (Ithaca, NY, 1983), pp. 176–8; Anthony Goodman, *Margery Kempe and Her World* (London, 2002), p. 67.

16 See Tara Williams, '"As thu wer a wedow": Margery Kempe's Wifehood and Widowhood', *Exemplaria*, XXI/4 (2009), pp. 345–62.

17 See Goodman, *Margery Kempe*, p. 19; David Wallace, *Strong Women: Life, Text, and Territory* (Oxford, 2011), pp. 113–20.

18 See Klaus Bitterling, 'Margery Kempe, an English *sterte* in Germany', *Notes and Queries*, XLIII/1 (1996), pp. 21–2.

19 On the prayers, see Barbara Zimbalist, 'Christ, Creature, and Reader: Verbal Devotion in *The Book of Margery Kempe*', *Journal of Medieval Religious Cultures*, XLI/1 (2015), pp. 1–23; Josephine A. Koster, 'The Prayers of Margery Kempe: A Reassessment', in *Encountering the Book of Margery Kempe*, ed. Laura Kalas and Laura Varnam (Manchester, 2021).

20 BMK, p. 358.

21 Gail McMurray Gibson has called Kempe's *Book* an 'autohagiography'; *The Theatre of Devotion: East Anglian Drama and Society in the Late Middle Ages* (Chicago, IL, 1989), p. 47; see also Katherine Lewis, 'Margery Kempe and Saint Making in Later Medieval England', CBMK, pp. 201–2; Laura Kalas, *Margery Kempe's Spiritual Medicine:*

Suffering, Transformation and the Life-course (Cambridge, 2020), pp. 217–18, on burial practices at St Margaret's.

8 Writing and Rediscovery

1 See the essays in Liz Herbert McAvoy and Diane Watt, eds, *The History of British Women's Writing, 700–1500* (Basingstoke, 2012).

2 Liz Herbert McAvoy, ed. and trans., *A Revelation of Purgatory* (Cambridge, 2017), pp. 80–83.

3 On Hull's life see Alexandra Barratt, 'Dame Eleanor Hull: A Fifteenth-century Translator', in *The Medieval Translator*, ed. Roger Ellis (Cambridge, 1989), pp. 87–101; David Lawton, 'Psalms as Public Interiorities: Eleanor Hull's Voices', in *The Psalms and Medieval English Literature: From the Conversion to the Reformation*, ed. Tamara Atkin and Francis Leneghan (Cambridge, 2017), pp. 298–317.

4 Alexandra Barratt, ed., *The Seven Psalms*, EETS o.s. 307 (Oxford, 1995), p. xxvi.

5 Ibid., p. xxxi.

6 On the limited extent of formalized women's education in England at Kempe's time see Nicholas Orme, *Medieval Schools: From Roman Britain to Renaissance England* (New Haven, CT, 2006), pp. 129, 166–7.

7 Rebecca Krug, *Margery Kempe and the Lonely Reader* (Ithaca, NY, 2017).

8 See Nicholas Watson, 'The Making of the *Book of Margery Kempe*', in *Voices in Dialogue: Reading Women in the Middle Ages*, ed. Kathryn Kerby-Fulton and Linda Olson (South Bend, IN, 2005), pp. 395–434.

9 Anthony Bale, 'Richard Salthouse of Norwich and the Scribe of *The Book of Margery Kempe*', *Chaucer Review*, LII/2 (2017).

10 Norman Tanner, *The Church in Late Medieval Norwich, 1370–1532* (Toronto, ON, 1984), p. 35.

11 Mount Grace evidently had a collection of mystical texts similar to Kempe's: a copy of the mystical treatise *The Cloud of Unknowing*; a translation, by Richard Methley of Mount Grace, of Marguerite Porete's *Mirror of Simple Souls*; Nicholas Love's *Mirror of the Life of Christ*, a text known to Kempe; and the Carthusian compilation *Speculum spiritualium* (*The Spiritual Mirror*). See Neil Ker, *Medieval Libraries of Great Britain*, at http://mlgb3.bodleian.ox.ac.uk.

12 On the manuscript's annotations see Joel Fredell, 'Design and Authorship in *The Book of Margery Kempe*', *Journal of the Early Book Society*, 12 (2009), pp. 1–28; Kelly Parsons, 'The Red Ink Annotator of *The Book of Margery Kempe* and His Lay Audience',

in *The Medieval Professional Reader at Work*, ed. Kathryn Kerby-
Fulton and Maidie Hilmo (Victoria, 2001), pp. 217–38; Katie
Bugyis, 'Handling *The Book of Margery Kempe*', in *New Directions in
Medieval Manuscript Studies*, ed. Kathryn Kerby-Fulton (South Bend,
IN, 2014), pp. 138–58.

13 Cambridge University Library Sel. 5, 27 (de Worde) and British
Library C. 37 (Pepwell).

14 A *veray devoute treatyse* (London, 1521), D6v–E3v.

15 See Ethan A. Shagan, 'Print, Orality, and Communications in the
Maid of Kent Affair', *Journal of Ecclesiastical History*, LII/2 (2001),
pp. 21–33; Diane Watt, 'Reconstructing the Word: The Political
Prophecies of Elizabeth Barton (1506–1534)', *Renaissance Quarterly*,
50 (1997), pp. 136–63.

16 See Julie A. Chappell, *Perilous Passages: The Book of Margery Kempe,
1534–1934* (New York, 2013). Chappell advances a convincing
case that the manuscript was at the Carthusians' London priory, and
removed from there circa 1535–8, by the former Carthusian monk
Everard Digby.

17 See Hilton Kelliher, 'The Rediscovery of Margery Kempe: A
Footnote', *British Library Journal*, XXIII (1997), pp. 259–63;
Chappell, *Perilous Passages*, pp. 63–6. The manuscript was in Butler-
Bowdon's family in the eighteenth century, as revealed by two
bookplates belonging to Henry Bowdon (b. 1754).

18 The missal is now the *Broughton Missal* (Lambeth Palace Library,
MS 5066), purchased by the Art Fund in 2015. Its history cannot be
connected with the Margery Kempe manuscript until it came into
Butler-Bowden family's ownership between the sixteenth century
and about 1845. This manuscript was held at the parish church at
Broughton (Lancashire), 24 km (15 mi.) from the Butler-Bowdens'
ancient seat at Pleasington Old Hall.

19 Hope Emily Allen, 'A Medieval Work', *The Times*, 27 December
1934, p. 15.

20 On Hope Emily Allen's immersion in, and Sisyphean pursuit
of, Margery Kempe, see John Hirsh, *Hope Emily Allen: Medieval
Scholarship and Feminism* (Norman, OK, 1988); Carolyn Dinshaw,
*How Soon Is Now? Medieval Texts, Amateur Readers, and the
Queerness of Time* (Durham, NC, 2012).

21 See David Wallace, *Strong Women: Life, Text, and Territory* (Oxford,
2011), p. 66.

22 *The Children's Newspaper* (London), 10 October 1936.

23 Bryn Mawr College, H. E. Allen collection 16, box 4.

24 Ibid., box 6.

25 See George Burns, 'Margery Kempe Reviewed', *The Month*, 171 (1938), pp. 238–44; Marea Mitchell, *The Book of Margery Kempe: Scholarship, Community, and Criticism* (New York, 2005), pp. 55–67.

26 Katharine Cholmeley, *Margery Kempe: Genius and Mystic* (London, 1947), pp. vi–vii.

27 Caroline Walker Bynum, *Jesus as Mother: Studies in the Spirituality of the High Middle Ages* (Berkeley and Los Angeles, CA, 1982), p. 172.

28 Robert Glück, *Margery Kempe* (London, 1995), p. 49.

29 Ibid., p. 48.

30 Ibid., pp. 160–62.

31 Ibid., p. 162.

32 Margaret Atwood, *The Testaments* (London, 2019), p. 139.

33 Matthew Kneale, *Pilgrims* (London, 2020).

34 Chris Kraus, *I Love Dick* (Cambridge, MA, 2006), p. 211.

35 Karl Ove Knausgaard, *My Struggle: Book One* [*A Death in the Family*], trans. Don Bartlett (New York, 2012), pp. 221–2.

36 Alicia Spencer-Hall, *Medieval Saints and Modern Screens: Divine Visions as Cinematic Experience* (Amsterdam, 2017), pp. 167–87.

Envoie

1 Fragments of the Norman doorway are now in the Lynn Museum.

2 Alexandra Walsham, *The Reformation of the Landscape* (Oxford, 2011), pp. 123, 147.

FURTHER READING

Arnold, John H., and Katherine J. Lewis, eds, *A Companion to the Book of Margery Kempe*, revd edn (Cambridge, 2010)

Atkinson, Clarissa W., *Mystic and Pilgrim: The Book and the World of Margery Kempe* (Ithaca, NY, 1983)

Bhattacharji, Santha, *God is an Earthquake: The Spirituality of Margery Kempe* (London, 1997)

Chappell, Julie A., *Perilous Passages: The Book of Margery Kempe, 1534–1934* (New York, 2013)

Fanous, Samuel, and Vincent Gillespie, eds, *The Cambridge Companion to Medieval English Mysticism* (Cambridge, 2011)

Gibson, Gail McMurray, *The Theater of Devotion: East Anglian Drama and Society in the Late Middle Ages* (Chicago, IL, 1989)

Goodman, Anthony, *Margery Kempe and Her World* (London, 2002)

Kalas, Laura, *Margery Kempe's Spiritual Medicine: Suffering, Transformation and the Life-course* (Cambridge, 2020)

—, and Laura Varnam, eds, *Encountering the Book of Margery Kempe* (Manchester, 2021)

Krug, Rebecca, *Margery Kempe and the Lonely Reader* (Ithaca, NY, 2017)

Lochrie, Karma, *Margery Kempe and Translations of the Flesh* (Philadelphia, PA, 1991)

Mitchell, Marea, *The Book of Margery Kempe: Scholarship, Community, and Criticism* (New York, 2005)

Riehle, Wolfgang, *The Secret Within: Hermits, Recluses, and Spiritual Outsiders in Medieval England*, trans. Charity Scott-Stokes (Ithaca, NY, 2014)

Staley, Lynn, *Margery Kempe's Dissenting Fictions* (University Park, PA, 1994)

Yoshikawa, Naoë Kukita, *Margery Kempe's Meditations: The Context of Medieval Devotional Literature, Liturgy, and Iconography* (Cardiff, 2007)

ACKNOWLEDGEMENTS

In the course of writing this book I have incurred many debts of thanks. I want especially to thank Michael Carter, Matthew Davies, Daniela Giosuè, Clare Griffiths, Shay Hamias, Celia Hatton, Kathleen Coyne Kelly, Joanne Leal, Josephine Livingstone, Hannah Lucas, Susan Maddock, Humphrey Ocean, Andreas Rehberg, James Simpson, Laura di Stefano, Nigel Tringham, Romina di Vizio, Nicholas Watson, Joanne Winning, Marius Winzeler and Barbara Zimbalist. Ruth Bale, Isabel Davis, Susan Maddock, Timothy Phillips and Marion Turner offered generous and perceptive feedback on drafts. The 'Medieval Lives' series editor, Deirdre Jackson, was an acute reader of the draft manuscript, and the press's readers gave constructive and incisive reports on the book; Michael Leaman, Alexandru Ciobanu and Phoebe Colley at Reaktion Books have been supportive and generous throughout. Any errors that remain in these pages are mine to deplore. I am grateful for the support of The Leverhulme Trust (International Research Networking Award, IN-2015-041), and the staff of the London Library and Bryn Mawr College Archives (especially Marianne Hansen). Much of this book was written thanks to Harvard University (Morton Bloomfield Fellowship) and the Huntington Library (Erika & Kenneth Riley Fellowship), whose generous support allowed me time and space to focus on Margery Kempe.

PHOTO ACKNOWLEDGEMENTS

The author and publishers wish to express their thanks to the below sources of illustrative material and/or permission to reproduce it. Some locations of artworks are also given below, in the interest of brevity:

© Anthony Bale: 1; photos Anthony Bale: 3, 5, 6, 10, 13, 14, 29; Bibliothèque nationale de France, Paris (MS Fr. 2810, fol. 255r): 15; British Library, London (Royal MS 6 E VI/1, f. 2r): 18; © British Library Board, all rights reserved/Bridgeman Images: 19 (Harley 5370, fol. 167r), 27 (Add. MS 61823, fol. 71v); photo Paul Brooker (CC BY 2.0): 8; photo Didier Descouens (CC BY-SA 4.0): 12; photo Amos Gal (CC BY-SA 4.0): 25; photo Julian P. Guffogg and Jenny Hannan-Briggs (CC BY 2.0): 26; © Shay Hamias and Anthony Bale: 2; photo © Neil Holmes/Bridgeman Images: 17; Hope Emily Allen Papers, Special Collections Department, Bryn Mawr College Library, PA (photo Anthony Bale): 28; Peter Horree/ Alamy Stock Photo: 21; Landesmuseum, Mainz: 20; © Museum of London: 9; The New York Public Library (Spencer Collection MS 32, fols. 138v–139r): 11; Pinacoteca e Museo Civico, Volterra: 24; photo Dmitrij Rodionov (CC BY-SA 3.0): 16; reproduced by kind permission of the Syndics of Cambridge University Library (MS Gg.4.27, fol. 433r): 7; © The Trustees of the British Museum (CC BY-NC-SA 4.0): 22; Walters Art Museum, Baltimore, MD (CC BY 3.0): 23 (MS w.188, fol. 100r).

INDEX

Illustration numbers are indicated by *italics*

A Coruña 94
Aachen 21, 93, 177, 189, 190, 193
Acomb, John 104
Adam 115–17, *18*
Agincourt 110
Alan of Lynn *see* Warnekyn, Alan
Alberti, Margherita degli 98
Alfonso of Jaén 62
Allen, Hope Emily 200–202
Alnwick, William, bishop of
    Norwich 47, 111, 183
Amsterdam 155
Amy, John 87
Ancrene Wisse 176
Andrew, Thomas 87, 161
Arabia 60
Arnesby, John 122–6
Arundel, Thomas, archbishop of
    Canterbury 53–8, 229
Assisi 68, 140, 142
Atwood, Margaret, *The Testaments*
    204
Avignon 59

Babthorpe, Robert 126–7
Bakthorpe, William 108
Bartholomew the Englishman, *On
    the Properties of Things* 155–6
Barton, Elizabeth 199
Baxter, Margery 183
Beaufort, Henry, cardinal 179,
    223
Beaufort, Joan *see* Neville
Beaufort, Thomas 110–11, 179
Bedford 25

Bedford, Duke of [John of
    Lancaster] 109–13, 183
Bedlam, *see* London, Bethlem
    Royal Hospital
Benedict XIII, pope 59
Benedictines 47, 52, 63, 87, 195,
    200
Berebreuer family 29
Bergen 28
Bethlehem 20, 43, 73, 146, 157
Beverley 21, 57, 109, 112–13
Bianchi 147–8
Birgersdotter, Birgitta *see* Bridget
Birgitta, St *see* Bridget
Birgittines 62, 98–9, 111, 180,
    190, 229
Bishop's Lynn *see* Lynn
Boanas, Guy 81
Bokenham, Osbern 123
Bologna 20, 63
Bonaventure, St 100, 102, 144
Boniscambi, Ugolino 68
Book of Vices and Virtues 32–3,
    148, 174
Boston 28, 125
Bowet, Henry, archbishop 104–9,
    112
Brenner Pass 59
brewing 20
Bridget of Sweden, St 21, 61–2,
    66, 70, 77–81, 82–3, 87–8,
    95–100, 108, 118, 119, 144,
    145, 148, 164, 170, 186, 199,
    219, 224, 225, *17*
    Liber celestis 61–2, 97–100, 144

Bridlington 106–10
Bristol 21, 93–4
Burchard of Mount Zion,
    Description of the Holy Land 165
Burnham, Isabella [Isabelle] 19,
    27–8, 29, 31
Burnham, John 19, 25–8, 31, 47,
    122, 150, 215
Burnham, John Jr 31
Burnham, Robert 31

Caiaphas 183
Caister, Richard 49–51, 87, 196
Calais 21, 98, 190
Calvary 18, 20, 71, 72, 103,
    163–5, 178, 186
Cambridge 25, 34, 104, 200
Canterbury 57, 93, 117
Capgrave, John, *Solace of Pilgrimes*
    76, 83
Carmelites 52, 62, 87, 88, 90, 91,
    219
Carthusians 57, 100, 196
Catfield, Joanna 91
Catherine of Siena 66, 80–81, 85,
    87, 91, 97, 108, 170, 176, 199
    Dialogue 108
Caulibus, Johannes de 224
Cawood 57, 104, 107, 183
Chaucer, Geoffrey 152
Chevele, Thomas 182
Chichele, Henry, archbishop 112,
    127, 129, 218
Cholmeley, Katharine 203
Christopher, St 142
Church of the Holy Sepulchre *see*
    Jerusalem
Cistercians 94, 229
Clowne (Derbyshire) 200
Cobham, Lord *see* Oldcastle, John
Constance 58–63, 78, 86, 114, 147

Constance, Council of 59–63,
    97, 118
Constance, Thomas 88
Courtenay, Richard, bishop of
    Norwich 47
Curzon, Colin 202–3

Despenser Retable 48
Despenser, Henry, bishop 47, 56
Devil, the 15, 18, 20, 35, 39, 42,
    51, 111, 113–20, 131, 152,
    178, 180, 190, 194, 225
Dives and Pauper 133
Dominicans 44, 57, 60, 87, 88,
    89, 91, 99, 104, 108, 138
Doomsday Book 208
Dorothea of Montau 85
Dover 98
Downside Abbey 200
Drye, Nicholas 182
Ducheman family 29

Easton, Adam 98
Ebner, Margareta 228
Edinburgh 28
Edward III, king 27
Egypt 60
Elizabeth of Hungary 97, 144,
    172, 223, 26
Ely 25
Ethiopia 60
Eve 115–17,18

Fabri, Felix 71–2
Florence 98, 100
Florentyne, Margaret *see* Alberti,
    Margherita degli
Francesca Romana 119
Francis of Assisi 170
Franciscans 21, 68, 70–73, 104,
    117, 135, 224

Frank, Arthur W. 173
'Friar Daw's Reply' 117

Gardner, Helen 202
Gdańsk 21, 28–9, 93, 187–9
George (ship) 29
Gerson, Jean, On Distinguishing
        True from False Revelations 118
    On the Examination of Doctrine
        118
    On the Proving of Spirits 118
Gibbs-Smith, Charles 200
Glück, Robert, Margery Kempe 204
Goodman, Anthony 52
Gower, John, Confessio
        Amantis 19
Great Ouse, river 19, 89
Gregory XII, pope 59
Greystoke, Elizabeth 93
Guy de Chauliac, Cyrurgie 171,
        185–6

Hailes 94–5, 121, 223
Hali Meithhad 176
Hampole 100
Hansards see Hanse
Hanse (Hansards, Hanseatic
        League) 28–31, 189
Harfleur 110
Hatmaker, Geffard 29
Hatmaker, Gysberd 29
Henry IV, king 56, 93, 104, 110,
        117, 194
Henry V, king 98, 104, 109, 110,
        111, 117, 195
heresy 13, 53–9, 104–13, 117,
        126–9, 134, 147, 182–3, 190,
        222
Hessle 21, 57, 89, 109–10, 112,
        183
Hevingham, Thomas 87, 89

Hilton, Walter 22–3, 58, 87, 100,
        144, 161
Holy Maid of Kent see Barton,
        Elizabeth
'How the Good Wife Taught her
        Daughter' 146
Huddleston, Roger 200
Hull 109
Hull, Eleanor 194–5
Humber, river 21, 109
Huntingdon 25
Hus, Jan 60–61, 11
Hussites 59–61
Huswyf, Roger 195

India 60
Ipswich 21, 92, 188, 190

Jaffa 64, 67–8
James, Montague Rhodes 200
Jericho 73
Jerome, saint 132
Jerusalem 20, 28, 48, 53, 59, 66–
        73, 76, 79, 97, 99, 112, 121,
        134, 135, 139, 159–65, 188
    Church of the Holy Sepulchre
        70–72, 160, 165, 15
    Muristan hospice 70
    see also Calvary
Joan of Arc 111, 118, 183
Joan of Navarre 117, 194
John of Bridlington, saint 109
John of Gaunt 93
John of Lancaster see Duke of
        Bedford
John XXIII, antipope 59
Julian of Norwich 90–92, 114,
        153, 193–4, 203

Katherine of Alexandria, St 82,
        111, 123, 125–6, 128–9, 19

Kempe, Agnes 216
Kempe, John 19, 20, 29, 31–2, 58,
    82, 122, 173, 176, 182–6
Kempe, John junior 21, 28,
    185–8, 193
Kempe, John senior 31
Kempe, Simon 31–2
Kendal, John 104
Kilkenny 119
King's Lynn *see* Lynn
Kingston-upon-Hull *see* Hull
Knausgaard, Karl Ove, *My
    Struggle* 205
Kneale, Matthew, *Pilgrims* 204
Konstanz *see* Constance
Kraus, Chris, *I Love Dick* 205
Krug, Rebecca 195
Kyteler, Alice 119

Lambeth 52–5
Lambeth Palace 55, 112, 129,
    205, 10
Lee, Hermione 10
Leicester 21, 89, 95, 101, 121–9
leprosy 80, 170–73, 186, 190
Lok, Margery 27
Lok, William 223
'Lollardy' 47–8, 56–8, 62, 64, 105,
    110–13, 117, 134, 182–3, 189
London 28, 52–6, 76, 110–11,
    117, 148, 177–80, 190, 195,
    197, 200
    Bethlem Royal Hospital
    ('Bedlam') 16
Love, Nicholas 87
    *Mirrour of the Blessed Life of Jesu
    Christ* 57–8, 100, 102–3
Lübeck 28–9
Lydgate, John
    'Ballade on an Ale Seller' 34
    'On the Image of Pity' 136–7

Lynn (Bishop's Lynn, King's Lynn)
    13, 19–24, 25–46, 47, 49, 54,
    56–7, 63, 76, 82, 87–9, 91–3,
    97, 99, 108, 111, 113, 122,
    128, 138–9, 144, 150, 154–7,
    175, 178, 179–81, 182, 183,
    187, 187, 188–90, 191, 215,
    223, 234
    Corpus Christi Guild 31
    Guild of the Holy Trinity 21,
    26, 31, 36–8, 154–7, 191, 195,
    197, 207–8, 217, 5
    Guild of St Giles 31
    Guild of St Julian 31
    Guild of Young Clerks 43
    Hanse *kontor* 28–31
    St Margaret's Church 28–9,
    31–2, 36–46, 47, 56, 87–9, 91,
    138, 150, 154–7, 191, 217, 6

McAvoy, Liz Herbert 145
Marcello of Rome 77
Margaret of Antioch, St 82, 97,
    111, 129, 142, 190
Margaret of Winchester 194
Margery Kempe Society 205
Marie d'Oignies 85, 97, 144, 170,
    224
Marshall, Thomas 121–3
Mary Knyght (ship) 29
Mary Magdalen, St 71, 172
Mechtilde of Hackeborn 85
Meech, Sanford Brown 201–2
Melton Mowbray 95
Methley, Richard 236
milling 20
Mintlyn 207–9, 29
Mirk, John 58–9
Mohammed 114
Moon, Hawise 182
Moses 134

Mount Grace 102, 196–7, 199, 236
Mount Joy 159–62
Mount of Olives 160, 164
Mount Quarantine 73–5, 16
Mount Zion 70

Nabi Samwil see Mount Joy
Netter, Thomas 62, 183, 219, 234–5
Neville, Joan, Countess of Westmorland 93, 179
Newcastle-under-Lyme 93
Niccolò di Tomasso 148
Nineveh 60
Norway 21, 93, 150, 188
Norwich 35–6, 47–52, 87–93, 98, 135–8, 147, 153, 162, 172–3, 180, 192–3, 196, 207, 217
 Cathedral 35–6, 48, 196, 4
 College of St Mary in the Fields 92
 St Peter Mancroft 172–3, 26
 St Stephen's Church 48–50, 196, 8
Novgorod 28

Oldcastle, Sir John see Oldcastle Revolt
Oldcastle Revolt 64, 110–12
Order of the Garter 111
Oxford 55, 100

'Parlement of the Thre Ages' 184
Paul, St 91, 107
Pentney Abbey 144
Pepwell, Henry 197
Persia 60
Perugia 134, 233
Peter of Limoges, De oculo morali 140

pilgrim badges 49, 50, 138
pilgrimage 20–22, 53, 56, 58–9, 63–8, 71–2, 79, 82–6, 92–4, 112, 121–2, 134, 138, 144, 146, 148, 155, 159, 162, 164, 177, 187, 189–90, 193, 223
Pisa 59
Ponziani, Francesca see Romana, Francesca
Prester John 60
Pseudo-Bonaventure see Bonaventure
Pula 67
Pye, Hugh 182

Raby Castle 93
Radegund, saint 173
Ramla 68, 72
Randolf, John 117
Raughton, Emma 223
Reginald the Hermit 87, 92, 188, 190
Repingdon, Phillip, bishop 53, 58–9, 147
Revelation of Purgatory 194
Rhodes 60, 69
Richard II, king 27, 148
Richard of Ireland 77, 87, 135
Richental, Ulrich 60–62
Riga 60
Rolle, Richard 86, 87, 100–103, 174
 The Fire of Love 86, 100–102
 The Form of Living 179
Romana, Francesca, saint 119
Rome 20, 28, 53, 59, 76–81, 82–5, 92, 95, 97–101, 119, 121, 132–3, 135, 141, 147–8, 152, 174–5, 187–8, 233
 Casa di Santa Brigida 77, 82, 98

Church of Santa Maria
    Maggiore 156–7, 24
Church of Santi Apostoli 82
English Hospice of the Most
    Holy Trinity and St Thomas
    77–8, 98
Pantheon (Church of St Mary)
    76
Roper, Lyndal 81
Rosenwein, Barbara 158
Rothley, Richard 129
Rouen 183

St Albans 195
Salthouse, Richard 52, 196
Sandringham 97, 17
Santiago de Compostela 20, 21,
    53, 93
Satan 114–15, 18
Sawtry, William 56–7
Scotland 26, 60
Sedgeford 218
Sheen 180
Sleightholme, William 86, 87,
    106, 109, 179
Smithfield 52, 87, 90–91
Sopwell 195
South Elmham 56
South Lynn 91, 217
Southfield, William 52, 87,
    90–91
Springold, Robert 86–90
Springwell, John 182, 234
Steedman, Carolyn 153
stockfish 150–52
Stralsund 29, 189
Sturdy Cunt (ferry boat) 90
Sutton, Geoffrey de 28
Swynford, Katherine 93
Syon 98, 111, 180, 190, 193

Talkyng of the Love of God 176–7
Teutonic Knights 189
Thames, river 55, 200, 218
Thomasson, John 77
Tottington, Alexander, bishop 47
Trotula 13–14, 214
Trussebut family 27

Ulfsson, Karl 186

Vadstena 97, 224
Van de Put, Albert 200
Vandepar, William 29
Vantoter, Henry 29
Vatican 76
Venice 20, 59, 63–8, 78, 135, 140,
    142, 148, 178
    Convent of San Zaccaria 63–6,
    12, 13
Veronica, saint 76, 178
Vitry, Jacques de 84–5, 87, 224

Waddon, John-William 182
Wadi Qelt 73
Wakering, John, bishop 47
Warnekyn, Alan 62, 86, 87–90,
    98, 133, 180, 234
Weaver, William 86
Wenceslas *see* Wenzel of Rome
Wenzel of Rome 80, 87
Wereham, John of 45, 217, 234
West Lynn 89–90
Westminster 27, 52, 54–5, 197
White, William 182, 235
Wilsnack 21, 155, 177, 189, 193
Windsor 111
Wisbech 128
Woolf, Virginia 9
Worde, Wynkyn de 197
Wycliffe, John 48, 55, 133
Wythe, John 182

York 143, 183, 184
York mystery plays 115
Yoshikawa, Naoë 85

Zadar 67
Zierikzee 59